SamulNori

CHICAGO STUDIES IN ETHNOMUSICOLOGY

A series edited by Philip V. Bohlman, Ronald Radano, and Timothy Rommen

SamulNori

Contemporary Korean Drumming and the Rebirth of Itinerant Performance Culture

NATHAN HESSELINK

The University of Chicago Press
Chicago and London

Nathan Hesselink is associate professor of ethnomusicology at the University of British Columbia. He is the author of *P'ungmul: South Korean Drumming and Dance*, also published by the University of Chicago Press, and editor of the volumes *Music and Politics on the Korean Peninsula* and *Contemporary Directions: Korean Folk Music Engaging the Twentieth Century and Beyond.*

The University of Chicago Press, Chicago 60637
The University of Chicago Press, Ltd., London

Printed in the United States of America

21 20 19 18 17 16 15 14 13 12   1 2 3 4 5

ISBN-13: 978-0-226-33096-9 (cloth)
ISBN-13: 978-0-226-33097-6 (paper)
ISBN-10: 0-226-33096-6 (cloth)
ISBN-10: 0-226-33097-4 (paper)

The University of Chicago Press gratefully acknowledges support of this publication by the Academy of Korean Studies of the Republic of Korea.

Library of Congress Cataloging-in-Publication Data

Hesselink, Nathan.
SamulNori : contemporary Korean drumming and the rebirth of itinerant performance culture / Nathan Hesselink.
p. cm. + 1 sound disc (4 3/4 in.) — (Chicago studies in ethnomusicology)
Includes bibliographical references and index.
ISBN-13: 978-0-226-33096-9 (cloth : alk. paper)
ISBN-10: 0-226-33096-6 (cloth : alk. paper)
ISBN-13: 978-0-226-33097-6 (pbk. : alk. paper)
ISBN-10: 0-226-33097-4 (pbk. : alk. paper) 1. 880–01 Samul-Nori (Musical group) 2. Folk music—Korea (South)—History and criticism. 3. Percussion ensembles—Korea (South) I. Title. II. Series: Chicago studies in ethnomusicology.
ML421.S25H47 2012
786.8′162957—dc23

2011027200

♾ This paper meets the requirements of ANSI/NISO Z39.48–1992 (Permanence of Paper).

To E. Park, who introduced me to the intricacies and joys of this art form;
to N. Abelmann, who reminded me of the dignity of scholarship;
to C. Park, who inspired me with the passion of performance;
and to S. Hwang, who makes it all worthwhile.

CONTENTS

ILLUSTRATIONS

ACKNOWLEDGMENTS

This journey began in earnest in Seoul during the summer of 1994, when I had the opportunity to take group *samul nori* lessons with the master drummer and educator Eun-ha Park (an honor I shared with Gustavo Aguilar, HK Chae, and Ann Yoshikawa). Part of our "education" included travel to concert venues via highways and byways through rural South Korea in the backs of vans and buses, and so from the very beginning I have associated the sounds of gongs and drums with life on the road.

During the ensuing years my work required me to travel to Korea on a regular basis (almost too many times to count now), for which I am grateful financially and institutionally to the Korea Foundation, the Academy of Korean Studies, SamulNori Hanullim, and the University of British Columbia's Centre for Korean Research. My time in Korea—not to mention the flights, buses, taxis, and train rides shared in getting there and back—was made not only enjoyable but intellectually stimulating by a regular and close-knit group of fellow travelers who I am privileged to call friends: Andy Sutton, Roald Maliangkay, Keith Howard, Hillary Finchum-Sung, Heather Willoughby, Josh Pilzer, Andrew Killick,

Katherine Lee, Lee So-young, Kim Su-youn, and Sheen Dae-cheol. I would like to think that *noraebang* served as a rite of passage into this community.

Back in North America I have been helped over the long haul by a group of remarkable individuals who are to me akin to a league of superheroes, for reasons academic, performative, and inspirational: Jonathan C. Petty, Chan Park, Andy Sutton (again!), Nancy Abelmann, Ch'oe Pyŏngsam, and Michael Tenzer. I add to this list my colleagues at the University of Chicago Press: Philip Bohlman, for continuing to surprise me with your patience and wisdom; Elizabeth Branch Dyson, who should now be considered a patron saint of Korean drumming traditions; Anne Summers Goldberg, for your diligence and humor (I wish you well in your new position); two anonymous readers; Ryan Li for another stellar job with the book's design; and Michael Koplow, for making my text look better than the original. Toward the end of this journey three long-time friends and fellow students came through in a significant way, to which I owe special gratitude: Donna Kwon, Kim Heesun, and Lee Yong-Shik. And this project would have never happened without the help and support of Master Kim Duk Soo.

I end with a secondary dedication to Kim Dong-Won, exemplary performer, pedagogue, philosopher, world traveler, "co-father," and beautiful human being. You're on every page of this book, and I couldn't have done it without you.

ORTHOGRAPHY AND PRONUNCIATION

In order for readers to be able to cross-reference the Korean terms found in this book with my earlier publications, as well as the related academic literature in English, I have maintained the use of the McCune-Reischauer system of Korean romanization. This includes the preference for the modified compound "shi" instead of "si," resulting in "*shijo*" and "*shikku*" rather than "*sijo*" and "*sikku*." In the bibliography, author's names are cited by the romanizations found in the original publications when applicable, but are identified by the McCune-Reischauer version in brackets immediately following (e.g., "Kim Duk Soo [Kim Tŏksu]"). Chinese terms are romanized according to the pinyin system, Japanese terms according to Hepburn. Foreign terms are italicized throughout, with the exception of proper nouns, titles of pieces, associations, government groups, buildings, and offices.

The vowels *a*, *e*, *i*, *o*, and *u* in Korean are essentially pronounced as their counterparts in Italian or Spanish. *Ŭ* is pronounced as the *ou* of "should," *ŏ* between the *ou* of American "ought" and *o* of "come," and the possessive marker *ŭi* is often pronounced like the Korean *e*. The vowel compounds *ae* and *oe* sound as *a* in American English "hat" and *we* of "wet" respectively. Consonants are roughly equivalent to English, with ʻ indicating greater aspiration; the consonant *r* is always a "flapped" *r* as in Spanish or Italian. Morpheme-initial or -final consonants *p*, *t*, and *k* when surrounded by vowels are pronounced as *b*, *d*, and *g* respectively (e.g., *kuk* + *ak* = *kugak*, or "national [Korean] music"). The same is true if the adjacent sound is a voiced continuant consonant, such as *l*, *n*, or *w* (*p'ungmul* + *kut* = *p'ungmulgut*, or "percussion music and dance").

INTRODUCTION

Pŏpko ch'angshin (Preserve the Old While Creating the New)

The Challenges of Tradition

Children of wandering minstrels—did they walk along dusty, sun-touched paths? Sitting by the sides of the elders as they drew on their cigarettes, their eyes look towards the distant hills: did they glance to see the play of light on the leaves, fluttering in the brilliant brightness? Did they know that it was the sound of their music which set in motion an entire village as they crossed its threshold? Did they hear the sound of furious applause erupting after a moment of stunned silence from an audience who has watched dancers drawing arcs against the sky with the long white ribbons of their *sangmo* [spinning-tasseled hats] as they spin almost into invisibility? After the harvest, as the rice patties [*sic*] lie fallow and dry branches pierce a chilly sky—did the children sense the approach of winter? These children of the wandering minstrels—did they see their shadows following them wherever the roads took them?

Time passes. The band of minstrels drift apart, leave and gradually disappear. But the children of their music grow up and talk of their dreams of the future.

KIM RIHYE 1988:5

It began with a small but expectant crowd in a cramped little basement theater in downtown Seoul, in February 1978. The fruition of a vision more than a decade in the making, the concert was billed as the celebration of the efforts of an intimate group of friends and musical colleagues who had come of age. The performers, inspired by mentors and artistic forebears borne of itinerant troupe performance traditions, were bound by the goal of saving Korean traditional music from obscurity in a nation threatened by Western cultural hegemony. Playing one each on the four core drums and gongs of the folk art known as *p'ungmul*, and employing rhythms and performance techniques directly inspired by this tradition, their adaptation of folk music to the stage was in many ways bold and without precedent. What the group had accomplished, almost literally overnight, was the repackaging and revitalization of a familiar yet declining age-old rural practice for the entertainment of city dwellers in the heart of the bustling capital.

That February evening might have been relegated to an academic footnote if the quartet had not created such a commotion. The group's youthful, dynamic, and contemporary approach to tradition seemed to have touched a nerve, tapping into an underlying generational zeitgeist waiting to be released. Choosing to call themselves SamulNori—*samul*: literally "four objects," a reference to the core instrumentation; and *nori*: folk entertainment—the newly formed ensemble soon took the traditional music world by storm. Over the next few years urban youth flocked to SamulNori performances, packing concert halls and even stadiums in a rock concert–like atmosphere. A leading academic and journalist at the time characterized SamulNori as new, fresh, and fast like contemporary life, not old, slow, and "backwards" like the music of one's parents (Han Myŏnghŭi 1992a:17–20).[1] Its energy, speed, and even sex appeal seemed to have matched the vigor of younger audiences and popular music being heard in the media, so that SamulNori audiences were able to forge an identity that acknowledged folk roots while maintaining a kind of urban, modern savvy (Hwang and Na 2001:209; Park, Shingil 2000:187–88). SamulNori grew with such a force and momentum that by the end of the 1980s there did not seem to be enough outlets for the phenomenon, so ubiquitous was their presence on television, newspapers, radio broadcasts, and commercial recordings. As a symbol of the characteristics and hopes of the decade, SamulNori achieved a kind of mythological status, spurring on traditional music's popularization and globalization while simultaneously inspiring the evolution of an entire genre—now romanized as *samul nori* or *samullori* (Han Myŏnghŭi 1992a:17–18; Sejong munhwa hoegwan chŏnsa p'yŏnjip wiwŏnhoe 2002:233; see also Han, Myunghee 1993:35).

SamulNori's popularity was not limited to domestic audiences. During the summer of 1982 they received their first invitation to perform abroad in Japan; their first American tour followed that fall, with high-profile appearances at Disney World's World Showcase Festival (Epcot Center) and the annual PASIC (Percussive Arts Society International Convention) Conference in Dallas, Texas. A second American tour was sponsored by the Asia Society in 1983, after which their touring took a frenetic pace. By the mid-1990s SamulNori had visited twenty countries, performances that introduced them to audiences at the Seoul Olympics, the Kennedy Center, WOMAD, the 1986 World Expo in Vancouver, and the Royal Albert Hall (BBC Proms), to name just a few.[2] Residencies were also established throughout North America, including the Smithsonian in Washington, D.C., the Lincoln Center for the Performing Arts, the University of California at Berkeley, and the University of Michigan. Their audiences and venues represented a kaleidoscopic array ranging from school children, college students, government dignitaries, priests, shamans, and even the pope, to stages in markets, plazas, temples, gymnasiums, concert halls, riverbeds, and mountainsides. Foreign media were nearly unanimous in their praise of SamulNori from the very beginning, showering them with superlatives such as "fantastic," "amazing," "mystical," "ecstatic," and "totally astonishing" (see Samstag 1988b:45–47 for an overview of the first decade of reviews).[3] As of 2007, SamulNori had performed nearly 5,500 times in fifty different countries on 3,000 stages worldwide (see figure I.1).[4]

By the 1990s, SamulNori/*samul nori* in various incarnations had become a prominent fixture of the Korean musical landscape, seen on television broadcasts and in concert halls, disseminated on CD, VHS, and DVD recordings, studied in chapters of music history and appreciation textbooks, and taught at the primary, secondary, and collegiate levels throughout the peninsula.[5] Regularly occurring training institutes and camps were established in South Korea, Japan, Germany, Switzerland, and the U.S., while the broader genre became the default traditional percussion choice at the government-sponsored National Center for Korean Traditional Performing Arts (Kungnip Kugagwŏn, hereafter "National Center") for all of its concerts, educational outreach efforts, and presentations on tours, both domestic and foreign. In 1993 SamulNori expanded to become SamulNori Hanullim, Inc., an organization that subsumed various touring groups, an instrument store, and an arts promotional society that was

Figure I.1 SamulNori concert tour promotional literature (© SamulNori Hanullim).

second only to the National Center in the offering of traditional music events in the 1990s (Park, Shingil 2000:181). *Samul nori* festivals and competitions were held throughout the peninsula, often with major endorsements and financial backing. The musical theater sensation "Nanta" [Nant'a] (or "Cookin'" in English) was spawned (see Yi Yŏngmi 1997), while members of the original Samul-Nori quartet were invited to perform at the United Nations in 1995 and at the

2002 World Cup (Ku, Hee-seo 1994; Lee, Sang-man 1995).[6] By the late twentieth and early twenty-first centuries SamulNori/*samul nori* had become a national symbol of Korean culture (Kim, Jin-Woo 2003a; Nam Hwajŏng 2008:19).[7]

My initial exposure to Korean music in a live performance setting came during my first trip to South Korea the summer of 1992. Engrossed in Japanese language study and *shamisen* (three-string plucked lute) lessons in Kyoto that year—I bragged at the time (tongue in cheek) to friends at home that I would become the first white male geisha—I became increasingly frustrated with the social structure of the learning process and my dwindling financial resources (conditions that were related). And so I took on a higher-paying English-teaching job that would keep me in Japan a few more months to investigate some other traditional music forms. The new employment required a change in visa status; Korea was the closest foreign country where the paperwork could be completed, and I had the additional benefit of having (future) in-laws living in Seoul where I could stay for a few nights. Toward the end of my stay on July 4, I was invited to see a late afternoon performance of Korean traditional music and dance at the National Center (then called the Korean Traditional Performing Arts Centre), the highest-profile performing arts venue for traditional genres in Korea. The concert was part of the Regular Saturday Performance of Korean Music and Dance series, a smorgasbord approach to presentation with six representative excerpts drawn from court, aristocratic, and folk styles for an audience primarily of foreign adults and Korean schoolchildren. The last piece on the program featured the resident *samul nori* ensemble.

It has become cliché to describe an experience as having "made all the difference" (à la Frost), needlessly dramatic to say that in a single moment everything changed. I do not even know if it was one of their better efforts, and yet the performance of *samul nori* that afternoon was so moving—complex cycles with shifting meters, breathtaking crescendos and accelerandos, exacting discipline and virtuosity, an exquisite balance of high and low tones and the contrasting timbres of leather and metal—that I knew almost immediately that my research and future course of study would involve Korean percussion. Something was so completely satisfying about it all, a fullness and richness borne completely of rhythm. There was its beautiful economy of instrumentation and visual presentation, just four musicians seated on a mat playing on two drums—the larger hourglass-shaped *changgo* and the barrel-shaped *puk*—and two gongs—the small handheld *soe/kkwaenggwari* and larger suspended *ching*. And there was that special sense a discoverer must feel when believing s/he has witnessed something for the first time, so unfamiliar and unknown was *samul nori* to me at the time.

Some kind of supernatural force seemed to be in play when the National Center announced the inauguration of a program tailored for foreign students, academics, and performers to take place the summer of 1993. Classes on Korean music theory, history, and aesthetics would be complemented by group and individual lessons on traditional instruments and vocal genres, including sessions on *samul nori* (see Song Hye-jin 1994). I felt fortunate to be accepted, and so found myself back in Seoul newly invigorated by the thought of solidifying the direction of my future doctoral studies in ethnomusicology. As I began to discuss my plans of researching *samul nori* with local Korean academics and North American university professors in the program, however, I was almost uniformly discouraged from this course of action. It was then that I discovered that the formation of the genre by the original SamulNori group had only occurred in 1978; through others' and my own preconceived notions and prejudices I became convinced that something so popular, urban, and recent could not possibly be "traditional." I was instead encouraged to study the age-old, rural percussive art form known alternatively as *p'ungmul* (literally "wind objects," a reference to the core percussion instruments) or *nongak* ("farmers' music"), advice that satisfied my admittedly naive quest for "purity" and "authenticity" in Korean traditional percussion music.

My formal fieldwork on *p'ungmul* began the fall of 1995. That year spent out in the provinces in and around the North Chŏlla provincial capital of Chŏnju was a deeply engaging and transformative period in my life. I was impressed and humbled by the kindness and openness of my mentors and fellow students, and I felt a kind of holistic connection to music making through an integrated approach to drumming and dance that I had never experienced before. My research also supported the feeling that I was taking part in musical practices that extended centuries back into the country's rich cultural past, a window onto the "real" Korea. This perspective was not expanded or called into question by those around me, many of whom were not very sympathetic toward *samul nori*. One of my earliest interviews with Mr. Pak Hyŏngnae, a nationally designated *p'ungmul* cultural asset performer from Imshil P'ilbong Nongak, commented on the urban "contamination" of *samul nori*: "*Samul nori* is *p'ungmul* that has been popularized in urban areas for people with little knowledge of the past. It's like disco music—it doesn't have any slow rhythms which let you move in a distinctively Korean way" (quoted in Hesselink 1998:315). Later a close friend and teacher gave me a *p'ungmul* workbook that included one of the most extreme criticisms of *samul nori* I have ever encountered, ostensibly motivated by the perceived threat of Western influences on *p'ungmul* performance practice: "What we now call *samul nori* is only [the glittering of] Snow White's costume jewelry. We have eaten her apple, more venomous than pesticide, more poisonous than the word '*nongak*'" (An Pyŏngt'ak 198?:17–18; to be discussed further below).[8] Perhaps my mentors and classmates were just telling me what I wanted to hear; everyone I studied and performed with (minus the cultural asset teachers) knew the *samul nori* repertoire, and the main SamulNori group's popularity was just as strong out in the provinces as it was in the capital.

Over the years that followed I began to pay more attention to what was being said about SamulNori/*samul nori* in the academic literature, though again without really engaging what its practitioners were saying about themselves. Little I read changed how I had been conditioned to respond: detractors were quick to highlight the gap between what "real" *p'ungmul* performances were supposed to be—rural, amateur, participatory, dance-based, and timeless—versus SamulNori's "bastardized" style passing for tradition (Ch'oe Chongmin 2002:12; No Poksun 1993:18–19; Yi Sŏngch'ŏn et al. 1997:180–81; Yi Sŏngjae 1999:95–101; see also Stock 2008:199). Sometimes a nod was made to the traditional elements of SamulNori, but with qualifications in quotation marks (Nam, Sang-suk, and Gim, Hae-suk 2002:46–47); other times "neo-traditional" (Lee, Byong Won 1997:14) or "newly created traditional music" (Syn-Nara Record Co. n.d.:24) sufficed. And there was the specter of Hobsbawm, haunting us with SamulNori as "invented tradition" (Kim, Jin-Woo 2003b:818).

The first real challenge to this worldview came the summer of 2001. Increasingly perplexed by SamulNori's connection to older Korean culture, and wishing to expand the base of my knowledge of Korean rhythm, I made arrangements to undergo a two-month *samul nori* apprenticeship in Seoul with one of my first drumming teachers from the National Center. The most valuable revelation I took away with me from that experience was the discovery that my fieldwork and research to date had shielded me from an equally rooted, important, and compelling narrative in Korean music history. It was a story of professionalism, complexity, and cosmopolitanism, a realm broadly understood as itinerant troupe performance culture (*yurang yein chiptan munhwa*). During the eighteenth and nineteenth centuries this culture shaped, through invention, remodeling, and juxtaposition, much of what is today considered traditional Korean folk music (Shim Usŏng 1994; Song, Bang-Song 2001; Song Pangsong 2007:448–54). Numerous groups have marched under this banner, with distinctions often made based on religious affiliation, gender of the performers, and nature of the performance acts. The last of such troupes to survive into the early twentieth century (pre–cultural asset system) were the *namsadang* (literally "male temple groups"), historically all-male traveling artistic troupes associated with Buddhist temples that made a living from presentational music-making favoring technical mastery and innovation in an effort to please diverse and changing audiences. SamulNori represents the rebirth and logical outgrowth of the *namsadang*; the evidence of this will be the substance of this book.

As I began to digest the alternative reality presented by itinerant troupe performance culture, culminating in fieldwork conducted with the *namsadang* in 2006 (see chapter 1), I realized it was not only a historically flawed connection made to rural drumming practices that had misled so many of SamulNori's critics. What was at issue was a much deeper, more fundamental misunderstanding of the nature of a living tradition. In spite of overwhelming theorizing in nearly all academic fields on the fluid and transforming nature of the traditional,[9] SamulNori/*samul nori* as a specifically Asian art form was still shouldering the historical burden of Orientalism and the fallacies of an unchanging, untouched, and "pure" or "authentic" personage (Said 1979; see also Diamond et al. 1994:50 and Taylor 1997:125–45). Locally such biases were maintained on a practical scale through a cultural asset preservation system interested in finding original, "primary forms" (*wŏnhyŏng*) of performative arts that froze (contested) moments of time and history in a kind of artificially supported museum state (Maliangkay 1999; Hesselink 2004:406–12; Howard 2006b). Intellectually, this structure was supported by a nationalist and largely isolationist approach to cultural production known as the *minjung* (or "people's") movement, one that conveniently ignored centuries of foreign influence on the Korean peninsula and the activities of groups like the *namsadang* (for an overview of this movement, see Hesselink 2006:90–119). And there were always academia and the powers that be (aristocratic in a Korean context, but also European), distrustful of the "popular," the denial of artistic quality or value in "music that succeeds in the marketplace" (Rockwell 1999:97; see also Middleton 2003).[10]

To begin to understand the possibility of considering SamulNori as traditional, and to form criteria for establishing such a claim, we must jettison the artificially constructed dichotomies of the old and preservationist versus the innovative and modern (Nettl 1983:26–27; Titon 1995:439; Bohlman 2002:63 and 2008:104–7; Yi Soyŏng 2007).[11] While there are many sources of inspiration for such an interactive and organic approach, it is appropriate to draw on native conceptions of the traditional to culturally and historically ground the arguments that will follow. The *namsadang*—and itinerant troupe culture in general—began to flourish during the eighteenth century in a then-unified Korea. The nature of such activity was not lost on Pak Chiwŏn, one of the era's best-known and most progressive authors and literary scholars. Pak coined the phrase used for the title of this introduction and the conclusion, "Preserve the old [while] creating the new" (*pŏpko . . . ch'angshin* [reproduced in No Ŭnuk 1991:275]), an inclusive view of traditional art with a respected lineage extending back to the writings of Confucius.[12] In a workbook produced by SamulNori for Koreans living overseas, the recollection of their founding echoes perfectly Pak's sentiments: "These men were very much aware that 'tradition' and 'innovation' were merely two sides of a coin. This meant that the dance and the music of the past needed to be re-created to suit and to bear significance for the present" (Kim, Duk Soo et al. 1999:3).

Preserving the old while creating the new in fact describes the roots of most current and popular forms of traditional music being performed in South Korea today. SamulNori has commonly been seen in the same company as and completion of a trilogy of lasting folk music forms: "The eighteenth century was the era of *p'ansori* [narrative song accompanied by drum], the nineteenth century gave birth to *sanjo* [solo instrumental suite], and in the twentieth century SamulNori has been correctly recognized as the creative inheritors of tradition" (www.Korean.net web posting of May 21, 2005; see also Minsogakhoe Shinawi 1999). The importance of representing the traditional has not lost its currency in many parts of the world where links to tradition help guide performers, audiences, and governmental agencies to navigate the complexities and contradictions of modernization and commercialization (Livingston 1999; Rice 1994: 12–15, 18–20; Sutton 2002:3–27). For SamulNori this connection accounts for much of its livelihood, popularity, motivation for outreach, and sense of identity. The image they maintain and present to the outside world—the way they are perceived—also has significant ramifications for the choices that are made in the Korean diaspora and/or by cultural organizations overseas looking to present "traditional Korea" to local communities:

> The important thing to recognize from these repertoires is that these groups are taking their cues from the *samulnori* groups, not the student groups who are playing single beats over and over again [a reference to rural *p'ungmul*]. . . . This is interesting because of the complaints [other] student groups have had toward *samulnori* groups, that they are professionalizing the music too much, changing it too much from the way that it was played traditionally. If these claims are justified then it is somewhat contradictory for groups that are attempting to learn about

> and showcase "traditional" Korean music to be playing it in a way that has only existed since 1978. (Bussell 1997:43)

This statement, quoted from a B.A. thesis written at a midwestern university, aptly describes the sentiment of many student groups and arts societies in North America. There need be no conflict here; rural *p'ungmul* and *samul nori* represent two ends of the spectrum of the Korean percussion world—representative, overlapping, and complementary.

SamulNori as the rebirth of the *namsadang* and itinerant troupe performance culture embodies the natural extension of an evolving tradition steeped in the metaphors and realities of motion. Like all enduring and pertinent art exhibiting "the immanence of the past in the cultural certainties of the present" (Coplan 1994:19), SamulNori has remained close to its roots in allowing the current to inform a nevertheless distinctly traditional worldview, one that accepts and accommodates the arena of public scrutiny and taste. Carrying the mantle of their predecessors and a life on the road, they have become keenly aware of the necessity and benefits that movement affords. It is only through active social engagement, adaptation, and expansion of perspective that an art form moves beyond survival to flourish and eventually become worthy of emulation. For SamulNori it was a process many centuries in the making.

In spite of a fair amount of "common knowledge" about SamulNori/*samul nori* among the general Korean population, and also to a lesser extent by students and enthusiasts of Korean music and culture, a thorough sociological *and* musical-theoretical examination as I have assembled here in one volume does not exist in any language (in Korean, for example, one can contrast the rich biographical and historical content of Kim Hŏnsŏn's work [1994, 1995, 1998] with the analytical prowess of Ch'oe Pyŏngsam's volume [2000]). Although the immediate topic is contemporary South Korean percussion music, nearly all of the issues I address have direct parallels in the experiences and strategies of similar later developing and/or globalizing countries of the twentieth century. Governmental and educational institutions, cultural organizations, and individuals and groups in the performing arts in such societies who looked to discover, define, maintain, and/or promote the traditional during the twentieth century were faced with a number of challenges unique to the era. As Bruno Nettl has observed, such concerns seemed to gravitate broadly around the three constructs of nationalism (ideas of identity), cosmopolitanism (life in urban centers), and globalization (one's place in a new political, economic, and technological world), all derived from "the rapid musical [and cultural] interactions among ethnic groups, nations, classes, and world areas, and among musical strata (folk, classical, popular) once seen as distinct. They are processes that seem to be, at least in their magnitude, without precedent in world history" (2005:285).

Because of the vast range of theoretical issues these three constructs generate when accounting for a group like SamulNori, and also because of the sheer number of derivative groups, performances, and related commercial recordings that have come into existence and continue to be produced, I have limited the scope of my analysis to roughly the first twenty years of SamulNori's existence. This period is marked by their debut in early 1978 through to the completion of their Nanjang Cultures ventures in 1998 (the opening of the club), two decades of activity that set into motion nearly all of the major trends of the traditional music world of the early twenty-first century (to be addressed throughout this book, but more fully in the conclusion). While I have attempted to give space to individuals' accounts and narratives at every possible turn, the main thrust of this book is nevertheless the larger social, cultural, and economic processes that surrounded and helped support the origin and continuing relevance of SamulNori. And though there is always some overlap in meaning and usage between the group called SamulNori and the genre known as *samul nori*, for the title of this book and most of the discussion I am referring to the original organization, one that over time chose "SamulNori"—later "Kim Duk Soo SamulNori"—as the proper means of romanizing and distinguishing themselves from the many other related percussion teams.

In the first two chapters I set up the historical and contextual background that made the arrival of SamulNori a possibility. Chapter 1 is dedicated to itinerant troupe performance culture in Korea with specific details regarding the activities of the *namsadang*; without properly grounding our understanding of these "wandering minstrels" (cf. opening epigraph), the rest of this manuscript and its logic will make little sense. I begin with the early historical record and the *namsadang*'s role in providing mass entertainment, interpreting such data as part of a larger trend toward professionalization and presentational-style music making in the folk arena. The discussion then moves to the fate of these troupes in the early twentieth century, a period marked by the powerful confluence of Japanese colonialism and the encroachment of imported religious, philosophical, and societal attitudes. In spite of these drawbacks, however, the *namsadang* were able through the medium of performance art to loosen some of the restrictions and boundaries of regionalism that had worked against the nation during these times of internal and external conflict, planting the seeds of a fledgling pan-Korean identity that would bloom in the 1960s and '70s. The chapter concludes with the re-formation and reenvisioning of the *namsadang* as part of a fully modern South Korean society.

Nationalism and cosmopolitanism come together in chapter 2, where I examine the ascendancy of urban culture in South Korea in the 1970s, paying special attention to concert halls and arts organizations as the new loci of encounter, influence, and appreciation for traditional music. As SamulNori prepared for their debut in early 1978, they were faced with a number of difficult choices when adapting their previously rural tradition to the rapidly evolving city landscape and soundscape. Newly built Western-style concert halls brought new challenges and constraints regarding size, acoustic environment, and the arrangement of seating. More important, however, were the attendant artistic and societal transformations: on the heels of such construction came large Western symphony orchestras, opera companies, and ballet troupes, events that in tandem with the impressiveness and novelty of the halls conspired against the older, smaller, and often more humbly conceived performances of the countryside. Social hierarchy had existed for centuries in Korea, but with the elite nature of the concert hall—restricted primarily to residents of the capital, and those with the ability to purchase a ticket—such social distinctions were strengthened through attendance as a marker of class and taste. This whirlwind of activity occurred within the broader context of the search within political and academic debates by arts organizations of the 1970s for a renewed meaning of Korean identity as expressed through music, dance, theater, literature, and architecture.

Picking up on trends documented in chapter 2, chapter 3 further focuses on the sociological and historical currents underpinning SamulNori's adaptation of the rural performance to the modern concert hall stage. Organized around a core succession of rhythms viewed as symbols of continuity, my analysis looks at the strategies employed by SamulNori when transforming their performances to meet the demands of changing venues, audiences, and channels of distribution under the rubric of authenticity. This includes the influences of professionalism on interpersonal relationships (between audiences and musicians); the move made to the recording studio and its reliance on mediation, commodification, and cultural brokers; and the broader related concerns of monetary exchange and ownership as SamulNori performances—increasingly conceived for CD or DVD—became freed from their original performance contexts and frameworks of understanding.

Chapters 4 and 5 examine SamulNori's more creative and ingenious approaches to outreach in their attempt to engage the realities of globalization.

In chapter 4 I document and explain their integration of music theory and performance practice with East Asian cosmology in their pedagogical materials. Contrary to many other arts organizations in South Korea that consciously chose to "update" their texts, workbooks, and teaching methodology based on North American or Western European models, SamulNori boldly embraced an older but deeply shared way of relating to human society and the cosmos, at the same time looking at ways of translating this material for their growing non-Korean student base. Chapter 5 continues with this theme of the challenges of cross-cultural encounter in an evaluation of their fusion projects and recordings with the Euro-American jazz quartet Red Sun. I begin with sonic considerations of the nature of hybridity, looking at ways the stylistic and performative backgrounds of both sets of musicians either contributed to or hindered a "meeting of the minds." My analysis operates within levels of specificity, beginning with the general notion of hybridity as the recognition of separate or foreign sources, moving to the more closely defined realm of syncretism and the interrelationship of the sonic elements, and finally identifying any ground level, embodied cross-cultural resonances in feeling or groove, of mood or sentiment. Political considerations are then intertwined with these concerns, looking at power relations as played out in the composition, production, representation, and distribution of the recordings, all understood within the context of current debates of exploitation versus collaboration found in discussions of "world music."

In the conclusion I revisit the definition of tradition as presented by the example of SamulNori and its embodiment of the proverb "preserve the old while creating the new." At the simplest and most tangible level the story of the ensemble and the genre it spawned is one of unconditional success, in that nearly every decision they made with regard to presentation, repertoire, pedagogy, and cross-cultural collaboration and fusion has been mimicked or outright embraced in every corner of the South Korean traditional music world. SamulNori made tradition relevant again to modern Korean society, bringing prestige, fame, and economic viability back to generations of other traditional performing artists. They also provided a safe and equitable model for engaging the outside world, both abroad and at home. In their successes, however, SamulNori called into the question the *meaning* of tradition in the twenty-first century. As the logical outgrowth of itinerant troupe performance culture and a worldview inclusive of the foreign, current, and organic, SamulNori created a powerful alternative to the government's cultural asset system, policies that are emulated in other East Asian countries and by UNESCO. This alternative is one in which performers and creators are afforded agency, the power not only to adapt but to call into question those aspects of codified tradition with the potential for political, social, and economic domination. Acceptance of this new perspective has important and perhaps troubling ramifications for the fields of preservation, concert promotion, folklore festivals, and cultural tourism.

In previous paragraphs I alluded to negative responses generated by SamulNori's existence—criticized for its professionalism, popular appeal, recent history, cosmopolitanism, complexity, virtuosity, malleability, and supposed urban and Western/global contamination. Within this discourse there is an academic paper trail that can be characterized by an (unfair) comparison to rural *p'ungmul*, inspired primarily from an intellectual vantage point. The statement of my *p'ungmul* teacher and An Pyŏngt'ak's vitriolic comment (also from a *p'ungmul* source), however, point to a temporary but strong undercurrent of discontent experienced by rural percussionists and performers in the provinces. For many of these artists SamulNori was a philosophical and economic threat, a challenge to their way of life and their livelihood. In the early 1980s many student *p'ungmul* groups in the cities, as well as in the countryside, saw the potential for SamulNori to eclipse *p'ungmul*, perhaps even take its place in the cultural asset system as a marker of Korean identity (in early 1980 only one of the five currently recognized cultural asset *p'ungmul* teams had been so designated). Concrete evidence of such sentiment—a proper account of SamulNori's early reception history—unfortunately survives only in anecdotal form, and thus I have not been able to include this aspect of the historical record in this book.[13]

For those familiar with some of the more sensational aspects of SamulNori—the trappings of their fame and success as demonstrated by an oftentimes rabid fan base, personal rivalries, incarceration and drug use of some of the founding members, and suicide—this volume will also seem silent. Methodologically, I must reiterate that the topic of this project is the original SamulNori group as it has been envisioned and maintained by the founding member Kim Duk Soo. Early split-offs from the original quartet—Kim Yongbae to the National Center, Yi Kwangsu to a private ensemble—represent in significant ways separate lines of inquiry. The National Center as a government bureaucracy presented its own set of specific challenges (and opportunities) not relatable to Kim Duk Soo, and later derivative *samul nori* groups formed by members of the original quartet had their own concerns related to their authenticity *as samul nori groups*, obviously not a fear for Kim and SamulNori. I have also chosen for personal reasons not to travel along this path, not only because of the lack of reliable documentation—rumor and anecdote plague this arena as they do the history of SamulNori's early reception—but also out of respect for the private lives of individuals who have been tremendously candid and warm with me in all of our interactions.

The primary goal of this book is to establish and elucidate the links between SamulNori and the *namsadang* as part of the trajectory and grander scheme of itinerant troupe performance culture as lived and experienced today, understood within the framework of the challenges and meanings of tradition. What I hope to accomplish is a critical yet balanced account of the ways SamulNori have embraced preservation and innovation as the creative and spiritual inheritors of a presentational, professionally based art form. While these connections have been made, or at least intimated, in the critical and popular literature, in this work I have gone further to suggest that SamulNori represents the rebirth and flowering of the traditional in our very midst, acting as a potential beacon for other artists—Asians or not—in their search for ways to keep a musical tradition alive and relevant in a world that often conspires to thwart such attempts. SamulNori's story is in many ways that of modern South Korea, an old, venerated culture reinventing itself in the face of nationalism, cosmopolitanism, and globalization as it grasps onto aspects of its past that make it distinct, at the same time accepting change and the new as integral to remaining vibrant and pertinent (Cumings 1997:456–95). It is also a story that has changed the meaning of music and music making in my own life in surprising and profound ways; if this book succeeds in leading others to finding their own way with SamulNori and a love for Korean percussion music, I will feel doubly rewarded.

1

The *Namsadang*

Itinerant Troupe Performance Culture and the Roots of SamulNori

At the close of the Chosŏn period during the late eighteenth and nineteenth centuries there emerged from the shadows of official history a professional class of entertainers known as the *namsadang* (literally "male temple group"). Rooted in centuries-old traditions of enfolding ritual practices and itinerant troupe performance culture, the *namsadang* call to mind elements of the circus, carnival, and traveling gypsy group fused into a composite whole.[1] A society composed exclusively of males, they enchanted and inspired their rural Korean audiences through highly polished and artistically refined performances of percussion music and dance, bowl spinning, acrobatics, tightrope walking, mask dance, and puppetry.

The presence and activities of the *namsadang* suggest a number of important trends that anticipate major developments of the twentieth century identified in the introduction, namely nationalism, cosmopolitanism, and globalization (Nettl 2005:285). Loved by the populace and largely dismissed by the aristocracy, the *namsadang* were Korea's first true superstars, performers who served the role of mass entertainment long before the days of mediated experience (cosmopolitanism/globalization; Kim Wŏnho 1999:309). They supported or were part of a broader movement toward professionalization and presentational-style music making in the folk arena that was occurring at an accelerated pace in the fertile closing years of the Chosŏn period, including the genres of *sanjo* and *p'ansori* (cosmopolitanism; see Song Bang-song 2001 and Hesselink 2002). As such, their performances provide a window into the aesthetic sensibilities of the commoner classes. The *namsadang* also provide a much-needed explanatory logic for the existence of similar, if not identical, melodies and rhythms across the various provinces at a time when village inhabitants engaged in extremely limited travel and displayed strong regional alliances (Buzo 2002:5–8; Lee, Ki-baek 1995:184–85). As a cultural repository of early pan-regional identities, aspects of their costuming, acting, and musical repertoire influenced untold generations of local musicians, dancers, and actors (nationalism). And as early "fusion" artists, combining elements of Korean traditional music and performance practice with that of China and Mongolia, the *namsadang* prefigured cross-cultural encounters characteristic of late twentieth- and early twenty-first-century South Korea (globalization).

Equally important to the theme of this book—a focus on the challenges and meanings of tradition as presented in the twentieth century—is establishing the genealogical and philosophical connections between the *namsadang* and the founders of SamulNori. Long before it was popular or even advantageous to claim ties and allegiances to these performance troupes (for social and historical reasons; see below), SamulNori cofounders Kim Duk Soo (Kim Tŏksu) and Kim Yongbae were open and adamant about their involvement with the *namsadang* as a direct source of inspiration for the development of their new performance art (to be further addressed in chapter 2). Early and later commentators all picked up on this thread (Kim Hŏnsŏn 1988:100; Sohn, Tae-soo 1997; Ko, Susanna and Yi Chŏnggyu 2005:98–99; Nam Hwajŏng 2008:20), with the most direct evidence coming from the writings of Kim Duk Soo himself:

> I come from a tradition of professional performing artists. These artists in recent history banded together and while wandering in every nook and cranny of the country gave performances which included music, song, dance, tightrope walking and other artistic feats. (Kim Duk Soo 1992:7)

> This was due to the fact that the village band [*p'ungmul*] was maintained by non-professional musicians, who performed their music in the context of their everyday lives. The *Mu-kut* [shaman ritual music] on the other hand was performed by a professional shaman. The third performance group, the "professional entertainers," refers to the traveling artists such as the *Pongsan mask dance troupe* or the *Namsadang*. Not unlike the gypsies in the West, the members of this group possessed the best technical skills and artistic proficiency in their arts, on which they depended for their daily living and to acquire which they were most severely trained from an early age. Among them, the *Namsadang* are the direct forerunners of SamulNori. (Kim, Duk Soo et al. 1999:3)

A precise historical reckoning of the *namsadang* and their formative roots, however, is difficult to establish. Their performance and social habits during their heyday in the Chosŏn period placed them on the lowest possible rung of the social ladder, practices or conditions that included illiteracy, itinerancy, busking, and interracial marriage, to name just a few. By default this precluded them from any serious or sympathetic consideration in dynastic annals or other official literary accounts. And despite the immediate and potential value of identifying and understanding their place in the overall Korean traditional music landscape, textbooks and surveys of Korean music history make only passing reference to the *namsadang* (Chang Sahun 1986:476; Pak Kihwan 1987:111, 129) or none at all (Song Hye-jin 2000; Yi Sŏngch'ŏn et al. 1997), with one notable exception (Song Pangsong 2007:448–54).

The tantalizingly little we do know about the *namsadang*'s past comes almost entirely from the tireless efforts of Professor Shim Usŏng. A performer, arts promoter, folklorist, academic, political activist, and prolific author, Shim has dedicated most of his professional life to championing the cause of the *namsadang*. Based on extensive fieldwork with surviving troupe members in the 1960s, his primary writings on the topic include the initial cultural asset report submitted for the entire genre (Shim Usŏng 1968), the seminal book now considered a classic (Shim Usŏng 1994), and his work with the Office of Cultural Assets (Shim Usŏng and Song Ponghwa 2000; English translations of excerpts of these publications are found as Sim U-sŏng 1974 [part of the first chapter of the 1994 book] and Sim Woo-sung 1997 [a general overview]). In addition to writing on other aspects of Korean folk culture (1975, 1978, and 1998), Shim was also an organizational and motivational linchpin behind SamulNori's early concertizing and promotional efforts, to be further discussed in chapter 2.

Unless otherwise noted, all historical details in the discussion that follows are drawn from Shim Usŏng's 1994 classic *Namsadangp'ae yŏn'gu* (A Study of *Namsadang* Troupes). Shim's work stands alone in its diligence and thoroughness; no new substantive research has been conducted since its publication.[2] Current perspectives are based on my own brief fieldwork with the *namsadang* in Seoul in 2006, as well as a survey of the handful of master's theses written on the topic in the 1980s and '90s. This chapter is organized chronologically, beginning with the formative years of itinerant troupe performance culture, moving on to the *namsadang*'s heyday, decline, and finally revival. This account will provide not only the requisite historical and descriptive details of their existence and the nature of their activities for understanding subsequent references to the *namsadang* in this book, but also the broader context for interpreting how tradition as "preserving the old while creating the new" was achieved and passed on to its spiritual inheritors in SamulNori.

Formative Years (pre-1700s)

Written documentation on the *namsadang* during their formative years is sparse at best. Any mention of pre-Chosŏn (pre-1392) itinerant troupe performance activity is limited to passing references to puppet shows and theatrical groups accompanied by music, references found only in later writings of the Chosŏn period after the fact.[3] Shim Usŏng surmised that such folk entertainment groups were in existence already prior to the Shilla period (668 to 935), though he admits that this is speculation at best, gleaned from careful and at times creative ways of interpreting literary documents and dynastic annals. He also believed that these traveling artistic troupes were a mix of Korean and migrating tribes from other parts of Asia to the north, a supposition with some weight considering the numerous parallels between *namsadang* and early Chinese theatrical performance arts (Idema and West 1982; Mackerras 1983). In all cases such groups would have been made up of primarily the commoner classes.

Looking backwards from the material evidence of the eighteenth and nineteenth centuries, we can guess that performance troupes of the seventeenth century (if not earlier) were distinguished from one another by gender of membership (mixed troupes would have been unusual because of prohibitions against unmarried men and women traveling and living together), religious affiliation, means of support (sponsorship, fund-raising, or direct payment), nature of the performance art(s), and type of music used for accompaniment.

The Namsadang's Heyday (1700–1900)

By the beginning of the eighteenth century the *namsadang* were only one of a number of successful kinds of itinerant performance troupes traveling along the roads and byways of the Korean peninsula vying for the attention of the populace. Through more extensive documentation at the elite and commoner levels, it is now clear that at least three types of groups provided direct competition to the *namsadang*: *sadangp'ae*, *kŏllipp'ae*, and *kwangdae*. The first two groups were associated with Buddhist temples, while the third hailed from a long history of shaman-based arts.

Sadangp'ae (literally "temple group troupe"), also known as *yŏsadang* ("female temple groups"), were female fund-raising troupes that made their livelihood primarily through song and dance. Accompanied by drum and at times the flute, *sadangp'ae* had formal ties with Buddhist temples on whose behalf they would perform and sell charms. *Sadangp'ae* were unusual in that while their performance arts were strictly presented by females, they nevertheless traveled with male companions (*kŏsa*, literally "Buddhist devotees") who aided in organizational and financial matters. When fund-raising through performance was unsuccessful, these men were also responsible for supervising the fees paid (*hŏuch'ae*) for the *sadangp'ae*'s sexual services. Etymologically *sadangp'ae* and *namsadangp'ae* are closely related (one need only add the prefix *nam-*, meaning male), but according to Shim and a sizeable literature on *sadangp'ae* the two groups were actually quite distinct in their composition and scope of performance abilities.[4]

Also related to Buddhist temples, but with expanded skills and responsibilities, were *kŏllipp'ae* (also called *pinarip'ae*).[5] Literally meaning "fund-raising troupe," a typical group was composed of fifteen or so male members organized hierarchically under a top-ranking *hwaju* (leader). Their primary function was to perform household rituals for individual families on behalf of a local Buddhist temple. After a dramatic prelude or pre-show in which the troupe would perform percussion music and dance (*p'ungmul*), mask dance, and (depending on the skills of the members) bowl spinning, they would then engage in a series of propitiatory rituals for the deities of the living quarters, kitchen, and domestic well. Once the majority of the household rituals had been completed, the troupe would then conclude with a *sŏngju kut* (house god ritual). This performance of percussion and vocal music featured the recitation of a ritual offering (*pinari*); during and after this concluding ritual, grain and money were collected as payment. *Kŏllipp'ae* activity was absorbed into the local (rural) *p'ungmul* scene sometime during the Chosŏn period, and it continues to be an important component of student-based and community-led *p'ungmul* organizations in modern times.[6] The *namsadang* would take on many of the *kŏllipp'ae*'s roles in the early twentieth century (to be addressed further below).

All-male performance troupes that similarly emerged from the shadows of official history in the eighteenth century, the *kwangdae* were the closest relatives of the *namsadang* in terms of the scope and type of their performance arts. A full show by a *kwangdae* group included puppet theater, mask dance, acrobatics, and tightrope walking. Differences are marked by the shaman roots of most *kwangdae* activity, the use of percussion instruments in an accompanying role (unlike *kŏllipp'ae* and the *namsadang*), and the prevalence of vocal music and the use of wind and string instruments (a greater focus on melody). *Kwangdae* troupes are more famous for what they became in the nineteenth century: as the larger troupes disbanded, the vocalists went on to develop and refine a new solo genre (first known as *kwangdae* singers, later as *p'ansori*), followed soon thereafter by individual instrumentalists who went on to invent *sanjo* (solo instrumental suite) and contribute to the improvisatory (and later secular) ensembles known as *shinawi* (Song, Bang-Song 2000:219–44; Pihl 1994). *Kwangdae* troupes were all but extinct by the twentieth century.

With this brief survey of itinerant troupe performance culture in place, I now turn to the organization and performance activities of the *namsadang* at the height of their popularity.

Organization

The *namsadang* were all-male performance troupes organized hierarchically under a single powerful *kkoktusoe* (leader). The typical *kkoktusoe* needed recruitment skills, discipline, artistic vision, rehearsal acumen, diplomacy (negotiating with village elders), knowledge of geography (for life on the road), and the ability to secure housing and food, no mean feat considering the typical size of a troupe numbered between forty and fifty males ranging in ages from children to the elderly (see figure 1.1). *Kkoktusoe* were selected from the top level of performers (*ttŭnsoe*) and elected by a majority vote in a manner resembling modern democratic procedures; once in power, however, their authority was absolute. Membership in a *namsadang* troupe was rule-governed and often represented a lifelong commitment, with the ultimate decision of retention or dismissal residing in the *kkoktusoe*. Depending on the nature of an offense against the troupe,

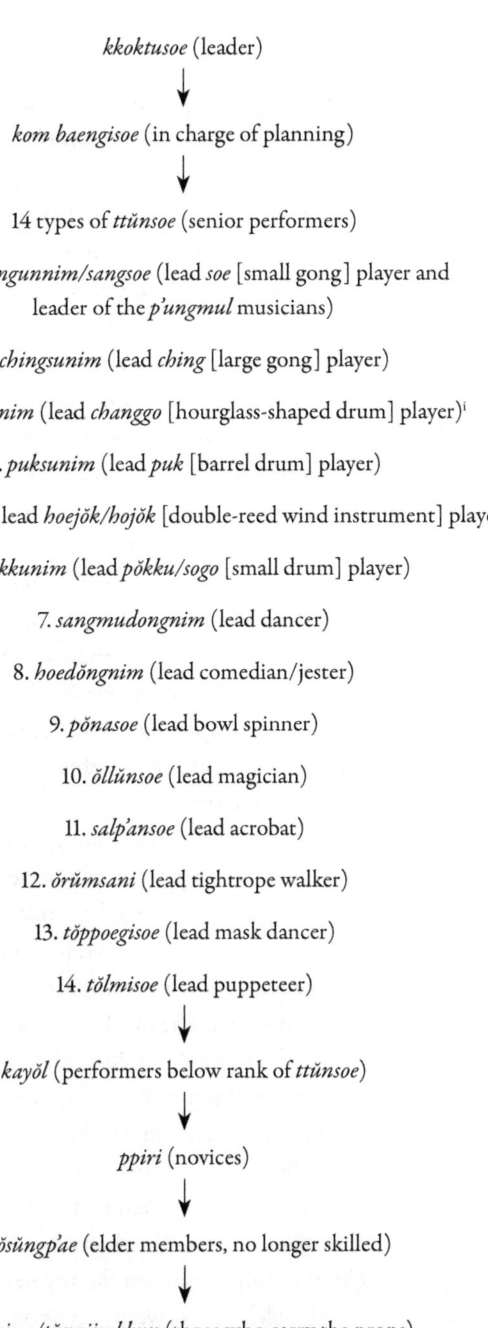

Figure 1.1 *Namsadang* organizational structure.

[i]For reasons of which I am unaware, the syllables for the name of the drum (*changgo*) are reversed when referring to this performer (*kojang*)

a *kkoktusoe* could assign flogging or the withholding of a meal; the most severe beatings were reserved for those who attempted to run away. Once a *kkoktusoe* lost the confidence of his troupe and/or was unable to perform at the requisite high level, a discussion and then vote would be called and a new leader elected.

Under the *kkoktusoe* was the *kombaengisoe*, an individual responsible for the organizational planning of all the performances. The *kombaengisoe* was also essentially the number two in charge when the *kkoktusoe* was unable to work, due to sickness or other more pressing matters. Below the *kombaengisoe* were the bread and butter of the troupe, the senior skilled performers known as *ttŭnsoe*. *Ttŭnsoe* were the public face of *namsadang* performances; the fate of the troupe was in their hands. These master artists were arranged into fourteen categories by performance type: musicians, mask dancers, comedians, acrobats, puppeteers, bowl spinners, and tightrope walkers (though everyone in the troupe was required to play a percussion instrument in the opening segment). The *ttŭnsoe* each had a number of *kayŏl*—skilled performers with less seniority—training under them whom they could choose to call upon in a performance (depending on the scale of the presentation), and the *kayŏl* in turn each had their own trainees (the *ppiri*). *Namsadang* troupes also took care of their elder members who were no longer able to perform, assigning them menial tasks (the roles of *chŏsŭngp'ae* and *nagwisoe*/*tŭngjimkkun*).

Competition for young *ppiri* was fierce among *namsadang* troupes. Any hope of longevity and financial security for a troupe resided in the successful recruitment of young boys who showed special promise (informally, members of a *namsadang* troupe were called *shikku*, literally "mouths to feed," an apt description of the most pressing concern for any *namsadang* performer of the eighteenth and nineteenth centuries). The ideal candidate had a combination of good looks, musical skills, and potential physical prowess. Recruits were drawn from children sold by poverty-stricken farmers, orphans, and runaways (Shim also cites instances of child abduction). In the beginning, *ppiri* were allowed to try their hands at all of the various performance arts; over time and under the watchful eye of the *kkoktusoe*, they were matched to a specific area. During this training period it was also common for the troupe to "lend out" *ppiri* and *kayŏl* to (male) village elders as companions under the names of *suttongmo* (male role) and *amdongmo* (female role).[7] There were exceptions, but in many cases the male roles were taken by *kayŏl* and the female roles by *ppiri*. Even when engaging in prostitution was not required, it was noted that in general the troupes with better-looking *ppiri* were more popular.[8]

Performance Activities

Because the primary audience of a *namsadang* performance was the inhabitants of fishing and farming villages throughout the Korean countryside, such performances were at their height from late spring with the planting of rice through the late fall at the end of the harvest. Every village owned a set of gongs (*kkwaenggwari/soe* and *ching*) and drums (*puk* and *changgo*) that were played by local *p'ungmul* musicians to help with the strain and tedium of labor.[9] By inviting a *namsadang* troupe, however, village inhabitants were promised the rare opportunity of a night of musical and acrobatic spectacle. The *namsadang* began by playing *p'ungmul* during the day while the farmers or laborers were working; after the labor was finished and dinner had been eaten, the inhabitants then enjoyed the *namsadang*'s show through the night to the light of cotton torches or pine knots set ablaze. Shim noted that such performances had two effects, not always complementary. Most commoners eagerly awaited the visitation by a wandering *namsadang* troupe, not only for the entertainment value but for the opportunity it afforded for social bonding and feelings of community. Village elders and/or landlords took advantage of this knowledge: although it cost them some money, they were able to work the farmers more efficiently, at the same time subduing any ill feelings their citizens might have been harboring.

Receiving an invitation to stay and perform at a village was not always automatic. Not all village heads were enthusiastic about the potential positive aspects of a *namsadang* presence; their itinerancy and rumors of interracial mixing and prostitution were often enough to keep them at bay. The typical procedure for the *namsadang* was to search for a village's communal labor flag (*yongdukki*, literally "dragon banner flag") flapping in the field during the season of communal labor. Once found, the *namsadang* would position themselves on a hill or embankment from which they could catch a bird's eye view of the village at a glance. They would then wave their signal flag (*yŏnggi*) and begin to play *p'ungmul* and display the more visually captivating elements of their performance repertoire. If they were successful in capturing the attention of some villagers, and the villagers were able to receive consent from their landlords, then the communal labor flag was waved as a signal to approach. The *kombaengisoe* would then enter the village and make a convincing case for his troupe in front of the village head and/or elder(s). According to interviews with surviving *namsadang* members consulted by Shim, in seven out of ten cases permission was not granted.

In the evening after the day's labor had been completed and dinner had been eaten, a torch or bonfire was lit in the large, wide-open communal meeting ground (*madang*) of the village, which became designated as the official performance space (a full performance by the *namsadang* was called a *madang kut*, literally "communal meeting ground ritual"). *Namsadang p'ungmul* musicians then marched through the village lanes collecting local inhabitants, forming a procession called *kil nori* (literally "road play"). While this took place, other *namsadang* members prepared the *madang*, including fastening the tightrope, setting up the stand and curtains for the puppet show, and laying out five or six straw mats in the center for the bowl spinning, acrobatics, and mask dance to take place (see figure 1.2). A troupe would perform their extended repertoire with even the basic assurance of a night's room and board, though of course some kind of additional financial remuneration was the ideal. It was also common to

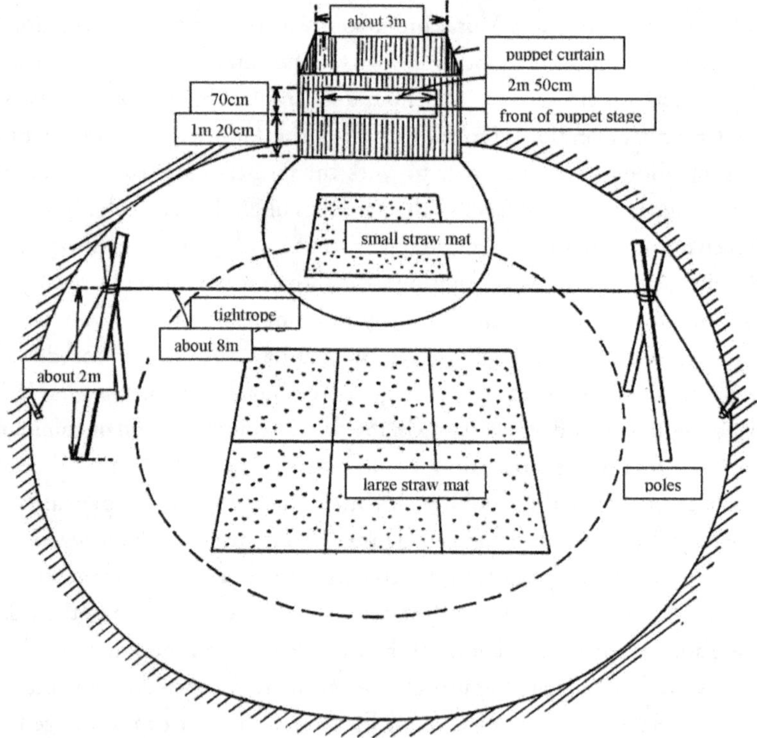

Figure 1.2 The performance space (*norip'an*) of a *namsadang* troupe (adapted from Shim Usŏng 1994:38).

Key for audience seating. Outer circle: boundary for *p'ungmul* performance; inner center circle (larger): boundary for bowl spinning, acrobatics, tightrope walking, and mask dance; inner upper circle (smaller): boundary for puppet theater.

receive traveling expenses from the village inhabitants out of personal gratitude when the troupe left the next day. It is worth pointing out here that the *namsadang* were not raising funds on behalf of a Buddhist temple, in spite of the etymology of their designation ("male [Buddhist] temple troupe").

During the high season of performance activity the *namsadang* traveled widely among the eight provinces of Korea, moving north when it became hot and south when it began to turn cold. A number of troupes went as far north as Manchuria, performing for and picking up influences from local audiences. Such itinerancy resulted in a show that was pan-regional and international in content (to be discussed further below under the specific performance arts). The most difficult time of year for a troupe, however, was during the winter. Reserves from the spring and summer months had to last during this period of inactivity; if supplies were insufficient, the troupe dispersed and went begging until the next spring, at which point they reassembled. This cycle was a vicious and self-fulfilling one: successful troupes were able to rest in *namsadang*-friendly areas throughout the country, where they could then recruit, rehearse, and teach the various skills to the junior members of the group.[10] *Namsadang* troupes unable to stay together during the winter months lost valuable time and opportunity to improve, and hence their competitive edge. This most likely accounts for both the decrease in number of troupes and the increase in professionalization and specialization within the surviving ones in the late nineteenth century.

Below are the six performance arts presented in a complete *namsadang* show. Typically the performance began around 7:00 PM and lasted until 3:00 or 4:00 the next morning. It should be noted, however, that not all troupes had enough skilled performers in all of these areas, and also that some troupes chose to withhold some of the more involved aspects of the performance—such as the puppet show or tightrope walking—if they felt their payment was too low.

Percussion Music and Dance (*p'ungmul*)

The *namsadang* always opened with a rousing performance of *p'ungmul* by all of the physically proficient members. Their skill and preference for percussion instruments put them in the same company as the *kŏllipp'ae* (Buddhist fund-raising groups) but distinguished them from the *kwangdae* and *sadangp'ae*. Shim acknowledges that his primary research consultants were from the *uttari* region of Korea—the central provinces of Kyŏnggi and Ch'ungch'ŏng, as well as the capital Seoul—and hence his data favored the rhythms and practices of this area. But even in this report he acknowledges the musical influences from other provinces, which is immediately apparent in his listing of rhythmic cycles that includes samplings from the southwest and southeast (Shim Usŏng 1994:39–40).[11] This influence went both directions: by the early twentieth century many local *p'ungmul* groups had fully integrated rhythms from beyond their immediate provincial borders as a direct result of witnessing and emulating the *namsadang* (see Shim Hyesŭng 1987).

This opening segment of percussion music and dance was called the *p'an kut* and it represented a tightly composed and choreographed succession of rhythms and accompanying ground formations (all musicians danced while they played; see figure 1.3). Once the entire troupe had performed as a unit, the performance then showcased dances by individual instrument families, followed by child acrobatics (*mudong*) and a dramatic conclusion that featured the manipulation of spinning-tasseled hats (generically referred to as *sangmo*). Unlike in local and predominantly amateur performances of *p'ungmul*, onlookers were not allowed to enter the performance space and dance or play along. The issue was in most cases a moot one, because villagers were apparently completely enthralled by the technical proficiency of the playing and spinning-tasseled hats. Master small gong (*soe*) and hourglass drum (*changgo*) players—top-ranking *ttŭnsoe*

Figure 1.3 *P'an kut* performance by *namsadang*, 2006 (photo by Nathan Hesselink).

members—have been immortalized in song and poetry (Kim Inu 1993:115–18), and it is now recognized that the ubiquitous presence of acrobatics and spinning-tasseled hats in modern *p'ungmul* groups of nearly all sizes and regional loyalties can be directly credited to the *namsadang* (see especially Hesselink 1998:317–18). Shim notes the small concession made to active participation by the allowance of two lucky villagers to become flag bearers—one carrying a signal flag (*yŏnggi*) and one a farming flag (*nonggi*)—as a small token of gratitude.

Bowl Spinning (*pŏna*)

Pŏna is the feat of spinning frames of sieves,[12] soup bowls, or wash basins on a stick made from cherry wood; in current times performers have added the use of a long tobacco pipe for heightened dramatic effect. In the past it was believed that *pŏna* included juggling as part of the act, but no modern troupes feature this particular skill. *Pŏna* is akin to Chinese dish spinning—a practice that continues to this day—and is theatrically rich, due to witty remarks and banter exchanged between the bowl spinner and a clown or jester character known as a *sorikkun*. The performance is classified according to the type of object being spun: soup bowl *pŏna*, knife *pŏna*, fishing pole *pŏna*, or frame of sieve *pŏna*.

Acrobatics (*salp'an*)

The acrobatic portion of the performance known as *salp'an* is so-named after the saying "If you're good at this you live (*sal p'an*), if you're bad at it you die." Originally one of the principal entertainments of shaman-based itinerant troupes (including groups directly related to the *kwangdae*), it has now also become part of the *namsadang* performance. For modern audiences *salp'an* resembles the floor routines of Olympic gymnasts, including cartwheels, hand stands, and back flips, with the exception of the jester character (*sorikkun*) who exchanges witty remarks with the lead acrobat. The various acrobatic feats are performed according to an established order and are matched to the rhythms of the percussionists. Performances are split nearly 50/50 between acrobatics and witty remarks, similar to the bowl spinning event.

Tightrope Walking (*ŏrŭm*)[13]

A performance of *ŏrŭm* was generally reserved for special guests by invitation only, often from a government officer or member of the aristocracy. *Ŏrŭm* was special in that there was no set fee—though some kind of additional payment was expected—and that its content and humor were organized completely according to the tastes of the villagers, in spite of the elite sponsorship. Korean tightrope walking (also known generically as *chult'agi*) is an example of slackwire, such that the tension on the rope is only provided by the performer and his prop (a fan in the Korean context). Visually the performance is dominated by a series of impressive steps, reversals, and bounces generated by a spreading of the legs and falling to the crotch. The tightrope walker also, however, sings and exchanges witty remarks with the jester—similar to the bowl spinning and acrobatics events—, conversation that can be characterized as direct and frequently crude. All elements of the performance are matched to the rhythms of the drums and gongs.

Mask Dance (*tŏppoegi*)

The designation *tŏppoegi* comes from "to see (*poegi*) double (*tŏp*)," a reference to the masks worn by the performers. As much theater as it is dance, the *namsadang*'s *tŏppoegi* (also known generically as *t'al ch'um*) is very much akin to regional mask-dance dramas throughout Korea in its biting satire and criticism of the ruling classes (including Buddhist monks). A full performance of *tŏppoegi* is composed of four movements: (1) *madang ssishi* (cleanse the ground); (2) *omt'al chabi* (literally "scabies mask performer"); (3) *saennim chabi* (gentleman scholar); and (4) *mŏkchung chabi* (apostate monk). In the first movement the performance space is established through a symbolic cleansing; in the second, foreign influences are removed; in the third, internal contradictions are resolved; and in the fourth, foreign (Buddhist) religion is rejected. Various masks are used, including *saennim* (gentleman scholar), *noch'inne* (aged parent), *ch'wibari* (prodigal servant), *malttugi* (servant), *mŏkchung* (apostate monk), *omjung* (monk with boil on face), *p'ijori* (niece), *kkŏksoe* (servant), and *changsoe* (servant).[14] The frame of the mask is made by gluing paper over a gourd; eye holes and a mouth hole are then cut out, after which a traditional form of glue paint—a mixture of glue, flour, and mineral powder—is applied.[15]

Puppetry (*tŏlmi*)

Tŏlmi (as it was called by *namsadang* performers), also known as *kkoktugakshi norŭm*, is Korea's only folk puppet theater. Phrases associated with *tŏlmi*, such as "*mok tŏlmi-rŭl chwigo*" (grasp the back of the neck [*tŏlmi*]) and "*mongdungi-rŭl chwigo*" (grasp the stick), indicate the prevalence of rod puppets, though in the past many other types were employed, including marionettes, glove puppets with strings, and puppets made from hemp sacks. According to Shim, the plays address three broad issues similar in scope to that of the mask dances: (1) resistance against the oppression and social structure of the ruling classes; (2) criticism of foreign religion as conveyed through satire focusing on an apostate monk; and (3) the simple and honest desires of the populace. A full collection by a successful *namsadang* troupe includes at least forty puppets and ten small props.

The performance area for the puppet theater is concealed on four sides by a curtain (refer again to figure 1.2). A space is left open in the front that acts as a stage where the puppets are manipulated. The main puppeteer (*taejabi*) sits in the center, while at his side are seated two assistant puppeteers (*taejabibo*) who help with the entrances and exits of the puppets. Out in front of the stage, slightly off-center, sits a vocalist (*sanbadi*) who converses with the puppets (similar in role to the jester), and next to him sit the accompanying musicians on gongs, drums, and the double-reed shawm the *nallari*. The performance is divided into two movements with seven independent yet related scenes.[16] Most puppets and props are carved out of paulownia or willow wood and are decorated with traditional glue paint. They range in size from twenty centimeters to one meter.[17]

Decline and Dormancy (1900–1960)

At the beginning of the twentieth century the popularity and hence demand for itinerant troupes began to wane. A combination of national internal strife, changing leisure habits, economic hardship, and eventual colonization of Korea by Japan in 1910 all conspired against the *namsadang* and similar performance organizations. In an attempt to keep afloat, a number of *namsadang* troupes joined together with *kŏllipp'ae* (previously mentioned fund-raising troupes), a move that on the surface was relatively easy due to both groups' reliance on percussion instruments.[18] Continuing under the banner of the *namsadang*, many such troupes established relationships with Buddhist temples, at the same time allowing for female members to join (some from the ranks of *sadangp'ae*). Shim lamented such indiscriminate mixing from the perspective of an academic looking to document the "true essence" of the previously separate institutions, but as a human being he understood the obstacles that were presented during the era. An early photo of a *namsadang* performance featuring *mudong* (child acrobatics) exists from around 1910 (figure 1.4).

Figure 1.4 Early *namsadang* photograph, c. 1910.

From Shim's research we now know that six *namsadang* troupes from the central region of Korea survived until the end of the 1930s, at which point the Japanese officially clamped down on such activity. These troupes were: (1) the Kaedari Troupe (also called the Paudŏgi or Kim Amdŏk Troupe), based in Kyŏnggi province and named after the female leader (*kkoktusoe*) Paudŏgi (previously a *sadang*); (2) the O Myŏngsŏn Troupe, based in Hwanghae province (present-day North Korea); (3) the Shim Sŏnok Troupe, based in Kyŏnggi province and which claimed later legendary *p'ungmul* performers Kim Munhak and Yang Toil (a teacher of SamulNori cofounder Kim Duk Soo); (4) the Ansŏng Pongmani Troupe, based in Kyŏnggi province and which claimed another famous teacher of Kim Duk Soo, Nam Hyŏngu; (5) the Wŏn Yuktŏk Troupe, based in Kyŏnggi province (the group disbanded in 1939 in Manchuria); and (6) the Yi Wŏnbo Troupe, based in Kyŏnggi province but which spent the majority of its time around the outskirts of the capital Seoul.[19] As I mentioned previously, Shim's research was largely confined to the central region of Korea. While we can assume that *namsadang* also existed in other provinces, the only hard evidence I have been able to locate is a 1934 black-and-white photograph taken in the west coast city of Kyŏngju, though there is nothing that indicates whether the troupe was locally based or was visiting from another province (see No Tongŭn 1995:206).

From 1941 (early in World War II) through roughly the end of the Korean War (1953), there was almost no *namsadang* activity, as performers either went into professional hibernation or decided to "get out of the business" altogether. Biding their time, a few revivalist groups in modified form—no more itinerancy, and mixed groups of men and women, for example—began to assemble in the mid-1950s. The first documented effort was in 1954 under the leadership of the renowned lead small gong (*soe*) player Nam Hyŏngu/Unyong. Joining with members of the earlier Kaedari Troupe in and around the city of Ansŏng (Kyŏnggi province), the group was initially identified as the Ansŏng Farmers' Music Group (Ansŏng Nongaktae). Nam left the group only a few years later to lead a different (and competing) troupe, and it would take nearly forty years for Ansŏng Nongaktae to become officially recognized as a *namsadang* troupe with full financial backing from the Kyŏnggi provincial and Ansŏng county governments (see below). SamulNori's cofounder Kim Duk Soo would also join a makeshift *namasadang* troupe formed by his father in the late 1950s.

Under the radar of many governmental officials and even performers during this period was a young man by the name of Shim Usŏng who had heard the tales of the great *namsadang* artists of yesteryear. The *namsadang*'s revival in the 1960s is in many ways the story of Shim's single-handed hard work and perseverance to bring recognition to the then little-known history of itinerant troupe performance culture, a story to which I now turn.

Revival (1960-present)

As a budding academic and political activist, Shim saw the need for a detailed account of older folk practices that were under threat of extinction in a country that had begun to look to the West for cultural models. A few years ahead of the curve (the South Korean government would promulgate the Cultural Asset Preservation Law in 1962), in the late 1950s Shim began to actively search out surviving *namsadang* members scattered about the countryside in an attempt to document and revive their performances from before the colonial period (pre-1910). While Shim was able to find a number of older famous performers who could help him with historical details and establish troupe lineages, he admitted that many individuals wished to conceal their past histories in an attempt to "cleanse" their family background while providing a blank slate for their children. Many of these men had become destitute, and so Shim began to invite *namsadang* who were willing and able to perform to come live with him in his home, all at his own personal expense. Over the next few years he attained a kind of critical mass, and so in 1960 he spearheaded the formation of the Minsokkŭkhoe Namsadang, or "Folk Theater Association Namsadang," based in Seoul.[20] Representing many of the finest musicians and performers of the day, this group has attained legendary status within current *namsadang* and *samul nori* circles (the 1960 roster is reproduced in appendix 1).[21]

In 1964 the *namsadang*'s puppetry element (*kkoktugakshi norŭm*) was recognized as National Important Intangible Cultural Asset No. 3 by the South Korean government (Pak Hŏnbong and Yi Tuhyŏn 1964). In the early 1960s Shim continued to carry on research while simultaneously lobbying for the inclusion of the entire performance under the name *namsadang*. Shim compiled and submitted the initial cultural asset report for the entire genre as early as 1968 (see Shim Usŏng 1968), and in 1974 he published the first edition of his monumental *Namsadangp'ae yŏn'gu* (A Study of *Namsadang* Troupes); it would take another fourteen years, however, for all six performance arts to be recognized and subsumed under this designation (in 1988). In spite of such official neglect, the Minsokkŭkhoe Namsadang—as well as the regional troupe based in Ansŏng—began to train a new generation of younger performers, including in the 1970s a then unknown percussion prodigy by the name of Kim Yongbae (cofounder of SamulNori along with Kim Duk Soo, who also studied with members of the Seoul troupe). Shim's relationship with both Kims is further discussed in chapter 2.

The nationally designated cultural asset *namsadang* team—as the Minsokkŭkhoe Namsadang would come to be known—currently includes three artists who enjoy the status of individual "holder" (*poyuja*) of a cultural asset: Pak Kyesun and Nam Kihwan (for puppetry, mask dance, and percussion music and dance), and Pak Yongt'ae (for mask dance).[22] The national troupe was featured at the 2002 World Cup in Seoul, and soon thereafter they established an office in Seoul, where regular instruction is now provided for the percussion music accompanying the various acts (to be discussed further below). An offshoot of this troupe also exists under the name of Namsadang Yemaek Yesultan (The Yea-Meak [Namsadang] Traditional Performing Arts Troupe). This group has extended the repertoire to include modern and Asian (non-Korean) elements, and in 1997 they released an instructional video for percussion music and dance (Nam Kisu 1997, *P'ungmul mit samul nori punsŏk*; Nam Kisu is brother to Nam Kihwan and son of Pak Kyesun, both cultural asset holders).

The previously mentioned regional *namsadang* troupe from Ansŏng was recognized as Kyŏnggi Province Important Intangible Cultural Asset No. 21 in 1997. Known more commonly as Ansŏng Namsadang (Ansŏng is a city located near P'yŏngt'aek), the group's official name is Ansŏng Shirip Namsadang Paudŏgi P'ungmultan (Ansŏng City's Namsadang "Paudŏgi Percussion Group").

Its namesake, Paudŏgi, was a famous female lead puppeteer who was born in Ansŏng and died at the age of twenty-three (Paudŏgi was with the Kaedari Troupe, one of the six surviving troupes from the 1930s; see also Chu Kanghyŏn 1996:188–207). Every year from late spring through the fall, Ansŏng Namsadang puts on a weekly Saturday evening performance of all the acts except the puppetry, and every fall they hold a special "Baudeogi [Paudŏgi] Festival." As of 2003 they also regularly perform a musical based on the *namsadang* repertoire called simply "Baudeogi."[23] In 2004, they were invited to the Athens Olympics, where they gave a 1.5-hour performance thirteen nights in a row.

With the completion of a *samul nori* apprenticeship in Seoul in 2001 came my desire to understand the historical and performative roots of the *namsadang* and their connections—if any—to current *samul nori* approaches and performance practices. I was already aware of Shim Usŏng's work, and so I began to explore and expand the scope of my search to include Korean research outside of music, as well as the work of foreign academics. Concentrated mostly within the late 1990s and early 2000s, Shim's work was the basis for the research of a number of Korean authors working on itinerant culture (e.g., Kim, Young Ja 1981 and Kim Hŏnsŏn 1995:27–73), as well as Western researchers in cultural studies interested in the dynamics of *namsadang* gender roles and sexual politics (Murray 2002:243–47 and Senelick 2000:30–31). Korean master's theses either focused on biographical studies[24] or on structural and pedagogical aspects of the percussion music and dance with the regionally based Ansŏng Namsadang (Yu Yŏngnyŏl 2000 and Han Pŏmt'aek 2003). No new historical research had been conducted since Shim's book, and almost nothing had been written on the national troupe in Seoul and any potential relationships they might have forged with Kim Duk Soo and other *samul nori* teams.

Few could have predicted the public response to the commercial film *The King and the Clown* (*Wang ŭi namja*) released late 2005. Featuring members of Ansŏng Namsadang, the story was a largely fictionalized account of a *namsadang* troupe invited to take residence in the imperial court during the Chosŏn period. Not looking to sugarcoat the more controversial aspects of *namsadang* history or their lower social class status, the film included scenes of extremely crude dialogue (appropriately held between performers and the jester character during mask dance or tightrope segments), prostitution, and an ambiguous homoerotic relationship between the two main characters.[25] In spite of such subject matter—or, perhaps precisely because of what it added to the underdog spirit of the narrative—the film was an overwhelming success, breaking all previously held box office records (12.3 million tickets were sold domestically). Its release accomplished what decades of research had not: an appreciation of the artistry of the *namsadang* was finally brought—or, more accurately, reintroduced—to the entire Korean population (Chin Nara 2006).

Suddenly and dramatically the *namsadang* were freed from the realm of isolated academic publications and conferences and thrust into mainstream consciousness. Most Koreans would not have recognized the actual tightrope walker engaged in the breathtaking stunts (the master artist Kwŏn Wŏnt'ae[26] from Ansŏng Namsadang), but many were impressed enough to search out *namsadang* teachers to study tightrope walking, as well as the art of bowl spinning.[27] Looking to capitalize on the subject of the film (and unaware of its eventual success), the national troupe in Seoul received special funding to produce a full performance of *namsadang* arts for the citizens of Seoul to coincide with the film's release date. Ansŏng Namsadang was quick to follow, opening a *The King and the Clown* museum only a few months later near the grounds of their troupe's weekly public performances in Ansŏng. Having been made aware of this flourish of activity by relatives living in Korea, my curiosity no longer allowed for me to ponder the *namsadang* from afar. By May 2006 I was enrolled in the national troupe's training institute in downtown Seoul, taking regular lessons in percussion and the *ch'ae sangmo* spinning-tasseled hat.

When I first began my study, staff at the institute assumed that I had seen the film and was interested in learning aspects of "traditional Korea." General enrollment at the institute had increased fivefold, a direct result of the film's success (according to the director and *namsadang* "master artist" [*isuja*] Kim Chinmu; personal communication, 2006). When I indicated that my real motivation was to look into connections between the *namsadang* and SamulNori, as well as gain some practical skill in some of the performance arts, the instructors were quick to highlight how indebted SamulNori was to the *namsadang*, but also how much the *namsadang* had in turn begun to incorporate elements of the SamulNori repertoire and its performance practices. My primary teachers, the master artists Kim Chinmu and An Chungbŏm, very early on pointed out that the founding members of both the original SamulNori group (Kim Duk Soo and Kim Yongbae) and the split-off team of the National Center for Korean Traditional Performing Arts (Kim Yongbae and Nam Kimun) were all from the official *namsadang* ranks (see further chapter 2). SamulNori's first piece at their premiere in 1978—"Uttari p'ungmul" (rhythms from the central region)—was a modified version of the main performance repertoire of the *namsadang*, and, in an interesting feedback loop, this seated version of "Uttari p'ungmul" had become the default piece for instruction at the *namsadang*'s training institute. On

August 2 that summer the *namsadang* even included a SamulNori-style seated portion on their program for the first time, a move I interpreted as a nod to SamulNori, who had begun including bowl spinning (a *namsadang* act) with its documented tour of France a year earlier in 2005 (see the DVD collection *Han'guk ŭi hon*).

With time, however, I realized that the changes that had been incorporated at the *namsadang* institute were only cosmetic; when I approached the institute's director the following year to look into the possibility of writing new music for their ensemble, or of incorporating non-Korean instruments into their lineup, I was told politely but quickly that such modifications were strictly against cultural asset policy. And there was the rub: for everything else positive that cultural asset policies had achieved, including financial security, raised social status, and a modicum of domestic and international recognition, the *namsadang* were nevertheless trapped in time, no longer allowed to expand and innovate as had their predecessors over the previous centuries. For the younger generation of *namasadang* performers—especially Kim Duk Soo and Kim Yongbae—this situation was unacceptable. And so in the next chapter I turn to the ascendancy of urban culture in South Korea in the 1970s and the challenges and opportunities that were presented to those who looked to reinvent and reinvigorate the original meaning of what it meant to be a *namsadang*.

2

Coming to the City

Urbanization, Scale, and New Loci of Cultural Authority

The 1970s marked a crucial turning point in the collective consciousness of a rapidly developing South Korean nation. A decade overshadowed by intense authoritarianism under President Park Chung-Hee (1961–79), brutal suppression of organized labor and student movements, and modernization trends that threatened older, inherited ways of relating to each other and the natural world, this period simultaneously witnessed a new confidence in what it meant to be "Korean," a "sense of ethnic pride in Korean achievement and potential after decades of subjugation to foreign standards" (Buzo 2002:140; see also Whang In-joung 1981; Cumings 1997:356–93; Buzo 2002:122–43). Increasingly emboldened nationalistic scholars, a burgeoning "people's" (*minjung*) movement, and sympathetic governmental cultural policies all converged in an effort at rediscovering and/or re-creating aspects of and practices related to traditional culture (Abelmann

1996:20–27; Yang Jongsung 2003:57, 97). The musicologist and critic Hahn Myong-hee [Han Myŏnghŭi], an early and faithful chronicler of the phenomenon of SamulNori, provides a succinct account of the potent confluence of nostalgia, late 1970s zeitgeist, and the emergence of the percussion quartet:

> SamulNori's formation in the late 1970s was one further manifestation of what cannot help but be regarded as a sociological phenomenon. By the end of the '70s, many Koreans had come to an important point in a process of self-awareness including a rise in interest in Korean Studies and the traditional performing arts. Politically it was a time when the power structure of our country was pressing heavily on our consciousness. It was these preconditions, so to speak, a newly emerging sensitivity to things Korean and the desire to release pent-up frustrations arising from the country's political situation, that found an effective release in the music of SamulNori. The music reminded listeners of half forgotten customs, mores, and the accompanying emotive life style. It awakened people to the cohesiveness of their own ethnic heritage. The music was superbly suited to the age. Exquisite and original, SamulNori's dynamic seemed to penetrate directly to the bone, spurring the release of built-up anger and frustration. In short, it was the perfect way to relieve the sorely tried hearts of the era. (Hahn, Myong-hee 1992:6; see also Han Myŏnghŭi 1992a:19 and Han, Myung-hee 1993:35)

Hourglass drum (*changgo*) virtuoso and SamulNori cofounder Kim Duk Soo was similarly aware of the timing of the group's appearance on this culturally and politically charged stage, an era when many believed that traditional Korean music was being lost and that the country had suffered for far too long under foreign rule (extending back in the consciousness of many Koreans to the Japanese occupation of the early twentieth century; Korean Conservatorium of Performing Arts 1992:9–10; An Hosang 1994:22).

Viewed through the narrow historical prism of SamulNori's successes and fame, however, accounts such as Hahn's overlook the existence of deep and strong sociopolitical movements connected to nationalistic musical activities that characterize the 1970s. SamulNori was only a small part of a much broader trend toward the promotion of Korean performing arts as a bulwark against the onslaught of Western cultural ideas and influences, an all-engrossing project to "re-establish a distinctive national identity" (Van Zile 2001:19). Artists and organizations under the banner of the *minyo undong* (folksong movement), for example, envisioned a society where traditional genres such as folksong and mask dance could be reintegrated into everyday life, efforts that complemented concurrent *minjung* (people's) theorizing (Koo, Hagen 1993:160; Howard 2006b:84). Progressive in outlook from its beginnings, the movement's revival of such genres went hand in hand with updating and producing new compositions for a general public that had become estranged from the sounds of traditional music (Yi Yŏngmi 1999:187–252; Howard 2006c:71–88). Recent analysis has suggested that similar stirrings in the folk percussion world (the *p'ungmul undong*, or drumming and dance movement) laid the groundwork for the possibility of SamulNori's breakthrough (Yi Soyŏng 2005:234–36).

A related feature that distinguished this period was the formal acceptance of traditional music in centers of higher learning. The founding of the Seoul Traditional Arts High School (Sŏul Kugak Yesul Kodŭng Hakkyo) in early 1960—the first such institution in South Korea—created generations of student-performers eager to continue their studies at the collegiate level the following decade (Sejong munhwa hoegwan chŏnsa p'yŏnjip wiwŏnhoe 2002:229). Following Seoul National University's lead beginning in 1959, the next three major universities to open traditional music departments did so in the 1970s: Hanyang University in 1972, and Ewha Woman's University and Chugye University of the Arts in 1974. In addition to supporting more established traditional genres, academia became the primary operating base for *ch'angjak kugak* (newly composed traditional music)—alternatively known as *shin kugak* (new traditional music)—, creative attempts at fusing the old with the new (Han Myŏnghŭi et al. 2001:267–69). Composers as passionate and motivated as their counterparts in the folksong and folk percussion movements similarly drew upon traditional materials in their search for a contemporary answer to the call to being Korean: "The rise of national pride and solidarity in the late 1970s, which called for Korean music with the distinctiveness and superiority of a Korean identity, . . . provided a paragon of the ideal for the new musical culture" (Ch'ae, Hyun-kyung 2000:151; see also Finchum-Sung 2003). An explosion of new works followed, fueling a slow but steady rise in public interest in the emerging art form and prompting students from various departments of Korean traditional music to commence regular performance series on campuses (Ch'ae, Hyun-kyung 2000:144–45).

Regardless of genre, motivation, or compositional approach, however, importantly the guiding orientation of these 1970s trends was an adaptation and reorientation to *urban* contexts and spaces. The city landscape and its changing frameworks of meaning began to challenge the countryside as the locus of Korean traditional music activity and authority. Focusing on Seoul as the administrative, financial, and cultural capital of South Korea, in this chapter I pay special attention to folk music groups and organizations and the precedents they set for SamulNori's genesis. Beginning with a background examination of the most active and influential concert halls of the period, the discussion will then move to the premiere folk music promotional society and its key players. There is little question that SamulNori appeared at the right place at the right time in a historically ripe moment; but as with all "new" forms of performative art, they could only do so by "standing on the shoulders" of those before and about them.

Concert Hall Culture

While broad societal support for traditional music within South Korea was still in its infancy in the 1970s, greater opportunities for folk musicians arose as a result of a flourish of concert hall construction and concert activity in the cities (Yi Sŏngch'ŏn 1980:335, 339–47; Lee, Byong Won 1997:10–12). The significance of the move from the fields and communal meeting spaces (*p'an*) to the stage cannot be overstated, signaling as it did a profound change in performance and reception aesthetics. Many of the original village contexts for folk music made little sense in the new urban environment. Institutionalized timetables favored the flow of money rather than the flow of the seasons, while paid admission to many events had implications for professionalism that were not always appropriate. A typical hall's construction frustrated communal participation—characteristic of many folk genres—with its focus on one-way communication from stage to audience, and the idea of a "piece" of music as an autonomous work of art subtly began to take hold (all further discussed in chapter 3).

On the heels of such construction came large Western performing ensembles to fill these predominantly massive spaces. Symphony orchestras, opera companies, and ballet troupes from the United States and Europe slowly but surely began to add South Korea to their itineraries; combined with the novelty and impressive nature of these structures, such performances began to undermine the appeal and even necessity for many of the older, smaller, and more humbly conceived events of the countryside. Such a drastic transformation of scale—promoting the "bigger is better" phenomenon—was not the only side effect of the transformed and transforming urban landscape. In the past when the *namsadang* came to a village (to cite a familiar example), both the commoner and aristocratic classes were able and willing to attend. Social hierarchies were still acknowledged and maintained, but access was not limited to one's social or financial standing. With the increasingly elite stature of the concert hall—restricted to citizens of the capital and those able to purchase a ticket—such distinctions were strengthened through attendance as a marker of class and taste, a trend accompanying concert hall construction in other parts of the world (Bourdieu 1984; Broyles 1992; Small 1998). Viewed within broader related trends of a rapidly modernizing South Korea, such practices contributed to the general population's ambivalent attitude toward folk culture and the increasing embrace of anything foreign (Hesselink 2002:720).

In the discussion that follows I describe the major folk music venues in Seoul that were available to SamulNori in the late 1970s. Beyond the historical significance of identifying these halls is the *nature* of the performances being mounted during this crucial time period. As will immediately become apparent, folk music groups and associations quickly adapted to the indoor stages in ways that often emulated their larger Western counterparts. SamulNori was not the first ensemble to present folk music in this new setting, nor even the first to evoke the percussive soundscape of the countryside. But what is central to understanding and appreciating the choices SamulNori made was how they distinguished themselves in contrast to such trends in their choice of a stripped-down ensemble, and in their preference for smaller and more intimate spaces.

Sejong Munhwa Hoegwan (Sejong Center for the Performing Arts) / Sŏul Shimin Hoegwan (Seoul Civic Center)

Construction on the Sejong Center for the Performing Arts, a prominent fixture of central Seoul located along Sejong Way just a few blocks south of Kyŏngbokkung Royal Palace, began in 1974. Named—like the road and the statue that now adorns it—after the legendary Chosŏn period king and cultural hero, the Sejong Center has remained the most high profile and prestigious venue of its kind in South Korea. Built on the site of the previous Sŏul Shimin Hoegwan (Seoul Civic Center), which burned down in 1972 on the evening of the Korean equivalent of the Grammy's, the Civic Center (and later Sejong Center) was home to and especially associated with the Sŏul-shi Kugak Kwanhyŏn Aktan (Seoul City Traditional Music Orchestra), Korea's first professional traditional music orchestra (their inaugural performance was on August 25, 1964). The idea of a "traditional music orchestra" was, of course, a direct influence of its Western classical counterpart, complete with a number of musicians to a part, performing on chairs with music stands (most of these instrumental genres would have previously been memorized), and a performance aesthetic that stressed uniformity of sound within the sections, generally without any improvisation or personal freedom of expression (uncharacteristic of many of the traditions from which these instruments hailed).

The Sejong Center, like its immediate predecessor, was an enormous enterprise organized around a large primary performance space. Sejong's Great Hall, designed initially for Western musical, theatrical, and dance productions, has three tiers with a total of 3,022 seats—the previous Civic Center had roughly 3,200 seats—and represents Korea's largest surviving hall. The hall also houses the largest pipe organ in all of Asia. From its inception, the Sejong Center has conferred considerable prestige on individuals, ensembles, and companies fortunate enough to grace its main stage. The Great Hall's size has naturally dictated the kind and scale of events that take place; by default, it favors large groups and grand spectacles. It is also a testament to the importance placed on public culture by a government and country that had not yet achieved its exponential rise in GDP as part of the "miracle on the Han River" (see figure 2.1).

Early experiments with staged folk music had already begun in 1965 with the March 2 performance of "Kwanhyŏnak t'aryŏng shinawi" (a shaman-inspired

Figure 2.1 Sejong Center's Great Hall, 2009 (photo by Nathan Hesselink).

large ensemble piece) and *sŭngmu* (Buddhist drum dance). By 1968 there was a regular rotation of traditional folk genres in smaller lineups—including *sanjo* (solo instrumental suite), *shijo* (short lyric song), *minyo* (folksong), and *p'ansori* (storytelling through song)—alongside elite ones, though newly composed works for larger ensembles such as traditional orchestra or dance troupe prevailed. A year later individual drum dances such as the *sogo ch'um* (small frame drum dance) and *changgo ch'um* (hourglass drum dance, albeit with *kisaeng* [female entertainer] influences) from the rural folk drumming and dance repertoire (*nongak/p'ungmul*) were introduced, and on June 29, 1977, a full staged version of *nongak/p'ungmul* with traditional music orchestra was arranged by the composer Yu Shin in a work titled "Nongak-kwa kugak kwanhyŏnak-ŭl wihan hyŏpchugok" (Concerto for *Nongak* and Traditional Music Orchestra), performed at a makeshift annex space (Sejong munhwa hoegwan chŏnsa p'yŏnjip wiwŏnhoe 2002:217, 229). It is worth mentioning here that the path of least resistance for SamulNori would have been to bring in, or at least evoke, a full-scale *namsadang/p'ungmul* troupe on the concert hall stage, something the above-mentioned concerto performance attempted in an imitation of two earlier such presentations at the National Theater (see below).

A partially completed Great Hall in the Sejong Center opened for performances in April 1978 (only two months after SamulNori's debut), with final construction of the entire complex completed in 1987; it now includes a small theater, chamber hall, art gallery, and outdoor performance space. The year 1978 was also significant for the folk music world beyond the founding of SamulNori: with the opening of the new space, there was now a concerted effort on the part of the organizers to have a more democratic balance of programs featuring aristocratic music (*chŏngak*), newly composed traditional music, and folk music. Joint concerts with the Kungnip Kugagwŏn (National Center for Korean Traditional Performing Arts; see below) were also mounted that year. After 1978 (the year the Great Hall opened) there was a marked increase in the number of traditional music concerts—with a heavy folk component—sponsored by the Center, as shown in table 2.1.

Kungnip Kŭkchang (National Theater)

Originally located in the trendy Myŏng-dong district of downtown Seoul, the National Theater opened its doors at its current site in Changch'ung-dong near Dongguk University in late 1973. The initial 820-seat theater was christened with traditional music by a performance of a *ch'anggŭk* (musical theater form)

Table 2.1: Traditional music concerts at the Sejong Center, 1974–84.

Year	Number of concerts
1974	4
1975	8
1976	6
1977	6
1978	6
1979	10
1980	10
1981	9
1982	10
1983	10
1984	8

Source: Sejong munhwa 2002:619–20.

rendition of "Ch'unhyang-jŏn" (Tale of Ch'unhyang) on March 21, 1962, marking the birth of the National Ch'anggŭk Troupe (Han Myŏnghŭi et al. 2001:82; Killick 2001:34). Between the late 1950s and the early 1970s, the National Theater expanded from featuring performances of Western theater and *ch'anggŭk* to include a mixed Western- and Korean-style dance troupe; in later decades a traditional music orchestra and an opera and ballet company were added (all large-scale troupes). The presentation of such large choreographed works was made possible by expanding the size of the proscenium stage in the new hall, and by increasing audience seating to 1,563 arranged on three floors.

Two productions from the mid-1970s are especially important in the context of staging folk percussion in an urban setting. The first took place over the two evenings of October 16 and 17, 1975, when *nongak* ("farmers' music") dance by the esteemed Kim Hyanggŭm Dance Troupe was a prominent feature of the program. A year later, October 4–6, 1976, a much longer segment of *nongak* dance was provided by troupes belonging to the master artists Kuk Suho and Son Pyŏngu.[1] Critically, these were not actual *nongak/p'ungmul* groups from rural areas, but rather were grounded reinterpretations by choreographers interested in evoking the sounds and imagery of provincial experience. Throughout the 1970s, in fact, many traditional forms of dances were staged at the National Theater—*salp'uri* (shamanist dance of purging) and *mudang ch'um* (shaman's dance) being related examples—making SamulNori's break from movement and spectacle and their primary focus on the music (rhythm) all the more remarkable (see Yu Minyŏng et al. 2000:683–84).

Kungnip Kugagwŏn (National Center for Korean Traditional Performing Arts)

The impressive and highly venerated Kungnip Kugagwŏn, currently translated as "National Center for Korean Traditional Performing Arts," has served as the artistic hub of traditional music and dance activity in Korea since before the liberation from the Japanese. A symbol of the perseverance of generations of musicians, dancers, scholars, government officials, and sympathetic members of the general public, the "Institute," as it was more commonly known, has done more for the study, documentation, performance, and promotion of Korean performing arts than any other such institution throughout the entire peninsula. From 1968 through 1988, the Center, in a more humble state, occupied a small space at the National Theater in Changch'ung-dong, though it had access to its Great Hall (the National Theater was also used in lieu of the Seoul Civic Center after its fire in 1972); after 1988 it was moved to its current location south of the Han River along the base of a mountain range in Sŏch'o-dong. The Center has since blossomed into a beautifully laid out complex subsuming rehearsal rooms, two concert halls, an open-air theater, a museum, a bookstore, and a radio station.[2] Its two halls—one large and one small—with proscenium stages contain 794 and 521 seats, respectively.

The first Center-sponsored concert of folk music was a performance of solo zither accompanied by drum (*kayagŭm sanjo*) in September 1949, though until 1961 programs of traditional music were weighted heavily in favor of court and aristocratic (*chŏngak*) genres. Concerted folk music activity began only after 1961, largely due to the efforts of the esteemed *p'ansori* singer Pak Tongjin (Kim Kyŏnghŭi 2001:452). While the earliest concerts of newly composed traditional music took place during the 1950s (the terms *shin kugak* and *ch'angjak kugak* were used somewhat interchangeably at that time), in 1974 a new group and series was inaugurated under the name of the Han'guk Ch'angjak Ŭmak Palp'yohoe (Society for Korean Newly Composed Music), a name change from the previous 1965 designation of Shin Kugak Chakkok Palp'yohoe (Society for New Traditional Music Composition). In 1979 a formal separate subgroup—the Minsok Ŭmak Yŏnjuhoe (Folk Music Performance Society)—was established, with a special memorial concert marking this important occasion in 1981. And although *samul nori* as a genre was not yet a part of the regular rotation at the

Center, from the early 1980s onward folk music had secured a place in the official and public consciousness (Kim Kyŏnghŭi 2001:211–16).

On August 1, 1979, a number of "human cultural assets" (*in'gan munhwajae*) from the Minsok Ŭmak Yŏnjuhoe formed their own group, the Muhyŏng Munhwajae T'ŭkpyŏl Yŏnjudan (Intangible Cultural Asset Special Performance Troupe). Early the next year a number of younger, non–cultural asset or lesser status performers joined them, including SamulNori cofounder and small gong (*soe*) player Kim Yongbae, an addition that foreshadowed the formation of the primary and most longstanding rival *samul nori* team to that of Kim Duk Soo (Kim Yongbae was still the small gong player of the original SamulNori quartet at this time; see below and refer to appendix 2). In 1983 a kind of pre-official *samul nori* concert was held on April 4 featuring the composition "Samul-kwa t'aep'yŏngso shinawi" (Improvisations for *Samul Nori* and Shawm), and on March 9, 1984, a newly formed Center *samul nori* team (Kungnip Kugagwŏn Samulnori) presented their inaugural concert with Kim Yongbae at the helm, signaling his split from Kim Duk Soo (Kim Kyŏnghŭi 2001:206–9).[3]

The initial lineup of the Center's team included Kim Yongbae on *soe*, Chŏn Sudŏk on *changgo*,[4] and Pak Ŭnha on *ching* (large gong) and *tchaksoe* (interlocking *soe*), the only female performer of *samul nori* during the first decade of its existence.[5] The impetus behind the decision to establish a *samul nori* group and program at the Center was mainly the scholar and administrator Han Manyŏng, then director of the Center. Han saw the artistic and commercial value in the quickly emerging art form; he was also instrumental in recruiting the fiddle (*haegŭm*) player Pang Sŭnghwan to play barrel drum (*puk*) to fill out the ensemble (a picture of this first Center *samul nori* team is reproduced in Kim Hŏnsŏn 1998:51).[6] Their first performance, on March 9, 1984, was held in the Taegŭkchang (Great Hall) of the National Theater—the opening of the current Center located in Sŏch'o-dong was still four years away—where they performed the standard repertoire of three regional pieces plus a recomposed work for four hourglass drums (discussed further in chapter 3); the press singled out Kim Yongbae for his advanced skill (Kim Kyŏnghŭi 2001:435, 454). Two months later, on May 18, 1984, the new team gave a concert as part of a series sponsored by the parent group the Intangible Cultural Asset Special Performance Troupe, and since that time at least one *samul nori* concert has been featured every year at the Center.

Over the next three years the Center's team would undergo two substantial personnel changes. In 1986 Chŏn Sudŏk left and was replaced by Nam Kimun, a *namsadang changgo* performer who has remained a stalwart in the Center's

Figure 2.2 Kungnip Kugagwŏn Samulnori lineup (1986), from left to right: Pang Sŭnghwan, Kim Yongbae, Nam Kimun, and Pak Ŭnha (Ch'oe Pyŏngsam not pictured) (© Jigu Records).

teams' development over the years (see figure 2.2).[7] Nam solidified the connection with itinerant troupe performance culture, at the same time lending weight to the Center's ensemble through his cultural asset status. Nam brought Pusan-based *p'ungmul* performer Ch'oe Pyŏngsam on board as a second *puk* player, a fellow graduate of the Seoul Traditional Arts High School (discussed below) and a friend from their shared days with the Little Angels, a children's touring troupe that claimed members from both the original and Center's *samul nori* teams.[8] The second rearrangement was a direct result of Kim Yongbae's tragic and unexpected suicide on April 23, 1986.[9] After a period of complete disbandment, only Nam and Ch'oe returned in 1987 to reboot with two other Pusan musicians, most likely because of Ch'oe's regional allegiance (see appendix 2 for the first decade of SamulNori/*samul nori* activity with regard to personnel changes and overlapping allegiances).[10] Significantly, through all of these upheavals and transitions, the various Center teams never strayed far from the original vision of *samul nori* as a small and intimately conceived performance art.

Konggan Sarang (Space Theater)

"Konggan" (literally "Space") was initially the name of a multifaceted and politically involved artistic group created in 1960 by the widely admired and emulated architect Kim Sugŭn. A cultural activist with a lifelong concern for Korean identity in the face of threats from modernization and Westernization, his singular vision and integration of older Korean cultural practices and spaces was called upon for designing Olympic facilities, countryside museums, and the Masan Cathedral. November 1966 saw the launching of *Konggan* magazine (which continues to be published today), a venue in which Kim and other members of the group could express, through prose and poetry, a worldview that privileged modern contexts for and reinterpretations of Korean tradition. "Tradition was meant to authenticate the present: it could be modernized" (Delissen 2002:252). This organic and self-reflective approach to history and culture was memorialized in the hundredth issue of *Konggan* in 1975:

> *Konggan* turns over and revives the tradition and history of a field that covers arts, environment, architecture. Turned to the future we judge desirable, we do record, set in order and criticize what our present is made of. For the Koreans to know Korea better and better, *Konggan*'s content, even when embedded in the most contemporary issues, enriches the spirit of present day Koreans and the more brilliant it is, the more it enhances the dignity of Koreans' lives. Our ambition is to bear witness of our values to the distant future. (from the original English passage)

In the mid-1970s Kim Sugŭn became especially interested in connecting the past to the present through live performance arts, and so on April 2, 1977, the Konggan Sarang (literally "Love of Space") theater-gallery was opened as the physical face of his grander design (Yi Hyŏngyŏng 2004:36; see figure 2.3 later in the discussion for its interior). Located in the basement of the Konggan Office Building in Wŏnsŏ-dong (near the entrance gate to Ch'angdŏkkung Palace), the roughly 120-seat box-style space was striking in its simplicity and intimacy—when compared to the grand designs of the Sejong Center and National Theater—and was more akin to a larger room in an aristocrat's home of yesteryear.

Kim's friend and collaborator Kang Chunhyŏk, dramaturge and artistic director of the Konggan Sarang in its early years, similarly envisioned the hall as a fresh and healthy new place to showcase traditional and "modern" (*hyŏndae*) approaches to composition and performance. The humbler dimensions of the Konggan Sarang enabled smaller-scale performances—solo or small chamber works—and combined with the growing support and resultant popularity of its offerings, the hall was of tremendous consequence for the development of Korean traditional performance arts culture in the later twentieth century (Yi Haerang 1985:467–68). The Konggan Sarang was also host to the first SamulNori performance in 1978, an event that has elevated the importance of this hall to mythic status.

Urban audiences of Seoul had access to a much broader palette of music and dance offerings in the late 1970s than they did even a decade earlier. While the ascendant forms were based on the Western models of the symphony, opera company, and ballet troupe—not to mention the inroads of jazz and rock music—, traditional music and dance were available and poised to embrace and/or challenge these newer developments in sound, presentation, and performance contexts (especially the concert hall). Discovery, experimentation, and expansion went hand in hand with folk music performance and composition and its adaptation to these urban spaces, both large and small. SamulNori's vision was special but not unique, owing to the activities of like-minded and sympathetic individuals in theater (Kang Chunhyŏk), architecture (Kim Sugŭn), and folk music promotion (the Minsogakhoe Shinawi).[11]

The Folk Music Society "Shinawi"

If concert halls were the physical face of music making and urban life in the South Korea of the 1970s, especially in and around Seoul, then folk culture/music associations represented the spiritual and motivational side of the equation. As was previously discussed, in the late 1960s and early 1970s many Koreans were left with a continued sense of failure over the outcome of the Korean War, and with related questions of national and racial identity as a result of leftovers of Japanese colonialism and the encroachment of Western cultural practices. The concerted efforts of the *minjung* (people's) movement, the activities of the folksong and percussion movements, and the acceptance of traditional music in academic and governmental circles paved the way for a newer, healthier view of traditional culture and its transformative potential, albeit now centered in urban institutions removed from the rural contexts where most of these traditions were initially rooted. And yet folk music and musicians were frequently victims of intense prejudice, scorned and despised as "backwards" or "low-class" and associated with "superstitious" dealings, because of the close ties of much of the music to shaman ritual. And so on March 15, 1969, a group of graduates and faculty from the Seoul Traditional Arts High School (Sŏul Kugak Yesul Kodŭng Hakkyo) formed the Minsogakhoe Shinawi, or "The Folk Music Society 'Shinawi'" ("Korean Folk Music Group Sinawee" in a 1973 program), as a remedy to this societal malaise (see Chŏn Chiyŏng 2005:293–94). Rooted in a deep love of and respect for Korean folk music, the society hoped to provide a solution to this long-standing rejection, hostility, and sense of frailty (Ch'oe T'aehyŏn 1991:29).

According to Ch'oe T'aehyŏn, an original member at its founding and SamulNori's first *ching* (large gong) player, the society in the beginning had no written forms or manifesto, but rather reflected a group of like-minded individuals with similar goals ("like a family") who naturally gravitated toward one another. Although the founding members had all been friends at school, early gatherings were problematic and challenging, largely due to financial concerns. Struggling to exist in the general world of traditional music in the 1970s, they were also keenly aware that fellow members represented their direct competition within the even smaller sphere of folk music. They recognized that only the elite few would survive and that the payoff would be modest at best, hoping to improve on the situation of other more senior artists who had dedicated their lives to folk music but were rewarded with poverty and humiliation (Ch'oe T'aehyŏn 1991:29–31).[12]

The society chose a three-pronged strategy of research, teaching, and performance to promote their broader agenda, a vision with two separate yet crucially related components. The first was to unearth and rediscover traditional folk music that was deemed to be on the verge of extinction, forming the foundation of all of their activities. From there the society would create and promote new traditional music based on this knowledge that met the changing needs of the times. In their view, for folk music to become and remain viable, preservation must evolve appropriately into re-creation that corresponds to current societal and artistic trends. Positioning themselves in direct opposition to the cultural asset preservation system and the search for "authentic" archetypes—i.e., static, museum relics—, the goal became the popularization of folk music as a healthy part of the new Korean society, "popular" being understood to indicate the public's attitude toward this music becoming positive (not a commercializing or "dumbing down" of the art forms; see Yang Jongsung 2003:115–16). In this idealized world, the new folk music culture would reconnect the modern with the traditional, the current with the historical, and re-creation with preservation, always with an eye for the progressive (Ch'oe T'aehyŏn 1991:30, 45–46).

A key player and driving force behind the formation of the society was Professor Shim Usŏng, the folklorist and champion of the *namsadang* discussed in chapter 1. Shim had already formed the Minsokkŭkhoe Namsadang, or "The Folk Theater Society 'Namsadang,'" in 1960 with the intent of reviving the latent tradition into a "living folk" (*sara innŭn minsok*) reality (Ch'oe T'aehyŏn 1991:32). Such involvement caught the attention of Pak Hŏnbong, principal of the Seoul Traditional Arts High School at its opening that same year and a fellow researcher of potential cultural assets for the South Korean government. Pak initially hired Shim to teach traditional music theory (*kugak iron*) at the high school, though later he would call on Shim's help and expertise to recruit graduates of the school in early 1969 to form the Minsogakhoe Shinawi ("The Folk Music Society 'Shinawi'"), a name Shim coined (Minsokkŭkhoe became Minsogakhoe, the character change of *kŭk* to *ak* signaling the change in emphasis from theater to music). Shim was instrumental in the choice and practicing of repertoire, and it was his preference for small ensembles and theater spaces that would influence nearly all practical and aesthetic choices made over the following decades. He was also cognizant of the role that the South Korean youth would play in his plans, a target audience of students whom he respected for their vitality, intelligence, and seriousness. Shim nurtured early society members and encouraged these qualities in them in an effort to instill pride in what they were trying to accomplish (Shim Usŏng 1999; Ch'oe T'aehyŏn 1991:32).

The first performance of the society took place on October 31, 1969, at 8:00 P.M. at the Seoul YMCA, located near the intersection of Chongno-2-ga in central Seoul.[13] The YMCA venue was really just a rectangular room converted into a makeshift concert space; about 100 seats were set up with a small area reserved in the front of the room for the performers, similar in layout and dimensions to the Space Theater that would open in 1977. According to the firsthand account of Ch'oe T'aehyŏn, the evening's concert was packed wall to wall with enthusiastic students, with many famous traditional musicians attending to lend their support. The performers' efforts and sweat were rewarded with applause that "sounded like thunder"—the concert was immediately understood as a watershed moment in the modern history of Korean folk music, a real turning point for the young artists who could now walk with their instrument cases out in public "with their heads held high" (1991:33). This success would prompt

Shim and the society to begin to look for proper alternatives to the large concert halls that were under construction or in the planning stages at this time to enhance their more human-scale projects.

Six more concerts were mounted during 1969–70, all but one held at the YMCA (see table 2.2). The society then went through a period of disorganization from 1971 to 1977 as members were either called into military service or spent time pursuing individual careers. This trend reversed itself in 1977, when Chi Yŏnghŭi and Sŏng Kŭmyŏn, two famous traditional musicians who had immigrated to Hawai'i, returned temporarily to Korea. Under their guidance and inspiration the society was infused with new life; a special concert was held in their honor on June 24, 1977, at the National Theater, after which the society

Table 2.2: First decade of concert activity for the Folk Music Society "Shinawi."

Date of performance	Program title	Venue
October 31, 1969	1st Regular Concert	YMCA
November 20, 1969	2nd Regular Concert	YMCA
December 4, 1969	3rd Regular Concert	YMCA
December 6, 1969	Korean Youth Group Conference Sponsored Youth Cultural Festival	Ehwa Women's University
February 2, 1970	4th Regular Concert	YMCA
March 2, 1970	5th Regular Concert	YMCA
April 6, 1970	6th Regular Concert	YMCA
May 22, 1971	7th Regular Concert	Shimin Hoegwan (Civic Center)
September 12, 1973	8th Regular Concert	National Theater (in Myŏng-dong)
June 24, 1977	Chi Yŏnghŭi/Sŏng Kŭmyŏn Invited Concert	National Theater
December 24, 1977	9th Regular Concert	Korean Culture and Arts Foundation
February 22 & 23, 1978	1st Konggan's Evening of Traditional Music (SamulNori's debut concert)	Konggan Sarang (Space Theater)
March 1, 1979	10th Regular Concert	Konggan Sarang
October 21 & 22, 1979	11th Regular Concert	Konggan Sarang

Source: Minsogakhoe Shinawi 2000 (all venues in Seoul).

regrouped and began in earnest their regular efforts at performance and promotion (Ch'oe T'aehyŏn 1991:35). Over the next few years the society's activities became much more ambitious in scope, in tandem with their increased public profile and popularity, though in hindsight the genesis of SamulNori in 1978 would overshadow these efforts in the coming decade of the 1980s.

The 9th Regular Concert of the society, held on December 24, 1977, at the Korean Culture and Arts Foundation (Han'guk Munhwa Yesul Chinhŭngwŏn)—the last formal event presented before SamulNori's debut February the next year—, focused on music that had not yet been presented on stage, including original and expanded approaches that were specifically modified for the new performance space (the Foundation stage was closer in size and scope to the Sejong Center and National Theater with a proscenium stage and over 600 seats). The program was:

1. "Ch'wit'a han pat'ang" (military processional music)
2. "Kŏmun'go sanjo" (solo instrumental suite for plucked zither)
3. "Taep'ungnyu" (aristocratic chamber music)
4. "Taegŭm sanjo" (group instrumental suite for transverse flute)
5. "Shinawi hapchu" (shaman ensemble music) (from Minsogakhoe Shinawi 1977)

The opening piece represented a large ensemble court genre that was historically performed outdoors in courtyards and public thoroughfares. Pieces two, three, and four were borne of aristocratic music parlors of the late Chosŏn period, with the *sanjo* compositions (2 and 4) now accepted as a kind of "art" folk music. Where "Kŏmun'go sanjo" (2) was realized in the traditional manner of a single soloist with drum accompaniment, "Taegŭm sanjo" (4) featured five flutists playing as a unified ensemble, a then novel approach which has since become standard practice in many concerts given at the National Center for Korean Traditional Performing Arts (one strategy in adapting smaller group performance to a larger venue that has remained from this period).

The fifth piece, "Shinawi hapchu," is worth highlighting for philosophical as well as personnel reasons. A shaman-inspired dance music form brought in from ritual contexts based in the southwestern provinces, the embracing and regular programming of *shinawi* by the society from this date forward would serve to elevate this historically downtrodden genre over the coming years to the status of "concert music" (many years ahead of the curve of institutions such as the National Center and the National Theater). By the end of the 1970s—in keeping with the society's commitment to the discovery and re-creation of folk music—all programs of the periodical concerts consisted of either (1) "transmitted pieces" (*chŏllae kok*), such as the various instrumental *sanjo*, folksongs (*minyo*), *shinawi*, and (later) *samul nori*; or (2) "newly created pieces" (*ch'angjak kok*), works identified with a composer but rooted in folk music idioms. It is significant that the contrast made here with "newly created" was the category of "transmitted," not "traditional" (meaning both were seen as equally occupying the realm of the "traditional"; see Ch'oe T'aehyŏn 1991:34–38). The lineup on this final piece is also noteworthy in that it brought together three of the four musicians who would form the original SamulNori group only two months later: Yi Chongdae on *p'iri* (who would play *puk*), Ch'oe T'aehyŏn on *haegŭm* (who would play *ching*), and Kim Duk Soo (Kim Tŏksu) on *ching* (who would play *changgo*). Chang Tŏkhwa, who played *changgo* on "Shinawi hapchu," would later be active with Kim Yongbae (the fourth member of the original quartet) at the National Center, though for reasons unknown was not asked to play with the original SamulNori group or the National Center team that would form in 1984.[14]

And so the foundations had been laid for SamulNori's debut on February 22, 1978, to a packed house at the Space Theater. Billed as the "1st Konggan's Evening of Traditional Music," the as yet unnamed percussion quartet composed of the *namsadang* member Kim Yongbae on *soe* (small handheld gong), previous *namsadang* performer Kim Duk Soo on *changgo*, Yi Chongdae on *puk* (barrel drum), and Ch'oe T'aehyŏn on *ching* (large gong)[15] performed "Uttari p'ungmul" (Rhythms of the Central Region, a condensed version of the nationally designated *namsadang* troupe repertoire) as part of a larger program sponsored by the society.[16] Kim Duk Soo and Ch'oe T'aehyŏn had known each other from their days at the Seoul Traditional Arts High School, while Kim Yongbae was newly brought into the society in 1978 by Shim Usŏng, who knew him from his involvement with the *namsadang* (see Park, Shingil 2000:177). Their performance was an unconditional success; soon thereafter it was decided by the entire quartet that the two nonpercussionists (Yi and Ch'oe) would need to be replaced, so as to not hold back the prowess—and charisma—of Kim Duk Soo and Kim Yongbae. And there was the issue of naming their new approach to performance, because what they were doing was clearly not *p'ungmul* as it had been conventionally conceived or practiced by amateur troupes and the *namsadang* (see further Kang Chunhyŏk 2009).

By the 10th Regular Concert on March 1, 1979, SamulNori now had its distinctive name,[17] though its membership was still in transition.[18] The "classic"

Figure 2.3 Photo featuring classic SamulNori lineup (1979), from left to right: Yi Kwangsu, Kim Duk Soo, Ch'oe Chongshil, and Kim Yongbae (©SamulNori Hanullim).

lineup—one that is frequently referred to (incorrectly) as the "original quartet" in the mainstream Korean media—that now featured Yi Kwangsu (a previous *namsadang*) and Ch'oe Chongshil (a *p'ungmul* performer from South Kyŏngsang province) would not solidify until two months later (Kim Hŏnsŏn 1995:123; the photo in figure 2.3 that documents this coming together of talent and vision has achieved an iconic status in the traditional music world similar to the image of the Beatles arriving in the U.S. for the first time.).[19] With the final pieces now in place, SamulNori set out on the broader project to translate the outdoor medium of *p'ungmul* into an indoor stage art, initially ignoring the dance component altogether and extracting and refining characteristic rhythms of entertainment-oriented performances (the *p'an kut*) under the rubric of "reorganizing" or "recomposing" (*chaegusŏng*) traditional music (see further chapter 3). SamulNori's creed in those early years was twofold: (1) the current state of *p'ungmul* and public attitudes toward it as an art form are disgraceful (only one of the currently recognized five cultural asset *p'ungmul* troupes was designated in 1979); and (2) rhythms and movements from the *p'an kut* that had become neglected over time must be preserved and defended (Ch'oe T'aehyŏn 1991:40).

This newly found pride in folk music by Samu1Nori and the society was reinforced when the Korean musicologist Song Bang-Song (Song Pangsong) became the director of the National Center. Song was instrumental in that institution's opening of a folk music section in 1979, a kind of recognition and national status considered almost unbelievable only a few years previous. This was both shocking and tremendously exciting for the entire folk music world; many of the core members of the society at that time were asked to join the National Center (including, eventually, Kim Yongbae to form a rival *samul nori* team). This interface between the society and the National Center bore many fruits, including a number of important collaborative recordings.[20] Over the years the activities of the two institutions would prove to be mutually beneficial.

As of 2000—the last formal concert I could find under their auspices—the society had presented a total of fifty-seven concerts. The 2000 event was part of a festival titled Passage of Life held at the Namsan Folk Village (Namsan-gol Hanok-maŭl) in Seoul, in which the society was joined by a *p'ungmul* group led by Yi Kwangsu (Yi moved from *puk* to *soe* after Kim Yongbae's death). A year earlier, writing on the occasion of the society's thirtieth anniversary, Shim Usŏng would connect the dots between the *namsadang*, the society, and the emergence of SamulNori to form the picture of "the large house of the people's art (*minjung yesul*)," with Shim clearly positioned as a kind of master artist or creative midwife. While he admitted that the society had had its ups and downs over the years—there wasn't always a clear direction for the group, and they weren't always in step with the times or prevailing mood, for example—, they nevertheless must not have regrets, be narcissistic, or avoid current realities. He also expressed his concern from the late 1970s, when SamulNori split off from the society, fearing their popularity would threaten the very existence of that institution, but then admitted such fears were unfounded due to the opening of the folk music section at the National Center in 1979 alongside other work opportunities for folk musicians that arose in the early 1980s. In all their efforts, however, the ultimate goal was "beauty through creative music," meaning the re-creation of Korean traditional music in new contexts but with living roots (Shim Usŏng 1999). In later years the society would change its focus to larger newly composed works (1980s) and shaman ritual traditions (1980s and '90s; Ch'oe T'aehyŏn 1991:41–43), while Chang Tŏkhwa (*changgo*) would continue to hold lessons under the society's auspices in a third-floor studio located near the art district of Insadong in downtown Seoul (Yi Ch'ŏljin, personal communication, 2009).

Conclusion

The 1970s signaled the dawn of the rebirth of a distinctive Korean consciousness and an increasingly positive view of traditional culture and the role it could play in the transformation of Korean society. Individuals and collectives worked together to bring about this change, a multifarious yet often unified front made up of government officers, academics, political theorists, and other cultural brokers; various arts movements and societies; and, of course, the performing artists themselves. It was a challenging and exciting time to be involved with the traditional music world, an era characterized by a general sense of possibility. This was especially true for folk music and musicians, a diverse and resilient group of personalities who helped pave the way for the appearance, appreciation, and continued support of *samul nori*, arguably the most influential traditional music genre of the twentieth century.

Folk musicians and their promoters at some point had to come to terms with the urban relocation of much of Korean life. The burgeoning concert hall industry in the cities presented perhaps the greatest challenge—or opportunity, depending on one's perspective—to the original contexts and modes of presentation for traditional music. Against the backdrop of new folk music series and subgroups formed in the 1960s and '70s, as well as a growing scene for "newly composed" traditional music (*shin/ch'angjak kugak*), five performances in particular stand out in importance for properly understanding folk drumming's transition from the fields to the stage. The first four are large-scale productions presented for large concert hall spaces: individual drum dances from the *p'ungmul* repertoire performed in 1969 at the Seoul Civic Center; choreographed representations of *p'ungmul/nongak* music and dance by professional dance companies at the National Theater in 1975 and 1976; and the 1977 "Concerto for *Nongak* and Traditional Music Orchestra" staged at the Seoul Civic Center Annex. The fifth, SamulNori's debut at the Space Theater in 1978, drew on many of the same rhythms and aural markers yet was distinctively different in its conception—choosing a smaller, intimate setting (four musicians playing for only 120 people)—and in its changing of the focus of the concert away from dance to music.

"Modernization" and "urbanization" are really just abstract concepts masking what is really the realm of human intention. It was specific individuals operating in a specific time and cultural context working together toward the common goal of "re-creation (*chaech'angjo*) grounded in tradition" (Ch'oe T'aehyŏn 1991:30) that made the conceptualization of SamulNori possible. Chronologically, we can look to the founding of the Seoul Traditional Arts High School in 1960 as a primary instigator of this process. Numerous administrators, faculty, supporters, and students dedicated their time and efforts toward the advancement, transmission, and promotion of folk music at a moment in Korean history hostile toward such efforts. The year 1960 also marked the founding of the

Konggan (Space) Group by the architect and cultural activist Kim Sugŭn, who, together with the theater director Kang Chunhyŏk, would collaborate with Shim Usŏng in the mid-1970s to promote the alternative performance venue of the Space Theater, Shim acting as a kind of creative and spiritual linchpin. Professors Song Pangsong and Han Manyŏng, as directors of the National Center for Korean Traditional Performing Arts, also played a crucial role with their opening and continued support of a folk music division at an institution that had historically neglected such activity. It is worth noting that it took only two decades for the locus of such traditional music transmission and authority to change to urban spaces.

In a sense the *namsadang* had already established themselves "in the city," because Seoul had served (and serves) as the economic, political, and cultural capital of Korea during the many centuries of the Chosŏn period (fictionalized accounts such as the film *The King and the Clown* help visualize such a presence). SamulNori was not so much the urbanization of the *namsadang* art of *p'ungmul* as it was the *further* adaptation to the changing nature of the city (see Williams 2001:4–11). A crucial hidden ingredient in this success story—admittedly with the strong backing of the society and Shim Usŏng—may very well have been the seriousness with which SamulNori took the interests and tastes of Korea's urban youth. By allowing the "current" and hence relevant to play a part in their more inclusive vision of tradition, they were able to once more bring the experience of traditional music back to a general public, not just an older sector more concerned with nostalgia and reminiscing (to be further addressed in the next chapter). SamulNori was not the first to usher folk music from the countryside onto a concert hall stage, nor even the first to evoke the sounds and sentiments of gongs and drums in the city soundscape. But in light of the historical record and their many and devoted fans around the world, they were apparently the best.

3

On the Road with "Och'ae chilgut"

Stages, Professionalization, and Mediation

It is now widely accepted in the field of musicology that a great deal of music's interest lies beyond its purely sonic arrangement of events (DeNora 1995; Leppert and McClary 1987; Small 1998; Wolff 1987). So-called extramusical factors such as space, dress, gender, historical period, and other symbolically encoded devices very much determine the ways in which a particular piece or event is performed, understood, and appreciated. Ethnomusicologists in particular have focused on musical change as part of this overarching totality, examining the roles played by urbanization, Westernization, industrialization, and the emergence of technology (Kartomi 1981; Keil 1984; Lysloff 1997; Nettl 1978). In this chapter I look to the sociological and historical currents underpinning adaptations made by SamulNori when putting *p'ungmul* on stage and in the recording studio, with special attention to performance practice and aesthetics. While much of this has to do with the changing demands of the city (documented in chapter 2), I also engage related trends borne of globalization and its reliance on mediation and commodification.

My primary organizational strategy is to focus on a single musical unit, the rhythmic cycle and/or movement known respectively as *och'ae chilgut* and "Och'ae chilgut" (literally "five-stroke road ritual"). This building block can be found at every "stage" of SamulNori's development, both literally in the space where it is performed as well as conceptually in its development by genre. Concentrating our gaze in such a manner will bring into relief the complementary aspects of the tradition's reliance on continuity and expansion, reminding us of the flexibility of music as a sound system and gestural language. In the context of this discussion, a core rhythm or succession of rhythms will remain stable and recognizable, even as the context for the performance and its attendant set of relationships change. And while I am borrowing the title of this chapter from an earlier publication of mine (Hesselink 2001), the analogy of the road is a common one, one that is directly reflected in three *samul nori* CD recordings: Cho Sanghun's *Kil: The Road* (2004), Kim Duk Soo's *Kil: On the Road* (2007), and Kim Dong-Won's *Kil-ŭl kara: On the Road* (2008).

This chapter is organized around four distinct yet related stages in the development of SamulNori/*samul nori*, understanding a performance space—tangible or imagined—as privileging certain kinds of relationships and mediations at the expense of others. The categories for this analysis are based on Small 1998:194–96. First category is that of location: the demands and challenges of outdoor events versus indoors, the vagaries of acoustics, the use of boundaries as marking something as rarefied, and the implications of the recording studio and commodification. The second consideration is the performers: the proximity and the nature of their interactions with each other, the role of memory and/or musical scores, and issues surrounding membership and leadership. The audience is the third category: their personal relationships to the performers and other audience members in terms of professionalism and idealization, monetary exchange relationships, and the quality of their attendance and interactions with the performers from beginning to end.[1] It is only for the sake of convenience that I present the four stages in discrete sections; for many Korean performers and listeners, the imagery and sound of the gongs and drums creates a rich amalgam of emotions and experiences that traverse any single historic, aesthetic, or narrative thread.

Country Roads (Rural *P'ungmul* and the *Namsadang*)

I first saw Iri Nongak perform in Seoul during the summer of 1994 while attending the second special program for foreign researchers and performers offered by the National Center (Kungnip Kugagwŏn). Iri's leader, Kim Hyŏngsun, had founded the group in the early 1960s in Iri, then a little village in the southwest province of North Chŏlla; the village is now subsumed within the larger city of Iksan. While his group was and continues to be composed mainly of local provincial players, they nonetheless have from their very modest beginnings set their sights on touring and national exposure. Years of hard work and consistent lobbying in the capital Seoul have paid off; today Iri Nongak is designated Important Intangible Cultural Asset (*chungyo muhyŏng munhwajae*) No. 11 (folk percussion and dance) by the South Korean government, one of only five regional ensembles to have received such recognition.[2] Iri Nongak became one of two primary groups I focused on during doctoral fieldwork beginning in 1995 (see further Hesselink 2006).

Iri Nongak hails from a long tradition of folk percussion music and dance, known in the Korean language as either *nongak* or *p'ungmul*(*gut*).[3] Predominantly a rural phenomenon until only the past couple of decades, *nongak/p'ungmul* served within village society as musical accompaniment to communal labor teams (*ture*), shamanistic rituals (*kut*), and large celebrations held at the end of harvesting or ritual fund-raising (*kŏllip*). Many of the older contexts for intensive manual labor and ritual events have disappeared, however, and so Iri Nongak has over the past twenty years or so abandoned these types of performances in favor of entertainment-based gatherings known generically as *p'an kut* (*p'an*: communal meeting space in a village; and *kut*: ritual and/or performance). The *p'an kut* traditionally came after a long day of communal labor or fund-raising and would last three or four hours into the middle of the night. The performance I saw that summer in 1994—and most since—was, in contrast, roughly an hour and a half in length, performed during the day, and divorced from any direct work or ritualistic contexts, trends that define almost all active *nongak/p'ungmul* groups today.

A performance of the first movement of the *p'an kut* by Iri Nongak in 1996 will serve as the first stage for the present discussion. Iri Nongak's *p'an kut* consists of four movements (*madang*), each a self-contained unit made up of a set series of rhythmic cycles or patterns (*karak/changdan*) and ground formations (*chinbŏp*) that are performed without fail. The title of the opening movement, "Och'ae chilgut," refers both to the entire movement and to the opening

Table 3.1: Comparison of rhythmic patterns by stage (titles have been regularized and rhythmic variations and transitions omitted to provide visual clarity at the deep structural level).

Name of group	Iri Nongak	Kungnip Kugagwŏn Samulnori (CD track #1)	Samulnori Chŏnsoe	Kim Duk Soo SamulNori & Red Sun Group (CD track #2)
Movement/ composition	"Och'ae chilgut"	"Honam udo kut"	"Honam udo p'ungmulgut" (1st mvmt)	"The Road Ahead"
Rhythmic patterns	*och'ae chilgut*	*och'ae chilgut* (0:00–)	*och'ae chilgut*	*och'ae chilgut* (0:00–)
	ujilgut	*ujilgut* (1:55–)	*ujilgut*	*ujilgut* (2:04–)
	chwajilgut	*chwajilgut* (2:41–)	*chwajilgut*	*chwajilgut* (3:42–)
	chilgut	*p'ungnyugut* (3:47–) (*chilgut*)	*p'ungnyŏn'gut* (*chilgut*)	
		kutkŏri (4:15–)	*kutkŏri p'ungnyŏn'gut* (*chilgut*)	
	yangsando	*yangsando* (6:27–)	*yangsando*	
	samch'ae	*samch'ae* (7:38–)	*samch'ae*	
	maedoji	*maedoji* (11:03–)	*maedoji*	

rhythmic cycle (refer to table 3.1). This rhythm is considered a microcosm of this particular regional tradition's musical subtlety and complexity; for this reason, as well as to provide a visual representation for means of comparison across the various four stages in this chapter, I have provided a simple reduction of *och'ae chilgut* (the cycle) in figure 3.1.

For this figure, like the ones that will follow in this book, I have chosen to use a modified form of Korean box notation. Each box represents an equal unit of time; boxes are arranged in paired horizontal rows and are read from left to right, with beats marked by bold vertical lines. Symbols within the top row of each

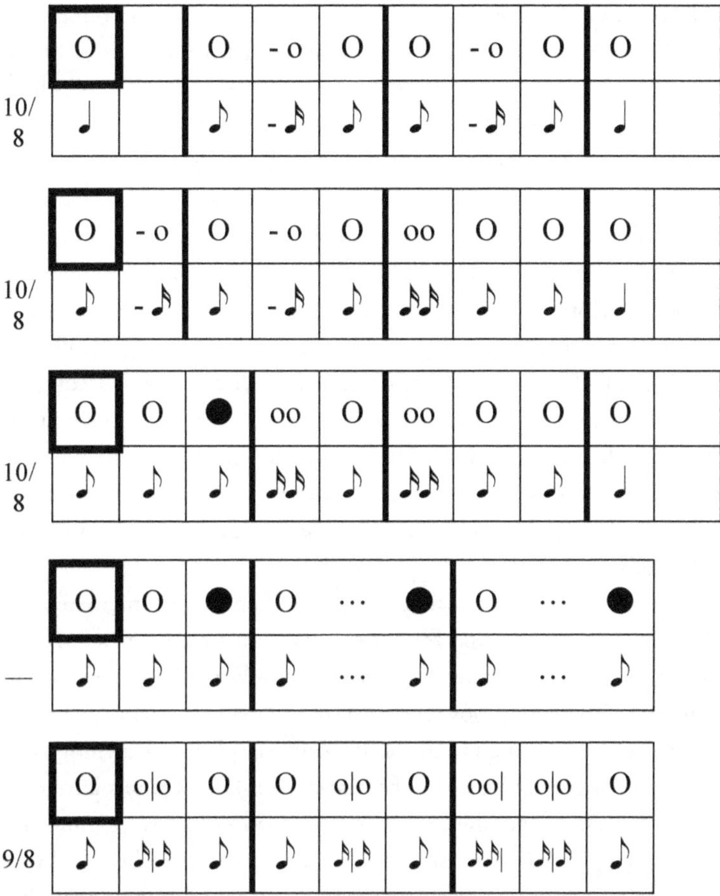

Figure 3.1 Iri Nongak's *och'ae chilgut* (*p'ungmul* version).

horizontal pair indicate small gong (*soe*) strokes: O = loud stroke, o = weaker stroke, ● = fully damped stroke. Bolded boxes—generally found at the beginning of each row marking a new phrase—identify strokes on the large gong (*ching*). Below the small gong row is a rough approximation of the rhythm realized in Western notation with the equivalent meter indicated at its head. Figure 3.1, therefore, represents a cycle composed of five phrases: phrase I, divided into four beats (in Western terms 10/8, grouped by eighth notes [individual boxes in this case] as 2 + 3 + 3 + 2); phrase II, four beats (10/8, 2 + 3 + 3 + 2); phrase III, four beats (10/8, 3 + 2 + 3 + 2); phrase IV, three unequal "beats" (the first measured compound meter beat is followed by two metrically free passages played as a quick succession of strokes akin to a roll); and phrase V, three beats (9/8, 3 + 3 + 3, with the second eighth note [or middle box] of the first two beats and the first two eighth notes of beat three subdivided into three).

Like the first outing of theirs that I saw back in 1994, Iri Nongak's 1996 performance took place at the Seoul Norimadang, an outdoor venue sponsored by the Seoul city government and the Ministry of Culture and Sports that features free live performances of Korean traditional music, dance, and theater during the spring and summer months. While the Norimadang was constructed specifically as a performance space for music and dance, it is meant to resemble the *(nori)p'an*, or communal village meeting ground, which is generally a multipurpose location for various often unrelated functions (see Chŏng Pyŏngho 1988). Performances by Iri Nongak at home and throughout the countryside tend to coincide with significant lunar calendar holidays—determined by agricultural and religious cycles—yet their cultural asset status requires them to travel to Seoul for nearly half of their yearly season, generally regardless of other considerations.

Nearly forty musicians, dancers, actors, and flag bearers interacted in close proximity in a circular ground formation, with most members at any particular time looking inward (true of many first movements by *p'ungmul* groups; see figure 3.2). The entire movement was danced—instruments or props were held in the hand or strapped to the body—and was played by memory, creating increased eye contact and a sense of intimacy. Ranking was recognized within individual instrument families, such as lead small gong player (*sangsoe*), second small gong player (*pusoe*), and so on, but ensemble members on the whole retained a fair amount of autonomy. Although leadership was maintained by the lead small gong player, who signaled beginnings and endings of rhythmic patterns, regulated tempi, and led the group through the elaborate ground formations, he did not monopolize the creative act, thereby allowing performers a degree of freedom with regard to the type and placement of footsteps as well as rhythmic variations.[4] Membership in Iri Nongak was and is set and has to be checked regularly with members of the Office of Cultural Assets, who approve or reject new recruits.

Rural performances in the past were largely amateur, communal participatory events, with little or no distinctions made between performers and onlooker-participants, who either danced along and/or exchanged instruments with ensemble members to try their hand at the rhythms. Such performances would have been attended primarily by close personal friends and relatives, creating a supportive and tight-knit atmosphere. The majority of Iri Nongak was

Figure 3.2 *P'ungmul p'an kut* (photo by Donna Kwon).

either semi- or full-time employed in other professions with only a few leadership positions receiving pay, a situation that under normal conditions would have preserved this nonhierarchical worldview and practice. Cultural asset status, increased touring, and oversight by the Cultural Assets Committee, however, had bestowed upon them a specialist air that discouraged such spontaneous interaction. While a number of friends, family, and former students were in attendance at the Seoul Norimadang re-creating the warm atmosphere of the countryside, audience members attempting to enter the stage during the performance proper to dance along with the musician-dancers were quickly and curtly escorted back to their seats (though see below).

Before a roof was constructed in 2005 on account of inclement weather, the Seoul Norimadang was a transitional space typical of many outdoor environments in which an audience member might only vaguely listen to the concert while attending to a conversation, a meal, or a game of chess. Such forms of social behavior are not usually noticeable in outdoor locales, where sounds and attention tend to spread out and dissipate. The audience could choose to sit close by at ground level or slightly above, with no formal barriers separating them from the grassy clearings behind them or the ongoing performance in front of them.

Partitioning was not necessary because admission was never charged, either in the countryside or in metropolitan centers; outings at the Norimadang were subsidized by local and national governmental agencies. Interaction occurred among the audience at all stages of the performance (in many different places), with members of Iri Nongak being visible and accessible before the commencement of the day's event. At the end of the day—a concession to older practices—the audience was allowed to join the troupe briefly by dancing or playing along in the performance space.[5]

Iri Nongak represents a transitional stage between rural *p'ungmul* as practiced in the past and their more professional counterparts in the *namsadang*. It is now common knowledge that ideas of touring, the use of spinning-tasseled headgear, increased rhythmic complexity, and unified concert attire employed by many, if not most, cultural asset *p'ungmul* teams were all direct legacies of interactions with the *namsadang* at the end of the nineteenth century. With rural *p'ungmul* and many of Iri Nongak's performances, dance created a virtual stage; by the late 1800s the *namsadang* were already formally marking off their performance areas in ways that would anticipate the boundaries of the modern concert hall (refer again to figure 1.2). Because of their hectic traveling schedule and low social status, the *namsadang* were almost uniformly regarded as strangers in the communities they visited, a situation that also played to their benefit as their success relied on a balance of the familiar *and* the exotic (unlike rural, grassroots *p'ungmul*, which established a sense of the local and of community). This distinction between amateur-based and locally grounded percussion music and dance and the professionalized, presentational, and pan-Korean style of performance art of the *namsadang* is a crucial one: many researchers (including myself some years ago) attempted to compare SamulNori/*samul nori* with rural *p'ungmul* with results that were often misguided and unflattering, rather than understanding SamulNori as the logical extension of the *namsadang* and a centuries-old itinerant performance tradition.

We can briefly characterize this first stage of percussion music and dance—Iri Nongak as a kind of midpoint between rural *p'ungmul* and the *namsadang*—by its reliance on closeness. This is true physically in the intimate spaces created among musicians, within the audience, and between musicians and the audience, as well as in its connections to life cycles that link these performances (at least in the countryside) to larger agricultural and spiritual events. Related to this proximity is a high density of social relations, defined by the number of different people one has relationships with who also have relationships with each other. This density is associated with strong feelings of solidarity and community, in contrast to the large metropolis with correspondingly low-density social relations (see Boissevain 1974 and Mitchell 1969).[6] Underpinning this closeness is a sense of openness, twin modes of social interaction encouraged through the lack of formal barriers, the placement of seats, and accessibility to the performers. While Iri Nongak has begun to approach the rarefied status of the *namsadang* of yesteryear and current-day *samul nori* ensembles, it nevertheless draws much of its enduring success and popularity from its close associations to the "earth"—literally and metaphysically conceived—and its regional place of origin.

Fo(u)rward Marching (SamulNori)

I have already outlined the emergence of SamulNori and the move it heralded from the countryside to the city. If one understands SamulNori as the artistic and philosophical inheritor of the *namsadang* tradition, the transition to the concert hall stage was as predictable as it was aesthetically sound. From a broader cross-cultural perspective, there is a long and established history behind traveling entertainers being sensitive to the local (unpredictable) acoustics, and hence constantly changing and adapting their instruments, tempi, and visual appeal to match and therefore enhance the ever fluid circumstances of their performances (Blesser and Salter 2007:101–2). The parallel development of the new ensemble alongside rapid urbanization in South Korea during the 1970s was not lost on Kim Duk Soo, here speaking in retrospect:

> More recently I have seen the birth of something that perhaps can be best described as mass culture. Yet in the same way that the culture which arose from our agrarian lifestyle gave structure to that society, so too, does this newer, urban mass culture define our now almost exclusively urban society. This relationship has interesting ramifications for a person like myself engaged in "traditional" music, but very much living in the 20th century. (1992:7)

The first and most obvious adaptation was SamulNori's choice to perform one each on the core percussion instruments from a seated position on the floor (referred to in Korean as *anjŭnban*). While the practice of a *changgo* (hourglass drum) player performing from this position was already established in court and literati circles, as well as aristocratically influenced folk genres, the full complement of gongs and drums from *p'ungmul* had never been formally presented in this manner.[7] It is important here to remember how visually captivating rural *p'ungmul* was (and is) with its costuming, ground formations, and flags; this appeal was increased exponentially when applied to the highly polished and artistically engrossing spectacle of the *namsadang*. Over time SamulNori would transfer the energy of the dance into exaggerated and highly stylized movements of the head and upper body, gestures codified in one of their earliest workbooks (Korean Conservatorium of Performing Arts 1992:18–19). Within a few years of their formation they reintroduced a danced portion to their concerts (*sŏnban*, literally "standing form"), appropriately called "P'an kut" in deference to the *namsadang*'s opening percussion-based performance act (see chapter 1). But it was by the development of the art form "from the floor" that they made their most significant mark on history.

The next task for SamulNori was to find a way to consolidate and condense the *p'ungmul* repertoire into performable units appropriate for a concert hall stage and its associated expectations for length (with the exception of Western opera, single "pieces" or events lasting two to four hours are not the norm; see Aubert 2007:35–36). In chapter 2, I showed how SamulNori was interested in specifically reviving the *p'an kut*, and elsewhere I have gone into considerable detail how technical prowess and the virtuosic manipulation of tempi and dynamics became coupled to musical-structural choices (Hesselink 2004). But for the present purpose it is sufficient to note that SamulNori soon established a canon of seated pieces, each averaging ten to twenty minutes, which were either mimicked or copied directly by other percussion quartets in the years that followed as the term *samul nori* increasingly came to denote a genre.[8]

One of these canonical works is the entertainment-based composition known by the alternative titles of "Honam karak" (Rhythmic patterns of Chŏlla province) or "Honam udo kut" (Chŏlla-province "right side" ritual/performance), direct references to the rhythmic patterns and style of playing characteristic of *p'ungmul* ensembles hailing from the western counties of Chŏlla province (represented officially by Iri Nongak). In this particular case, SamulNori faithfully reproduced the first movement of the *p'an kut*—"Och'ae chilgut"—in nearly every musical detail (the exception is an extra rhythm *kutkŏri* inserted between Iri's fourth and fifth cycles; see table 3.1).

As a direct point of reference for comparison with the *p'ungmul* version in figure 3.1, as well as to aid the reader in hearing this rhythm as it is played on track #1 of the accompanying CD (performed by a *samul nori* team from the National Center for Korean Traditional Performing Arts [Kungnip Kugagwŏn Samulnori], a rival group started by Kim Yongbae of the original 1978 quartet), I have provided the SamulNori/*samul nori* model of the rhythmic cycle *och'ae chilgut* in figure 3.3. We see here essentially identical numbers and lengths of

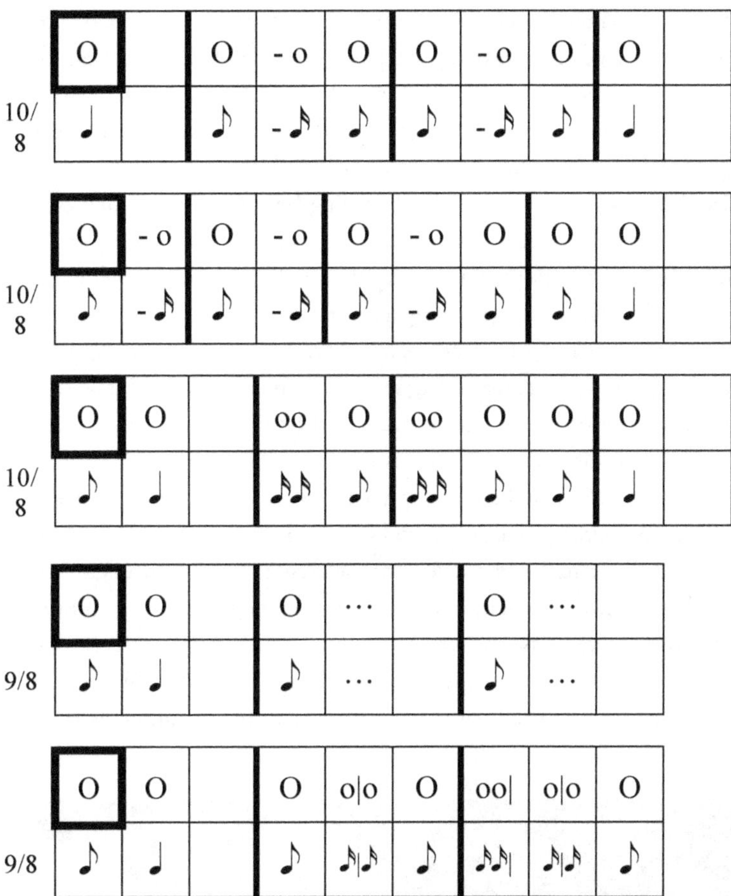

Figure 3.3 Kungnip Kugagwŏn Samulnori's *och'ae chilgut* (CD track #1, 0:00–1:54). Key: O = loud *soe* stroke, o = weaker *soe* stroke.

phrases, number of beats, and stroke order in the gong lines. Beats in phrase II are organized internally only slightly differently from the equivalent *p'ungmul* phrase (*p'ungmul*: 2 + 3 + 3 + 2; *samul nori*: 2 + 2 + 3 + 3), and the metrically free passages in *p'ungmul*'s fourth phrase are regularized in the *samul nori* version to create a phrase of 9/8. The first time this rhythm is played the listener will notice that the initial large gong stroke is omitted; as the performance continues, the small gong and hourglass drum player add embellishments on the basic model (timings for all of the cycles are provided in table 3.1).[9]

This second stage in the development of Korean folk percussion is very much an urban phenomenon, at least among the more professionally established groups. Performances are generally indoors in concert halls or arenas and are held on dates or at times that have no particular seasonal or religious significance—and this most often means on the weekend, in conformity to urban cycles.[10] As in most *samul nori* compositions, the performers are seated in close proximity, facing each other in a semicircular formation. A fair amount of eye contact is required because of the demands of playing by memory, the lack of a formal conductor, and the need to be attuned to small tempo and dynamic fluctuations, as well as transitions, signaled by the small gong (*soe*) player (a role taken from rural *p'ungmul* and *namsadang* performance practice; see figure 3.4). This close interaction over a number of years—membership is set among professional *samul nori* groups—fosters a strong sense of intimacy among the performers.

The introduction of the concert hall and its distinctive setup and rules for access have complicated ramifications for the composition of the audience and the manner in which it listens and participates. With performances moving away from community-building social functions common in the countryside to mostly clock-governed and convenient gatherings for city dwellers (and hence profitable for concert organizers)—cycles following the flow of money rather than the flow of the seasons (see especially Simmel 1950)—a level of anonymity becomes increasingly acceptable. Friends and family of the performers are always present, so personal ties continue to exist for the musicians, but because

Figure 3.4 A *samul nori* ensemble (© National Center for Korean Traditional Performing Arts).

the ability to pay admission determines the right to attend, not membership in any particular community group, audiences become more and more strangers to each other. The exchange of money immediately establishes a degree of professionalism (which always implies hierarchy), and *samul nori* performers are frequently employed full-time in the music business, further separating themselves from their rural *p'ungmul* counterparts. This distancing from the audience, however, characterized interactions with the *namsadang*, and so we must be careful not to valorize the more amateur variants of the folk percussion tradition.

Critics of the concert hall are quick to reveal the problematic symbolic and social elements embedded in its construction and attendance etiquette. Aubert has more recently reminded us of the predilection for one-way communication, with artists bathed in special lighting while an audience seated in the dark is reduced to passive spectators with an almost religious receptive attitude (2007:35). Blesser and Salter take this a step further, claiming the acoustical properties of an auditorium "should lower the aural status of the listeners," and that this design "therefore includes, intentionally or incidentally, the aural symbolism of dominance" (2007:53). While much of the eating and socializing that were found in the Iri Nongak performance is of course absent in a hall, on many occasions I have been part of an audience that "transgresses" concert rules by banging their feet, clapping their hands, and calling out to the performers on stage (I even recall one *samul nori* concert I attended in 2001 at the National Center where I was convinced that our row of chairs was going to rip out of the floor). In many ways I believe a typical *samul nori* audience adapts to the elevated stage and confinement of arranged seating in a manner analogous to a Western rock concert; and at most *samul nori* concerts, access before and especially afterward to the performers is expected and eagerly anticipated.

For the first generation of *samul nori* attendees, the sound and imagery of the percussion instruments on stage evoked for many a life left behind in the countryside, one still powerfully linked to ideas of community, nature, and ritual. As the critic Hahn Myong-hee noted in chapter 2, this confluence of nostalgia and the new drew in audiences from many different social and generational backgrounds (1992:6). Even with all of the trappings (and benefits) of the concert hall taking over urban Korean social life in the late twentieth century, audiences were not prepared to completely give up on feelings of closeness, evident in their unbridled enthusiasm and desire to be heard by the objects of their affection. The foundations of the "rock star" status enjoyed by Kim Duk Soo and others had already been firmly laid by their *namsadang* predecessors, and many *samul nori* practitioners in the future will continue to draw on this legacy.

The "Right" Way (In the Studio)

In the spring of 1996, when I was well into the second half of my doctoral fieldwork period, I encountered a third stage of the movement and rhythm *och'ae chilgut*. I had driven with one of my principal *p'ungmul* mentors from the North Chŏlla provincial capital of Chŏnju—my home base for research—to the city of Kunsan to attend a SamulNori concert. The event itself did not present anything I was not already familiar with, but a stand set up outside after the performance selling various SamulNori paraphernalia offered, among other things, a newly released, double-CD set with the enticing title of *Kim Duk Soo SamulNori: The Definitive Edition, Volumes I and II* (the original Korean title is *Kim Tŏksu SamulNori: Kyŏlchŏng p'an, I & II* [King SYNCD-114, 1996]; see figure 3.5). My teacher grabbed up a set on the spot, and we spent the drive back to Chŏnju

Figure 3.5 *Kim Duk Soo SamulNori: The Definitive Edition* [Korean text in center], *Volumes I and II* (© SamulNori Hanullim).

listening to it on the car stereo, engaged in lively debate over the relative merits and drawbacks of the new purchase.

The CDs and program notes contained a number of interesting new developments and ambiguities. In addition to most of the core repertoire was added, for the first time, a composition made up of rhythmic patterns from the eastern counties of North and South Chŏlla provinces, the so-called left side school or way (*Honam chwado*). But more importantly, the standard "right side" piece based on the *p'ungmul/nongak* movement "Och'ae chilgut" had undergone a name change to "Honam udo p'ungmulgut karak," or "*P'ungmulgut* Rhythmic Patterns of the Right [Western] Counties of Chŏlla Province." Did the inclusion of "*p'ungmul(gut)*" in the title now mean that the piece no longer belonged to the *samul nori* repertoire, but was in fact in the older tradition of rural percussion music and dance? A quartet still performed the piece, but noticeable and significant augmentations included a double-reed *t'aep'yŏngso* player[11] and condensed renditions of the second and third movements, sets of rhythmic patterns absent in every other recording or performance up to that time.[12] A listening to the track, however, revealed an essentially *samul nori* version of the "Och'ae chilgut" movement with the subsequent two movements of the *p'an kut* given only seven minutes out of a total twenty-one minutes and fifteen seconds (the content and order of the first movement is provided in table 3.1; the cycle *och'ae chilgut* is identical to the version notated in figure 3.3).

The piece was recorded by Samulnori Chŏnsoe, a regionally based quartet ostensibly from the "right side" school employed under Kim Duk Soo's umbrella SamulNori organization. The performers were in the same room (the studio) and seated in typical *samul nori* style for the recording, but these particulars are irrelevant in terms of live audience reception as the work in this version only exists on CD (you cannot, to my knowledge, go and see a performance of it). The audience of this digitized presentation is obviously consumers of the physical product; nevertheless, the liner notes and packaging are almost exclusively in Korean, suggesting a local target group. We may also assume that most purchasers are themselves amateur *samul nori* players or enthusiasts, due to the narrow scope of the selections, and that they will view the performers on the CD as specialists, especially with the title "definitive edition." Money is paid for the right to listen, or at least for the opportunity of sharing it with others, yet we can only surmise as to where and under what conditions the CD is heard. And there is of course no direct interaction with the performers; individual musician names are not listed in the liner notes, in the event someone wanted to correspond with the musicians in a more personal manner.

CDs and other such forms of recorded, commodified art define distinctively—though not exclusively—urban forms of listening and reception. There is certainly the sense that "accessibility replaces the festival" (Attali 1985:100) with the unique, exceptional event of the live concert being freed from performing human agents, so that the piece can be heard at any time, in any place where there is a CD player, and in any manner the listener sees fit (Durant 1984:5; Feld 1994:258–60). Original social functions are frequently forgotten or obscured, with the danger of "isolated, self-contained works intended as the objects of disinterested contemplation" (Small 1998:107). Physicality in the form of dance or visual motion is erased, signaling perhaps a change in values towards a more Western classical music aesthetic (McClary 1991:136). Recordings also valorize an aesthetic of cleanness, hyper-focused on a kind of perfection that "excludes error, hesitation, [and] noise," a "vision [that] gradually leads people to forget that music was once background noise and a form of life, hesitation and stammering" (Attali 1985:106).

And yet even if the listener-receiver of a CD knows or cares little about the original cultural context for the recording, s/he can still construct and reference meaningful experiences that are both "nonnative" while simultaneously containing some element or grain of the tradition that is embedded in the mediated source (Rice 1994:4–5). In the world of academia and the study of "world music," where there is considerable anxiety over commodified forms of musical expression, we can often lose sight of those who partake in emotionally engaged listening, that the sound of a single instrument—even its timbre—can evoke a tremendously diverse range of meanings and associations (Blesser and Salter 2007:13). This is especially true for fan groups and diasporic communities, where "the act of putting a cassette or CD into a machine evokes and organizes collective memories and present experiences of place with an intensity, power and simplicity unmatched by any other social activity" (Stokes 1994:3; see also Bohlman 2002:145). Driving with my drumming mentor back from the SamulNori concert that spring afternoon, there was the tangible sense that we were equally invested in the recording and its meanings, sharing in its agency. Far from characterizing our relationship with the piece in terms of distance, I prefer the oxymoron *displaced closeness.*

The Road Ahead (Beyond Borders)

In 1997 I returned again to Korea to participate in the Seventh World SamulNori Competition, sponsored by Kim Duk Soo's organization.[13] These events were always a great way to meet other foreign performers and enthusiasts, check out who was "hot" among the up-and-coming local talent, and observe what new trends and developments had resulted as an outgrowth of Kim Duk Soo's imagination. There seemed to be an unspoken, almost karmic connection between the various *samul nori* groups that competed each year with regard to the piece they chose for presentation before the judges: in the Sixth Competition (1995) it was overwhelmingly "Yŏngnam karak," or the rhythmic patterns of Kyŏngsang province, and this particular year it was "Honam karak," the piece based on "Och'ae chilgut," which has been examined numerous times throughout this chapter. More important, however, was that a new CD had just been released.

The recording, titled *From the Earth, to the Sky: Kim Duk Soo Samulnori & Red Sun Group* (Samsung/ak SCO-123NAN, 1997), was a collaborative effort with the Austro-American jazz/avant-garde ensemble Red Sun, the fourth of such joint projects dating back to 1989.[14] The goal of the collaboration, according to the liner notes written by the coproducer and composer Wolfgang Puschnig (also the leader of Red Sun), was to combine "*yin* and *yang*, east and west, rhythm and melody, harmony and modality," with special attention paid to improvisation. The recording claimed to have achieved a new unity, covering a "vast field of musical possibilities and expressions by giving and taking from each other." Complementing the core Korean percussion quartet were an alto saxophone, an electric guitar, an electric bass, and a number of supporting vocalists.

The titles of the various tracks were somewhat atmospheric—e.g., "Burdens of Life," "Going Places," "Another Step to the Sky"—and did not really suggest what type of compositions these might be. As I began listening to the CD upon my arrival back in the United States, however, I discovered to my delight that the second track, titled "The Road Ahead," was in fact melody and harmony layered over the first three rhythmic patterns of the "Och'ae chilgut" movement (see table 3.1). It was cleverly disguised and took some reorientation on my part to hear these patterns with Western voices and instruments, but the overall mix and effect quickly grew on me and did not (in my opinion) jar the listener with any awkward moments or juxtapositions (further discussion and analysis of this album is found in chapter 5). And in the program notes to the track there was the familiar metaphor of the road: "The road is always a metaphor for life. Though it is long, it is one we must travel. The rhythmic pattern used in this piece is rightly *kil kunak* [literally, "road military music"]. It is a characteristic military march of Korea. Red Sun, understanding this meaning exactly, performed a new road music of their own" (translated from the Korean).

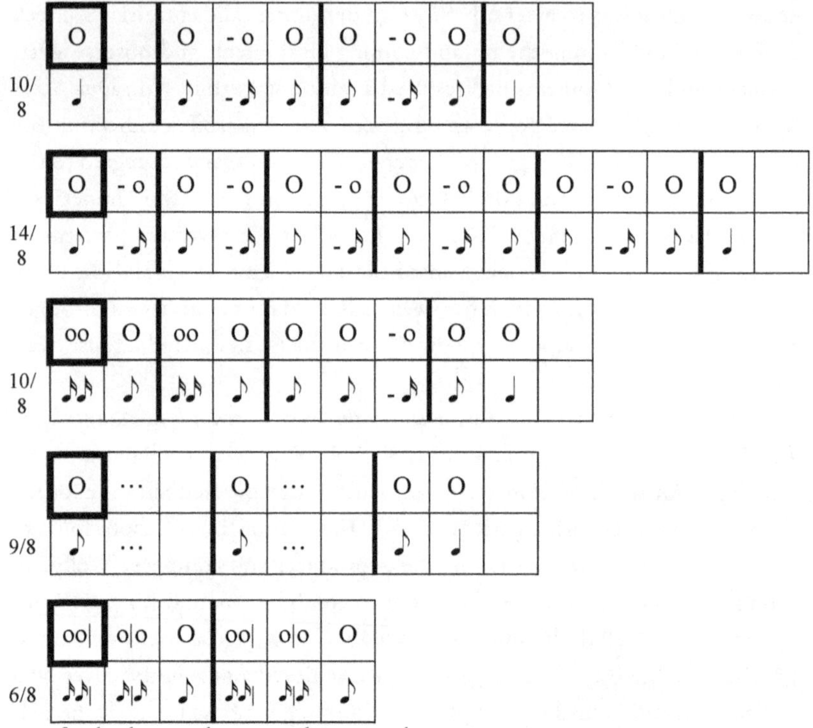

Figure 3.6 Kim Duk Soo SamulNori's *och'ae chilgut* (CD track #2, 0:00–2:03).

Key: O = loud *soe* stroke, o = weaker *soe* stroke.

Figure 3.6 provides the model of the first cycle *och'ae chilgut* as it is heard on track #2 of the accompanying CD ("The Road Ahead"; timings are listed in table 3.1). On first glance the rhythm appears to have undergone some significant modifications: what in the *p'ungmul* and earlier *samul nori* versions had essentially represented a cycle of five phrases organized as 10/8, 10/8, 10/8, 9/8, and 9/8 was now played as 10/8, 14/8, 10/8, 9/8, and 6/8. If I reconfigure this rhythm to match the earlier versions by stroke content, however, one sees that all that has really happened here is that Kim Duk Soo has added one eighth note (or box) in phrase II, and has then shifted the large gong stroke over by one beat in each of the remaining phrases (see figure 3.7). The important point here is that continuity with tradition is maintained, so that Korean percussionists and aficionados of the genre immediately recognize the way this older rhythm has been used and reinterpreted in a modern context (to be further addressed in chapter 5).

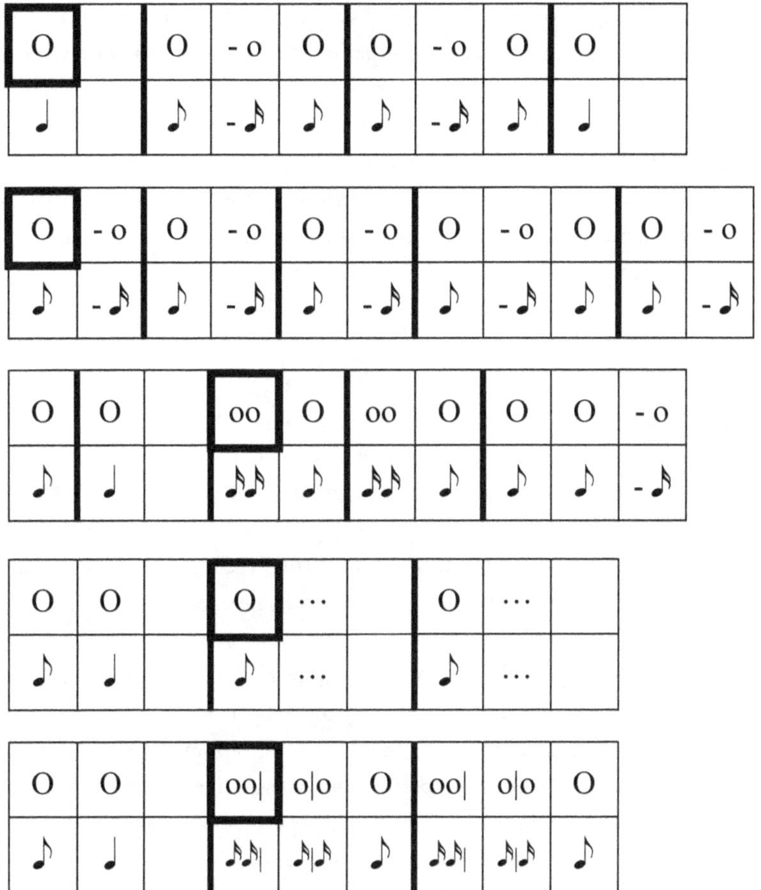

Figure 3.7 Reconfigured *och'ae chilgut* from figure 3.6 (compare with figure 3.3). Key: O = loud *soe* stroke, o = weaker *soe* stroke.

Most surface details of this recording parallel those of the previous collection discussed earlier. The musical work exists in digital format only as a commodity, so that its reception is very open-ended in terms of time, place, and the conditions under which it is listened to. The audience is again consumers of the physical product, yet with a broader and more international target group in mind due to the CD's instrumentation, sound, and case and liner notes in both Korean and English. Unlike the previous three manifestations of "Och'ae chilgut," this new context is now nearly completely divorced from a traditional Korean folk percussion aesthetic. Most nonspecialist listeners, especially foreigners, will miss the *p'ungmul/nongak* connection altogether, and, more significantly, the rhythmic patterns have for the first time been reduced to the role of accompaniment. Ironically, this distance has probably served to bring on board a large segment of Korean youth society not raised on *p'ungmul* or even *samul nori*, one more at home in the realms of popular and fusion musics. For these listeners the sound alone of Korean drumming is enough to remind them of their ethnic heritage, while at the same time not threatening their sense of cosmopolitanism and membership in a globalized community.

Conclusion

By examining the various parameters of location, performer, and audience and their contributions to the construction of a performance space, I hope to have revealed the multifaceted nature of the larger activity we call music. The constant throughout this chapter was a consistent, recognizably related rhythm or succession of rhythmic patterns found under the heading of "Och'ae chilgut"; yet as it traveled among the various stages of folk percussion music and dance in the late twentieth century, it came to mean different things to an increasingly diverse set of musical participants. "Och'ae chilgut" began in the countryside as entertainment for villagers after a hard day of labor or ritual fund-raising, and even as the older contexts began to disappear contemporary groups continued to honor these events by holding performances on dates of particular agricultural and/or religious significance. Similar such performances were codified and professionalized by the *namsadang*, though without the same concern for coordination with life cycle events. As urbanization on a large scale took place in the 1970s, bringing with it a characteristic set of constraints on time, place, and appropriate behavior, so too did the context for this piece change toward more urban cycles and modes of presentation and reception. Commodification of the tradition was soon to follow, with variously packaged CDs creating new frameworks for listening and understanding both domestically and abroad.

Musical performance and reception as a complex design formed by various angles and perspectives creates overlapping and often conflicting relationships. As "Och'ae chilgut" made its journey from the village to the city and beyond, its nature transformed rapidly from one exclusively of closeness to one that began to incorporate elements of distance. In social terms this reflected the move from a tight-knit, communal society characterized by high-density relationships to one that included a more scattered, international makeup of low-density relationships. In the past I was content to see this trajectory tracing a unilateral arc away from conceptions of proximity, but now I believe that a feeling of community has always been there, just in modified terms that are harder to quantify. What is certain is that as "music" continues both to shape and to adapt to new social structures and technologies of the twenty-first century, so too will Korean percussion music and dance and its practitioners, whoever and wherever they might be.

4

Cosmological Didacticism

Sacred Geometry and Educational Outreach

> Through scientific understanding, our world has become de-humanized. Man feels himself isolated in the cosmos. He is no longer involved in nature and has lost his emotional participation in natural events, which hitherto had a symbolic meaning for him. Thunder is no longer the voice of a god, nor is lightning his avenging missile. No river contains a spirit, no tree means a man's life, no snake is the embodiment of wisdom, and no mountain still harbors a great demon . . . His immediate communication with nature is gone forever, and the emotional energy it generated has sunk into the unconscious.
>
> JUNG 1976:255

Media accounts and academic analyses of SamulNori's enduring popularity have focused almost exclusively on its aesthetic dimensions (Kim Taegyun 1990; Chang Kwangyŏl 1996), yet from its genesis SamulNori has invested considerable time, effort, and resources on education and the promotion of its Korean cultural heritage. Here again the connection to the *namsadang* is telling, as Kim Duk Soo has directly credited his time with itinerant performers to fueling his desire to travel, teach, and spread the *samul nori* word throughout the world (Kim and Yun 1994). In the introduction I outlined SamulNori's early foreign touring schedule, beginning with Japan in 1982. By 1987 a camp had been opened in Miasamura, Japan, and from there other camps throughout Japan and South Korea were established to serve the needs of the growing number of *samul nori* enthusiasts (photo documentation from Miasamura in 1987 and '88 is found in SamulNori 1988:125–45). In chapter 3 I briefly mentioned the SamulNori competitions (*kyŏrugi*) that began in 1989, which expanded to become an international event with foreign teams competing every other year (1995 was the 6th World SamulNori Competition, 1997 the 7th competition). The brochure given out at the 6th World SamulNori Competition (figure 4.1) plainly lays out the group's educational and motivational philosophy:

> For almost fifteen years, SamulNori has gone to all parts of the world not only to perform, but to conduct its workshops which it considers as important as its concerts. This investment into education has created a great body of Samulnorians around the world. Witnessing the increasing popularity of SamulNori in many countries, we at SamulNori Hanullim have agreed it is time to gather the many players and groups from Europe, North America, and Asia in Korea. Furthermore, we have renamed the title of our competition to the World SamulNori Competition. In response to this increased demand for Samulnori classes we have also opened our Puyo [Puyŏ] SamulNori school, dedicated to the teaching of samulnori. (1995 competition brochure, English original)

SamulNori's Puyŏ Training Institute (SamulNori Hanullim Puyŏ Kyoyugwŏn)—as it came to be called—was established in September 1994, roughly a year after the founding of the larger umbrella organization of SamulNori Hanullim. The location had historical and symbolic significance, as Puyŏ was the capital of the ancient Paekche kingdom (18 BCE to 669 CE, an area that encompassed modern-day Chŏlla province), an era acknowledged for its artistic and cultural merits. The institute was (and is) open to the general public—including primary, secondary, and university-level students, as well as teachers—with sessions held during the winter and summer breaks. Sessions lasted from one to one and a half weeks with a number of course offerings available, including learning

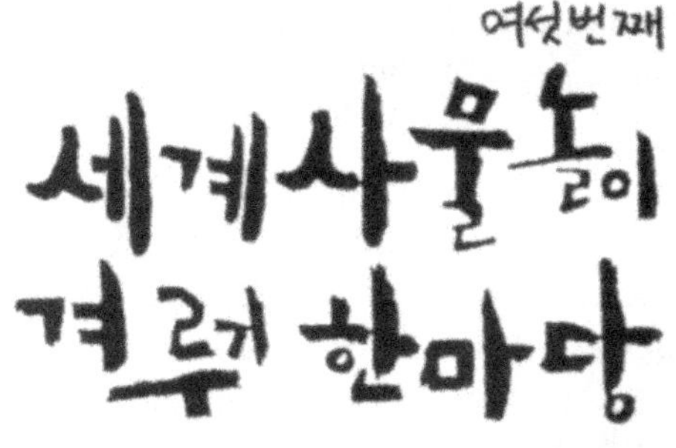

Figure 4.1 Brochure from the "6th World SamulNori Competition," 1995 (© SamulNori Hanullim).

any of the four core percussion instruments in addition to other elements of traditional culture (dance, flute, mask dance, etc.), a format modeled after similar *p'ungmul* training institutes (see Hesselink 2006:143–47 for the *p'ungmul* contexts). In 1995, when I was conducting fieldwork, the institute's fees seemed reasonable, organized into four tiers: non-Hanullim member, adult (US$185), Hanullim member, adult ($165), non-Hanullim member, student ($150), and

Hanullim member, student ($130); these fees included room and board. An ethnographic account of a summer session in 1997 is recorded in Park, Shingil 2000:204–18.

Early attendees of the institute knew what to expect because of a 1990 workbook released by SamulNori that has become a kind of bible in the *samul nori* world. First published in Korean under the title *SamulNori: Changgo ŭi kibon* (*SamulNori: Changgo Fundamentals*; Korean Conservatorium of Performing Arts, 1990), an English version was soon to follow, titled *Korean Traditional Percussion: Samulnori Rhythm Workbook I, Basic Changgo* (Korean Conservatorium of Performing Arts, 1992). Two more volumes in the series were published over the next three years (Korean Conservatorium of Performing Arts 1993, 1995), and in 1994 SamulNori created an in-house publication that complemented the notational efforts of the workbooks (SamulNori Hanullim Yŏn'gu Kyoyukpu 1994a, 1994b, 1994c, 1994d, 1994e, 1994f). As educational director, the renowned percussionist (and later Silk Road member) Kim Dong-Won (Kim Tongwŏn) published a musical-theoretical treatise on *samul nori* rhythms (1998), and with Kim Duk Soo's help they jointly released another English-language publication under the auspices of the Overseas Koreans Foundation, titled *Samulnori Textbook* (Kim, Duk Soo et al. 1999). This latter work was produced in conjunction with two VHS recordings (*A SamulNori Class with Kim Duk-Soo: Learning Korean Culture Series Tape 1 and 2*, 1999). Kim Duk Soo has also put together a brief practical guide to the *sangmo* spinning-tasseled hat (Kim Tŏksu 1998).[1]

This is all to say that there is a rich body of pedagogical material with SamulNori that is of considerable interest meriting a detailed investigation. What I have found to be consistent throughout their oeuvre—methods that distinguish their efforts from other traditional arts organizations in Korea—is their integration of music theory and performance practice with a distinctively pan–East Asian cosmology.[2] In this chapter I will elucidate these cosmological principles by focusing on the concept known in Sino-Korean as *wŏn-pang-kak* (圓方角 [원방각]), literally "circle, square, [and] triangle," and its application as revealed through the two series of instructional materials published by SamulNori in the 1990s. The broader task will be to understand the nature of the relationship implied by these mathematical building blocks, and the potential lessons they teach us about our connection and responsibility to the natural world about us.

While the roots of *wŏn-pang-kak* theorizing can be traced back conclusively to Shang dynasty China, over the centuries it was slowly absorbed and internalized by all of East Asia, at the elite and commoner levels alike (Baldinger

1954:49; Dilling 2001:175–79). As the twentieth century came to a close in South Korea, a time for many marked by confusion and conflicting values as Western culture and/or Christianity in many cases challenged or outright replaced older folkloric beliefs and religious practices (Yoon, Yee-Heum 1997; Buswell and Lee 2005), SamulNori boldly embraced this very deep, pan–East Asian worldview. A more complete story of their success can, therefore, be credited to their tapping into this shared ethos, a way of relating to the world still residing in many Koreans' collective subconscious. By pricking it and bringing it to the surface, then verbalizing and formalizing it in such a way through pedagogical materials, SamulNori found a way to make this knowledge accessible to the broader population. SamulNori thus is a fascinating case study in the reintroduction of traditional belief systems through the medium of education that has directly contributed to a music tradition's vitality and continuing pertinence to modern audiences.

These texts fulfill a number of additional important roles. For students and/or researchers of *samul nori*—both foreign and native—the workbooks provide a means by which to move beyond superficial technical skills by engaging with ways of conceptualizing the tradition, with ways of understanding the deep connections existing between cosmology, musical structure, physical embodiment, and energy. These issues speak to the underlying motives behind *why* this music is made and shared, not just how it is put together. The existence of such materials also suggests a way of satisfying, or at least assuaging, concerns expressed by nonnative directors and evaluators of world music ensembles in Western academia who are looking for meaningful and in some way "authentic" representations of the culture they are teaching and performing (see Solís 2004).

Sacred Geometry: Chinese Contexts

To make proper sense of SamulNori's interpretation and use of *wŏn-pang-kak*, it is necessary to first tease out the historical strands and precedents set in the Chinese contexts that gave birth to it. While the basic concepts are intuited by most Koreans—these theories would form the basis of a *p'ungsu* (*feng shui* in Chinese) worldview and methodology—this material and its relationship to drumming/music has not been fully explicated in either Korean or English. My discussion begins with its first two components, the circle (*wŏn*) and the square (*pang*). For reasons not entirely clear, due to nonexistent literary records, ancient Chinese apparently associated the shape of the circle with heaven and that of the square with earth. It has been suggested that such pairings might have already been in place in Neolithic China (3500–2000 BCE), because of the prevalence of jade ritual vessels found carved in the shape of a squared tube with a cylindrical bore (Barnes 1999:88, 114). Another source claims that in Neolithic burial sites each grave was rounded off at the head and squared at the feet, symbolizing heaven and earth (Shen 2001:14–15),[3] and in the subsequent Bronze Age bodies were found in rectangular tombs with circular vessels placed above the head (Barnes 1999:129).

Intent becomes clearer during the late Shang dynasty (c. 1200–1045 BCE), signaled by the first written records in China—the earliest in East Asia—in the form of oracle-bone inscriptions. From such accounts we see Shang cosmological thought envisioning the world as square, oriented to the four cardinal points (Ch.: *fang* 方) plus a central core area: "[This] concern with cardinality . . . was part of the deep structure of Late Shang religious and political cosmology, and its legacy was profound" (Keightley 2000:72; see also ibid., 66, 81). Derived from ancient Chinese ritual practices, this perspective of four sides *plus center* formed the basis of the later *wuxing* (五行, five elements) theory that has penetrated nearly every aspect of East Asian cultural practice.[4] This organizing principle is seen in the alternate Chinese character for earth 亞 (Ch.: *ya*)—a central square surrounded by four other squares—the design of which was prominent on ritual vessels and in the construction of tombs during this same period (Allan 1991:88–101).

The earliest direct association in print of the characters heaven/circle and earth/square (天圓 地方) appears in the *Zhou bi suan jing* (Mathematics Classics of the Zhou Gnomons), a revolutionary Chinese text on mathematics, astronomy, and cosmology completed around the first century CE, but reflecting a much older oral tradition (Allan 1991:57, with the Chinese text reproduced in Chen, Cheng-Yih 1996:151). Borrowing the circle and square characters from early mathematics and mapping them onto physical representations (Chen, Cheng-Yih 1996:182), the *Zhou bi* presented a square world composed of "basic numbers" (i.e., the cardinal points) coupled to a circular heaven represented by a celestial "rain-hat," or umbrella (the original text is reproduced in Cullen 1996:174).[5] In combination these shapes were imbued with tremendous power: "The square and the circle are of universal application in all activities of the myriad things. Making a circle within a square is called 'circling the square'; making a square within a circle is called 'squaring the circle'" (Cullen 1996:182; see figure 4.2).[6] Having said this, the *Zhou bi* does not explicitly claim that the actual shape of the earth was square, but rather that this was a stylized representation (true intent or belief is unclear). And, in fact, the earlier writer Zeng Can

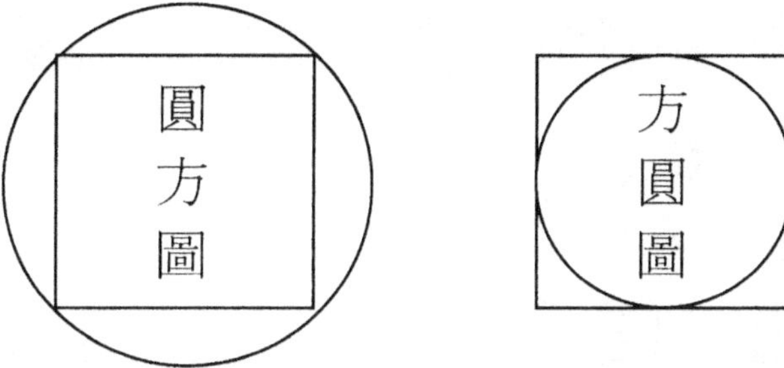

Figure 4.2 Circles and squares from the *Zhou bi*.

(505–440 BCE) stated in his *Zeng zi* (The Book of Master Zeng) that the sky was not *in reality* round, nor the earth square, but rather they exhibited those qualities (cited in Chen, Cheng-Yih 1996:152–53).

Critically it was during the Han dynasty (206 BCE–220 CE) that mankind entered as a central character on this cosmological stage. With the writings of the Chinese philosopher Xunzi—compiled during the first century BCE—heaven, earth, and mankind became bound together in a complementary and symbiotic relationship, a view that "became one of the seminal ideas in Confucian cosmological and ethical thought" (deBary et al. 1999:170).[7] Human agency became intertwined with the spiritual wellbeing of the country, so that "the ritual structure of society [was] part of a much larger weave, the ritual structure of natural process, and the Confucian ideal [was] for human community to dwell as an organic part of the cosmological weave of li [ritual]" (Hinton 1999:xviii).[8] At a time when *wuxing* and *yin-yang* were fully integrated into Han dynasty thought and practice (Guo 2003:29–30), Chinese scholars reinterpreted the interlocking *yin-yang* pattern (K.: *t'aegŭk* 太極) as three interlocking swirls (K.: *samt'aegŭk* 三太極; see figure 4.3) to accommodate the specifically heaven-earth-mankind worldview, a symbol of central importance to SamulNori musicians in the twentieth century (see U Shirha 2004:220–33 for the original Chinese texts with Korean commentary).[9]

The final component of our geometric composite—the triangle—appears in modified form during this era in the *Zhou bi*. Expanding the cosmological building blocks from the square and circle to include the trysquare (Ch.: *ju* 矩, two sides of a square at a right angle), the appropriate passage reads:

> The square pertains to the Earth, and the circle pertains to Heaven. Heaven is a circle, and the Earth is square. The numbers of the square are basic, and the circle

Figure 4.3 *Samt'aegŭk* symbol, South Korea (photo by Nathan Hesselink).

> is produced from the square . . . Thus one who knows Earth is wise, but one who knows Heaven is a sage. Wisdom comes from the base [of the right triangle] and the base comes from the trysquare. Through its relations to numbers, what the trysquare does is simply to settle and regulate everything there is. (reproduced in Cullen 1996:174)[10]

What this excerpt does not include is the crucial association of mankind with the trysquare (later interpreted as a triangle), the weakest link in terms of textual sources in SamulNori's *wŏn-pang-kak* theorizing. This missing piece would be filled in much later by an early twentieth-century Korean historian and philosopher.

Sacred Geometry: Korean Contexts

Material culture exists from earlier Korean dynasties that reveals direct influences from Shang and post-Shang Chinese cosmological thought. The architectural logic of the Buddhist Sŏkkuram Grotto, built in the mid-eighth century CE during the Shilla dynasty, exhibits the now familiar feature of a rectangular antechamber symbolizing earth space connected by a small liminal passageway—protected by the gods of the cardinal directions—to the seated Buddha in a circular chamber, crowned by a dome signifying heavenly space (Korean Overseas Information Service 2003:127–34). And in Koryŏ dynasty (918–1259) furniture, a common metalwork design was a circular shape imposed upon a square, representing "heaven-in-earth, [with] the circle [as] symbolic of heaven and the square, earth" (Wright and Pai 2000:157). But it was during the Chosŏn dynasty (1392–1910), when (Neo-) Confucianism was embraced officially, first by Korean elites and then eventually at the folk level, that the crucial belief in the interrelationship and interdependence of heaven, earth, and mankind took hold (Deuchler 1992; Yi Chongsul 1997:87; Choi, Changjo 2003). In Sino-Korean it is often reflected in the phrase *ch'ŏn-chi-in* (天地人 [천지인], heaven-earth-man).

State rites became the central locus of this cosmological drama, performed as obligations or moral indebtedness under the rubric of auspiciousness to the realms of heaven, earth, and the ancestors. Spirits honored at royal sacrificial rites were classified as heavenly (*ch'ŏnshin*), earthly (*chigi*), or of humans (*in'gwi*), and for certain ceremonies circular altars for offerings to heaven and square altars were constructed for offerings to earth, under the principle of *ch'ŏn-wŏn* (heaven-circle) and *chi-pang* (earth-square; Provine 1988:15; Chen, Cheng-Yih 1996:151; Yi Chaesuk 1998:3–5).[11] *Ch'ŏn-chi-in* cosmology was similarly referenced in the creation of the Korean alphabet, *han'gŭl*, in the mid-fifteenth century: authors of the *Hunmin chŏngŭm haerye* (Explanations and Examples of the Correct Sounds for the Instruction of the People) of 1446 stressed the ideological and linguistic roots of *han'gŭl*'s formation in *ŭm-yang* (Ch.: *yin-yang*), *ohaeng* (Ch.: *wuxing*), and the "Three Great Absolutes" or "Three Powers," i.e., heaven, earth, and mankind (Ledyard 1997:62–63). The three basic vowel elements included the • (round dot, symbolizing heaven), — (horizontal line, symbolizing earth), and | (vertical line, symbolizing man) (Kim, Jin-p'yŏng 1983:84). And the eighteen opening couplets of the sixth century CE Chinese poem the *Ch'ŏnjamun* (Korean for *The Thousand Character Classic*), read by all Korean scholars of the Chosŏn period, addressed heaven, earth, and man (see Han'guk chŏngshin munhwa yŏn'guwŏn 2002).

Central to the well being of the Korean state was the proper performance of music. Painstakingly planned and choreographed for specific rituals and occasions, at the elite level nothing less than the political, moral, and spiritual success of the nation was at stake: "In the Confucian idea of music, emphasis is clearly on the spiritual; stress should not be laid on superficial beauty of melody and specious notes. Furthermore, the Confucianist considers music to be intended for the purpose of regulating the state and perfecting the individual. In this classical conception of music there cannot be music for pleasure or entertainment" (Song, Bang-song 1980:35; see also Provine 1988:12–14). Ritual spaces were steeped in *ch'ŏn-chi-in* symbolism sonically and visually; a clear example is found in the clapper drums—a set of three instruments called the *nodo* (played for rituals honoring human spirits), *yŏngdo* (honoring deities for the earth), and *noedo* (honoring deities of heaven)—which had the *samt'aegŭk* painted on their drumheads, a pattern found on other instruments and architecture at the performance site (Chang Sahun 1995:139–42; see also Joo, Young-ja 2008). These Korean enactments harked back to an earlier fundamental notion in early Chinese philosophy and cosmology that music and the cosmos were inextricably linked: music reflected the movements of heaven and earth and the binary forces of *yin* and *yang*, hence music could be viewed as the universe in a microcosm, and that when properly executed had auspicious results for both man and his environment (Goldin and Mair 2005:130).[12]

The final piece of the puzzle—the association of mankind with the triangle (the Chinese character for the trysquare most likely misread)—is provided in the highly influential yet controversial *Handan kogi* (Chronicles on Korean History), a text complied in 1911 by the scholar Kye Yŏnsu outlining Korea's supposed ancient history (Kye Yŏnsu 2006). Historical accuracy and mixed academic response aside, Kye had access to or possessed considerable personal knowledge of scholarly Korean and Chinese sources, as well as similar commoner practices and beliefs (compare with Kim Ŭisuk 1993 and Kŭm Changt'ae 2000). Recognized as the primary (and perhaps only) source for linking *wŏn-pang-kak* geometry directly to *ch'ŏn-chi-in* cosmology (Kang Muhak 1991), the *Handan kogi* speaks of the ancient Korean kingdom performing heaven rituals on round altars (*wŏndan* 圓壇), earth rituals on square mounds (*panggu* 方丘), and rituals for deceased elders (humans) on triangular platforms (*kangmok* 角木; Kye Yŏnsu 2006:159).[13] The *Handan kogi* also stresses in numerous passages the interrelatedness and completeness of heaven-earth-man as a kind of sacred three-in-one, intelligible only under the guiding principle of *hongik in'gan*, or devotion to the welfare of mankind (Kye Yŏnsu 2006:84, 149).[14] SamulNori would similarly embrace this moral imperative, reinterpreting and applying it in pedagogically and musicologically novel ways.

Pedagogical Visions

From very early on in their professional development as an ensemble, SamulNori employed a two-pronged approach, looking to preserve and transmit traditional music to local Koreans while at the same time introducing this heritage to the outside world. What has been most beneficial to their at times missionary-like efforts, however, is two series of instructional materials from the 1990s that drew upon their extensive travels and teaching experiences, notably published in both Korean and English. The first collection, composed of three workbooks released by the Korean Conservatorium of Performing Arts/SamulNori Academy of Music between 1990 and 1995 (1990 [Korean version] and 1992 [English version], 1993 [both languages], 1995 [Korean only]), outlines in considerable detail SamulNori's history and philosophy, focusing on the central concepts of *hana-a* (literally "one," linked to breathing, playing technique, and movement), *wŏn-pang-kak*, *hohŭp* (breathing technique), and *umjigim* (movement; see table 4.1 for the table of contents of Workbook I).[15] The preface to the first volume, written by a former Korean minister of culture, provides a concise account of the significance of this work: "Aware of the necessity of preserving and teaching this music," they developed "teaching methods consistent with modern

Table 4.1: Table of contents, SamulNori Workbook I (1992).

Section	Page range
Preface (Lee, O-Young)	3
What Is SamulNori? (Hahn, Myong-hee)	5–6
Author's Introduction	7–11
Preliminaries	15–28
[includes sections on *hana-a, wŏn-pang-kak, hohŭp,* and *umjigim*]	
Changgo Touch Technique	29–176
Simple Changgo Rhythms	177–79
Advanced Changgo Touch Technique	180–84
Tasurim	185–99
Appendix I: Introduction to Dance Changgo	201–4
Appendix 11: Care of Your Instrument/Replacing the Leather/Tuning	205–8
Quick Glossary	209

Korean society and accessible to those outside our country. With their own experiences as a basis and with the development of a systematic approach that still manages to retain the essential Korean spirit of the music, they have successfully produced a sorely needed work" (Lee, O-Young 1992).

In 1999, an updated textbook and related two-part video series aimed primarily at Koreans living abroad, part of a broader Learning Korean Culture series, was copublished by The Korean National University of Arts and the Overseas Koreans Foundation. The promotional material reads as follows:

> Learning Korean Culture series is a special co-presentation by the Overseas Koreans Foundation and The Korean National University of Arts, aiming to provide a systematic teaching device for overseas Koreans in learning their cultural roots. We hope this series will serve their sincere attempts in seeking their cultural identity and strengthening their own national dignity. (Kim, Duk Soo et al. 1999:back cover; Kim, Duk-Soo, *A SamulNori Class with Kim Duk-Soo: Learning Korean Culture Series Tape 1 and 2*, 1999; see table 4.2 for the table of contents)[16]

Unlike other folk percussion workbooks/textbooks published during roughly the same period (e.g., Ch'oe Ikhwan 1995; Ch'oe Pyŏngsam 2000), SamulNori's books looked to integrate cosmological concepts with music theory and performance practice. Introductory passages to both series emphasized the close interrelationship on the Korean peninsula between music, ritual, and agricultural cycles. Central to such religious activity was and is percussion, in the Korean context reflected in the proper balance of leather and metal, drum and gong, earth and heaven, and, by extension, *ŭm* (Ch.: *yin*) and *yang*:

Table 4.2: Table of contents, SamulNori Textbook (1999).

Section	Page range
What Is *Samulnori*?	1–5
Learning the *Hohŭp*	6–11
Notation and Rhythmic Structure in Samulnori [includes section on *wŏn-pang-kak*]	12–14
Playing Techniques	15–20
Yŏngnam Nongak	21–49

> Korea has many folk instruments, but if one were to have to select the instruments whose sounds best express the innermost soul of the Korean, these would be the sounds of the *buk* [*puk*] (barrel drum), and *changgo* (hourglass drum); the *ching* (large gong) and *k'kwaengwari* [*kkwaenggwari*] (small gong) . . . In SamulNori's music their masterful rhythms produce this marvelous sense of release while at the same time raising our spirits. In short, the most elemental, the most essential part of our Korean spirit is captured in their music. Further, the two instruments made of wood and leather, the *buk* and *changgo*, are symbolic of the earth, while the two gongs are symbolic of the heavens. Thus even in the composition of the ensemble itself it is as if the sounds of the heavens and earth meet and create, in addition, a cosmic harmony. (Lee, O-Young 1992)[17]

While the connection between instruments, musical practice, and this ancient cosmic duality is common in other Korean musicological literature (e.g., Wi Hosŏn 1994; Chŏng Haeim 2004), SamulNori's further exploration and application of the sacred geometry of *wŏn-pang-kak* is unique in its scope and vision.

The exact intellectual pedigree of this principle within SamulNori's organization remains unclear. Interactions with the late Dr. Zo Zayong (Cho Chayong)—curator, musician, folklorist, and architect—in the mid-1980s certainly raised SamulNori's awareness of indigenous spiritual and philosophical matters (see Zo Zayong 1988). In Zo's 1982 classic on shamanism and folk art, he highlights what he calls the "shamanistic trinity" of heaven, earth, and man (minus the circle, square, and triangle), though this was common knowledge among anyone even tangentially associated with shamanism and/or Korean folklore during that period (Zo Zayong 1982:44). SamulNori's focus on and interpretation of the term *hana-a* (literally "one"; see above), in contrast, can be directly linked to Zo's writings (ibid.:44).

The encounter specifically with *wŏn-pang-kak*, however, is credited to Lim (Im) Tongch'ang, a composer and performer brought on to develop the notational system for SamulNori's first workbook in 1990. According to Lim (personal communication, 2006), it was his own research that formed such a link between music/rhythm and cosmology, an idea he then taught to Kim Duk Soo and Kim Dong-Won, then director of research and education (confirmed by Kim Dong-Won, personal communication, 2008).[18] There is little question, however, that Kim Duk Soo and Kim Dong-Won continued to develop and deepen their understanding and use of *wŏn-pang-kak*, as demonstrated in the later 1999 textbook (see discussion below). And while it is beyond the immediate scope of this chapter, Kim Dong-Won has outlined in considerable detail in his writings why this connection was important to him, both in its historical resonance and in its efficacy as a pedagogical tool for modern audiences (Kim Tongwŏn 1998, 2002, 2003).

In both the workbook and textbook series, the logic of these geometric shapes is introduced via the previously discussed *samt'aegŭk*, or interlocking "Three Great Absolutes" (see figure 4.3). Beginning with the first workbook published in English (Korean Conservatorium of Performing Arts 1992:16–17, under "Preliminaries"), this symbol of threefoldness is shown to embody the perfect balance of heaven (*ch'ŏn*), earth (*chi*), and mankind (*in*), reflecting universality in the number three. Heaven is associated with the Sino-Korean character *wŏn* (circle), the "largest encompassing entity"; earth with *pang* (square), the "first pillar" that divides this entity; and finally mankind with *kak* (triangle), a further smaller division. These three realms are then further mapped onto the performer's body as a physical entity, with heaven/*wŏn* located in the region of the nose and mouth, earth/*pang* in the knees, and mankind/*kak* in the abdomen. The final graphic of this section depicts the performer seated behind the *changgo*, now taking the role of human mediator between the lower-pitched drumhead, signifying earth (the mallet hand), and the higher-pitched drumhead, signifying heaven (the stick hand; see figure 4.4). The drummer and the instrument thus become the physical embodiment of the entire cosmos. It is worth noting that this workbook never directly reproduces a circle, square, or triangle, but only infers them through the appropriate Sino-Korean characters.

Wŏn-pang-kak is then brought back under the next subheading of "Changgo Rhythm Notation," the most distinctive application of SamulNori's theorizing on the topic (1992:27). The trifurcating nature of heaven-earth-mankind

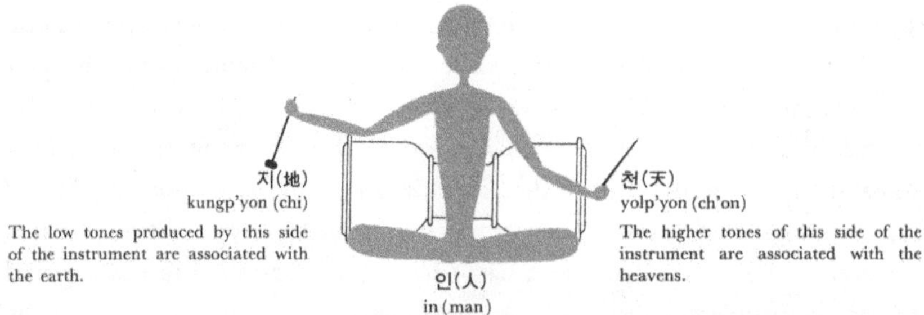

Figure 4.4 SamulNori *changgo* player graphic (© SamulNori Hanullim).

Figure 4.5 SamulNori metric visual indicator.

is directly applied to the visual and numerical representation of one iteration of a rhythmic cycle, the core building block of most Korean folk music genres. *Wŏn*, the "largest encompassing entity," now represents the cycle in its entirety, i.e., a *hanbae* (unit) or "one bar" (in Western musical terms). The next smaller division of *pang*, or "pillar which divides the entity," is equated with a beat or "pulse," called a small *hanbae*. Divisions of the beat or "units" are equivalent to *kak*, the smallest *hanbae* of a rhythmic cycle. These three aspects of the cycle are then placed within a *samt'aegŭk*-like symbol, as reproduced in figure 4.5. When placed at the beginning of a bar of notation, this figure indicates a single cycle (*wŏn* = 1) composed of four beats (*pang* = 4), each beat further composed of three smaller divisions (*kak*; 3 × 4 beats = 12), similar in surface structure to the Western meter of 12/8.[19] Importantly, this metric visual indicator reinforces in the sensitive learner the broader connections that exist between rhythm, the performer's body, the sound of the instruments, and mankind's place within the cosmos.

The 1999 textbook further develops and expands upon this *samt'aegŭk* performance and moral philosophy as realized through the concepts and geometry of *wŏn-pang-kak*. In the introduction to this work, "What Is Samulnori?," the author begins by explaining the significance of the transformation of the *yangt'aegŭk* symbol (*ŭm/yin* and *yang*, earth and heaven) into the *samt'aegŭk* (heaven, earth, and mankind):

> In [the] *samt'aegŭk*, nature is no longer an object, but has been incorporated into the subjective inner world of man. As [a] result, man is given a right as much as heaven or its counterpart. The *samt'aegŭk* thus reflects what Korean ancestors called the *samjaesang*, that it is nature's law that man must interact harmoniously with the sky and land. (Kim, Duk Soo et al. 1999:2)[20]

The passage continues by illustrating the role and power with which music was imbued in bringing about this harmony between these three realms. Ancient Korean rituals that integrated politics and religion are then referenced, with percussion being situated at the nexus of such spiritual and social activity (Kim, Duk Soo et al. 1999:1–3).

In a later chapter on notation and rhythmic structure, however, we are finally provided with the direct visual representations of the circle, square, and triangle. Reproducing the diagram from the textbook in figure 4.6 (Kim, Duk Soo et al. 1999:13), the first row provides the Sino-Korean characters and their Korean readings for the circle, square, and triangle.[21] The next row gives the appropriate symbol, with the corresponding number provided in the row directly underneath. From a Chinese or pan–East Asian cosmological view the dot in the center of the square is symbolically rich, for, as I previously discussed, ancient Chinese thought envisioned a world composed of five directions: north, south, east, west, and center. In the footnote to the Korean text of this chapter this connection is clearly laid out (1999:14), and when understood as part of the broader *ohaeng*/*wuxing* (five element) template and integrated with the ternary relationship of heaven, earth, and mankind, this SamulNori material harks to Chinese philosophical and musicological thought dating back more than a thousand years (Kuttner 1990; Li, Ying-chang 1994:xviii; Chen, Yingshi 2002).

In the last row of figure 4.6 the appropriate rhythmic concepts are listed.[22] A complete rhythmic pattern or cycle is equated with the number 1, and the smaller unit level of beat or pulse is matched with the number 5. While most Korean folk rhythms are composed of multiples of four-beat phrases, significantly a number of older ritual rhythms do employ five beats (Hesselink and Petty 2004:283–85). At the smallest level of beat division is the number 3, completely appropriate within a Korean context as most rhythmic cycles are made up of compound meters, or triple divisions of the beat.[23] I stress again here that SamulNori is the only musical organization in Korea to so reference and holistically adopt *wŏn-pang-kak* cosmology, itself a broader pan–East Asian conceptual framework that supports SamulNori's more inclusive worldview and pedagogical outreach. The only other such reference to *wŏn-pang-kak* imagery in the Korean musicological community is found in the name of the private music academy established by Hahn Myong-hee (Han Myŏnghŭi), an esteemed

	wŏn (원, 圓)	*pang* (방, 方)	*kak* (각, 角)
symbol	○	⊡	△
number signified	1	5	3
rhythmic structure	rhythmic pattern	beat	division of beat

Figure 4.6 *Wŏn-pang-kak* rhythmic realization (based on Kim, Duk Soo et al. 1999:13).

musicologist and critic who contributed "What Is SamulNori?" to the initial SamulNori workbook (Hahn, Myong-hee 1992). His institution, called I-Mi-Shi, was founded in 2003 and is named for the native Korean pronunciation of the geometric shapes: *i* (the circle, or ○ in the Korean alphabet, *han'gŭl*), *mi* (the square, or □), and *shi* (the right angle or trysquare, or ㅅ).[24]

In their efforts at cosmological didacticism, SamulNori created a body of innovative and highly integrated pedagogical materials with the purpose of bringing about harmony, in the fullest musical and spiritual sense of the word. With the musician as an active, human agent responsible for enacting such balance, and music (percussion) as the vehicle for bringing about its realization, a number of crucial links are established. The first is on the tangible level, as the drummer comes into physical contact with leather (earth) and metal (heaven). This connection is reinforced sonically by the complementary timbres of drum and gong forming a composite whole. Intellectually, the students and performers have been stimulated through the musical theoretical concepts and special notation to further understand their relationship to the natural world around them, the final spiritual bond with fellow members and the cosmos being felt on all of these levels when an ensemble convenes to make music together. *Wŏn-pang-kak* as outlook and theory might have been nurtured in Chinese soil and flourished throughout East Asia, but in the hands of SamulNori it came to signify a larger symbol of the possibility of embracing the West as well.

Conclusion

In this chapter I have sought to understand a key element of SamulNori's enduring success and influence through an analysis of their educational efforts. Focusing on the most distinctive aspect of their pedagogy, the traditional concept known as *wŏn-pang-kak* (circle/heaven–square/earth–triangle/humankind), I believe its explication and use took on a special meaning and power at a time in Korean history when Western cultural influences were threatening or eradicating older shared ways of relating to the physical and spiritual realms of human experience. The roots of this distinctive East Asian worldview began with ancient Chinese ritual practices that physically and symbolically joined heaven and earth with the shapes of the circle and the square. Later religious and academic thought added the human element—interpreted by some Koreans as a triangle—to create a kind of sacred trilogy in which mathematics, astronomy, and cosmology were synthesized. Imported into a Korean context, such theorizing was similarly embraced in rituals held by the court and by commoners,

Figure 4.7 "The Universe is a Friendly Place," by Kim Tae Wan [Kim T'aewan] (*ŭm-yang* symbol occupying the center of a five-element figure, itself further imbedded in a larger five-element space surrounded by a circular heaven disc imposed on a square earth plate; © Jeongak Gallery, Seoul).

with its additional visual representation in the figure of the *samt'aegŭk* ("Three Great Absolutes") being prevalent. There is little question today that such geomantic principles are intuited or outright acknowledged by the general Korean public, with practitioners of what is now called *p'ungsu* (*feng shui*) being in high demand. And its visual manifestation in the circle and square combined with *ŭm/yin-yang* and *ohaeng/wuxing* (five elements) remains a potent emblem for contemporary artists working in visual media as well (see figure 4.7 [with obvious parallels in the design of the Korean national flag]).

More significant, however, are the meaning of this material and the manner in which it was distributed. SamulNori's workbooks with *wŏn-pang-kak* at their core became the central methodological tool by which literally thousands of *samul nori* students all over the world have been introduced to the intimate relationship between Korean drumming and cosmology. These texts are found and used in every *samul nori* camp (from Asia to the U.S. and Europe), are distributed by the Korea Foundation to visiting foreign scholars, and are a part of nearly every major library in South Korea and Japan. For serious followers of the art form, the workbooks reveal the tremendously rich amalgam of physical, sonic, spiritual, and visual activity that takes place in the moment of drumming. This composite or holistic nature is of course true of many of the music-dance cultures of the world; but the detailed and comprehensive analysis SamulNori provides here is perhaps unique in the world's pedagogical text traditions. The choice to publish in English is also a significant factor in accounting for the group's loyal fan base in Europe and North America who treasure such efforts as a privileged window onto Korean drumming and its deeper meanings (and who continue to pass on such training to further generations).

SamulNori's methodology and message are one of integration, on many different levels: mathematics, music theory, performance practice, and cosmology; humanity and its natural surroundings; the past and the present (and future); and SamulNori and the rest of the world. It is also about teaching in the deepest, most moral sense of the practice and profession. Through their adoption and adaptation of *wŏn-pang-kak* theorizing, SamulNori provides a model for how to live our lives in harmony with the world and other sentient beings around us. Music again becomes imbued, as it did in Korea's past, with the power to rehumanize and reposition humankind emotionally and symbolically to nature and the cosmos. And in its embrace of non-Korean students and audiences, it also created spaces of possibility for cross-cultural encounter, the subject of the next chapter.

5

East-West Encounters in the *Nanjang*

Hybridity, Red Sun, and Cross-Cultural Collaboration

To attend a *nanjang* in its heyday was to experience rural Korean society at its liveliest and most boisterous. Over the course of a few days villagers gathered to eat, drink, purchase native and foreign wares, gamble, play folk games, have their fortunes told, attend wrestling matches, and be further entertained by performances of itinerant groups of musicians, dancers, and actors—increasingly the *namsadang* toward the close of the nineteenth century—all officially sanctioned by local authorities within an agreed-upon boundary and duration. The local and imported, the legal and unlawful (under ordinary circumstances), the violent and sometimes sublime, and even the sacred and profane, all coexisted somewhat artificially but in general harmony in this festival atmosphere (Chŏng Un'gil 1998:260; see also Yi Sangil 1987:138–40, Pak Sangguk et al. 1996:48–49, and O Changhyŏn et al. 2000:174–78).[1] For the traveling performers who accompanied such events, the *nanjang* offered valuable opportunities for artistic development, a place in both time and space to stretch and exercise creative inclinations. For those in attendance, it provided not only amusements but a window—admittedly opaque—onto cultural forms and practices beyond their immediate borders, the by-product of centuries of trading, interacting, and even intermarrying between wandering artists and merchants of Korea and those of China, Mongolia, and beyond (Shim Usŏng 1968:699–701; Kim Yang-kon 1967:5–7).

Nanjang formally came to a close during the Japanese occupation of the early twentieth century, though the idea and practice of Korean-foreign hybrid cultural expressions would take on a new and invigorated life during this period. The two earliest forms of musical hybridity on the Korean peninsula—here referring to the mixture of elements of Korean traditional music with Westernized popular music, the subject of this chapter—were both directly the result of this colonial encounter. By the late 1920s there emerged the "new folk song" (*shin minyo* in Korean), a trend defined by the composition and/or reinterpretation of traditional folk songs with Western melodic and other structural influences (Yi Soyŏng 2007; Finchum-Sung 2006). During the 1930s new folk songs joined the ascendant *t'ŭrot'ŭ* phenomenon (popular songs with Western dance band accompaniment and Japanese-Korean melodies)[2] in mainstream Korean consciousness, largely due to a nascent recording industry (Yi Yŏngmi 1999:57–98; Son, Min-jung 2004; Maliangkay 2008). Both styles continued to develop with the times, and both in modified forms can be found in "fusion" projects of the late twentieth century (to be discussed further below).

As South Korea emerged from the aftermath of World War II and a brutal civil war in its wake (1950–53), Korean traditional musicians found themselves in a society that had rapidly become apathetic or even intolerant toward most traditional music activity. The story of *kayagŭm* (twelve-string plucked zither) master Paek Inyŏng is representative and telling of the musical situation during these troubled times.[3] A musician coming of age in the late 1960s, his earliest jobs were as an accompanist for traditional singers on radio broadcasts and recordings (a direct legacy of the 1930s and '40s). To make ends meet, however, he also regularly played in hostess bars for clients who wanted to hear Western popular tunes alongside Japanese-era *t'ŭrot'ŭ* songs, genres of music in a performance venue that further lowered the status of traditional musicians. And though the situation would improve for some in the early 1970s with institutional support for "new traditional music" (*shin kugak/ch'angjak kugak*) at universities and the construction of concert halls that promoted some traditional music programming (as documented in chapter 2), for Paek and his contemporaries knowledge of a variety of performance styles and repertoire often made the difference between marginally surviving and complete destitution. Unlike most other musicians in his circumstances, however, Paek embraced such hybridity as a challenge and window of opportunity, so that even while he established himself during the 1980s and '90s as a leading proponent of the traditional zither, he also made time to release a number of popular and fusion recordings, including a collaborative improvisation-based CD that featured the composer-pianist Im Tongch'ang, the individual who worked with SamulNori on their first workbook (see chapter 4).[4] Paek's contemporary Lee Saenggang (Yi Saenggang), a human cultural asset for the transverse *taegŭm* bamboo flute, ruminates on a similar life in the program notes to his 2002 release *The Song of Hope*, a reinterpretation of Japanese-era *t'ŭrot'ŭ* songs for *taegŭm* and jazz quartet.[5]

Running parallel to these developments in the traditional music world was the planting of the seeds of rock music on Korean soil. The year 1962 is frequently cited as a watershed moment with the founding of Korea's first rock band, Add 4, by "the godfather of Korean rock," Shin Joong Hyun (Shin Chunghyŏn; Yoo and Choi 2002:42). Early experimentations with blues and psychedelic music quickly morphed into a more mature form characterized by the fusing of Korean traditional music elements onto a rock music aesthetic. The track "Beautiful Woman" ("Miin") from 1970 is a classic example of this style, Shin's electric guitar imitating the scales and plucking techniques of the aforementioned *kayagŭm* zither (Yi Yŏngmi 1999:231).[6] Later in the 1990s his references to traditional music became even more overt with projects such as the album *Shin Chunghyŏn Muwi Jayŏn* (*Shin Jung Hyun, Nature at Rest*, 1997), in which Shin directly transferred the solo genre of *sanjo* to the electric guitar (on the track "Chŏn'gi kit'a sanjo," or "Electric Guitar Sanjo").[7] Shin's worldview as expressed in a recent interview—one mirrored by countless other popular musicians in South Korea—perfectly fits within a SamulNori musical and philosophical aesthetic:

> Like all music, rock is a universal language. What's important is to put something of your own culture into the international style of rock. If you just imitate foreign music, you end up producing a rootless culture. Whether it be rock, jazz, or rap, Korean music should have a Korean flavor. (Yoo and Choi 2002:42)

At roughly the same time that Shin Joong Hyun was finding a voice with his Korean brand of rock, neighboring Japan was witnessing the flourishing of an "indigenous" jazz scene, one in which artists began to look to traditional Japanese music and culture for creative inspiration (Atkins 2001:226–60). Many of their ideas and musicians flowed into a receptive Korean progressive jazz movement in the 1970s and '80s, with typical early efforts represented by the activities of high-profile Japanese artists such as Yamashita Yosuke (piano) and Umezu Kazutoki (saxophone) playing with the Korean percussionist Kim Dae Hwan (Kim Taehwan), the original drummer for Shin's Add 4 back in 1962.[8] In 1978 Kim Dae Hwan joined his cousin Kang T'aehwan on alto saxophone and Choi Sun Bae (Ch'oe Sŏnbae) on trumpet to form the Kang T'aehwan Trio, Korea's first free jazz group. From there it was only a matter of time before Korean scales, rhythms, timbres, and approaches to improvisation would find their way into free jazz and improvisation circles, with Kim Dae Hwan leading the way for many by incorporating the *p'ungmul*/*samul nori* barrel drum (*puk*) into his standard drum kit. By the 1980s in the jazz and traditional music worlds it seemed that a kind of rapprochement had been achieved between Korea and Japan, albeit forty years after the end of the colonial period (Han Myŏnghŭi 1992b).[9] And so while SamulNori's forays into jazz during this period were not unique, just as their move to the stage in the late 1970s had been heralded by others, what set them apart was the nature and duration of their interactions with local and foreign musicians.

The Practice and Politics of Hybridity

The point of the previous discussion was to briefly demonstrate the length and depth of foreign cultural encounters on the Korean peninsula, a perspective that expands dramatically when including the new traditional music and classical music worlds (not discussed in this chapter). Such mixtures, of course, have been the norm, with almost everything considered "natural," "traditional," or complementary in a Korean context—court music, the vocal art *p'ansori*, even Coke with *kimch'i tchigae* (pickled cabbage stew)—being a direct result of cross-cultural hybridity. Theorists of hybridity have long recognized the identification of any particular music as "pure" or "authentic" as a selective historical act (Frith 1989:3; Mitchell 1993:335), so that one era's "mixed" or "bastardized" style frequently makes it into a later generation's collection of canonical works, even taking on the role of bearer of cultural identity. For the present analysis I choose to view hybridity in the abstract as a morally neutral term, as merely the acknowledgment of a process that has occurred for centuries in Korea and around the globe. There is nothing inherently "good" or "bad" when two or more cultures come together; it is the quality and conditions under which the meetings take place that define the nature of the interaction.

During the twentieth century such interactions between Korea, Japan, and the West took on an accelerated pace and level of intensity due to numerous wars, transfers of troops and technology, and exchange of cultural products as a result of "soft" diplomacy. By the late 1980s predominantly Korean-Western interfaces began to be referred to as "fusion" (*p'yujŏn* in Korean), a realm that extended beyond musical hybrids to encompass food, fashion, and architecture (Lee, So-young 2003). During and since that time there have been many approaches to fusion in the South Korean traditional music world, though a central defining feature according to the ethnomusicologist R. Anderson Sutton is that there should be "a mixture in which the identity of the components can still be perceived. In other words, the listening public, as well as the musicians, are conscious of the mixture as a major aesthetic element in the music" (2003:230). He further notes that the intention of many Korean fusion artists is to bring greater attention to traditional music, and that there be commercial appeal (2003:231–32). This certainly holds true for the earlier jazz fusion albums of SamulNori (to be discussed below), though the interpretation and appreciation of such projects often differ widely between domestic and foreign audiences (Sutton 2009).

Similar in language and usage to Sutton is the work of the ethnomusicologist Sarah Weiss, who, along with her university students, added further subtlety to the notion by choosing "the term 'intentional' hybrid [as] appropriate in particular because many of the products we studied advertised and acknowledged the fusion as integral to the aesthetic of the work" (2008:206). Weiss also noted that such mixtures did not generally lead to long-term genre development, but rather that the two (or more) styles remained distinct; this is true of SamulNori's relationship with the jazz quartet Red Sun (the topic of the next section). Where such terminology falls short is in describing the specific kind of interaction that takes place, the factors by which particular (musical) traditions are more easily able to fuse or come together. Surface considerations include the interrelationships—if any—between the sonic elements, instrumentation, staging, and timbres. At a deeper level one would look to shared religious or philosophical worldviews, as well as any ground-level, embodied cross-cultural resonances in feeling or groove, of mood or sentiment.

In spite of changing and competing understandings of the concept, I find the term "syncretism" as understood by Bruno Nettl particularly useful in analyzing the conditions under which SamulNori worked with foreign jazz artists.[10] For

Nettl, such culturally mixed phenomena are best described as syncretism when elements—musical or otherwise—between two or more different participating cultures or peoples are similar or compatible (2005:440–41). This means, hypothetically speaking, that cultures that share musical traits are more likely to interact and integrate, versus those who cannot find such matches. For Christopher Waterman, speaking from an African perspective, syncretism goes beyond mere surface or structural compatibilities to include human interpretation and agency: "It is ultimately tautological to explain musical dynamics in terms of the retrospective 'compatibility' of reified musical structures. Syncretism is fundamentally grounded in human actors' interpretations of similarity and difference, and in their attempts to make sense of a changing world in terms of past experience" (1990:9). As will become apparent in the discussion that follows, it was both existing structural features *and* the attitudes of SamulNori and their jazz cohorts—their openness and willingness to work together—that contributed to a "meeting of the minds."

Before moving on to the specific circumstances of SamulNori's cross-cultural encounter and the material products of their collaboration (audio recordings), it is worth briefly highlighting features and attitudes shared by Korean folk percussion and jazz musics, and by their practitioners. Language and other cultural obstacles notwithstanding, Korean folk percussion and jazz share a number of core structural traits. Each tradition operates within a cyclical framework: jazz with song forms and chord changes (at least historically speaking), Korean drumming with rhythmic cycles (*changdan* or *karak* in Korean). Rhythm in general is a prominent feature of both performances, as is a rhythmic base solidly rooted in compound meters (triple division of the beat), the latter observation not holding true for the neighboring countries of China and Japan. Both traditions place high importance on the ability and need to improvise, and, accounting for the special case of SamulNori (like their *namsadang*/*nanjang* predecessors), both groups of musicians have historically been at the cutting edge of their fields in their looking to other countries and traditions for new musical sounds and structures. And there are the timbral similarities between the jazz drum set and the Korean quartet, the balance and contrasts between leather and metal.

Beyond the generalities of hybridity and the kind of interaction specified by syncretism, however, lies the *quality* of the interaction, the politics and ethics that contribute to and maintain the cross-cultural encounter. Where do the various parties hail from? Under what historical conditions were they brought together? Is political or financial autonomy a key component? Hybridity and syncretism also do not speak to proportion, such as who or what instrument is placed in the foreground, which musical elements are dominant, or whether such elements mark cultural difference or social engagement (Stokes 2004:61). These issues make up the central discussion and analysis in the pages that follow, including concluding remarks that reflect upon power relations as played out in the composition, production, representation, and distribution of SamulNori's fusion recordings, all understood within the context of current debates of exploitation versus collaboration found in "world music" discourse. But first I must turn to the historical moment that brought SamulNori into contact with their future comrades-in-arms, inspired, appropriately enough, by their return to the road.

SamulNori and the Formation of Red Sun

Kim Duk Soo first met and performed with the saxophonist Kang T'aehwan of the Kang T'aehwan Trio in 1980. In 1985 Kim embarked on two projects with Kang that had lasting ramifications for both artists. The first was a tour of Japan with Kang and SamulNori that brought further exposure and recognition to the Korean groups, especially in the capital Tokyo (SamulNori's subsequent invitation and performance in 1987 at Suntory Hall, now captured on video,[11] has achieved a kind of mythic status). Later that year Kang and SamulNori were asked to join the inaugural performance of *Ult'arigut* (literally "hedge ritual"), a project that has been described as "the combination of stage and [musical] performances with multi-disciplinary artistic communication."[12] The brainchild of Kang Chunhyŏk, Konggan theater and METAA arts promotion and theater company director (introduced in chapter 2), *Ult'arigut* over the years featured a regular lineup that included the percussionist Kim Dae Hwan (of Add 4 and Kang T'aehwan Trio fame), the pianist and composer Kang Chunil (brother of Kang Chunhyŏk), the percussionist Kim Dong-Won (introduced in chapter 4), and the *changgo* player Chang Tŏkhwa (Minsogakhoe Shinawi member)—a group that touches on nearly every theme elucidated in this book. As of 2003, there had been nine *Ult'arigut* performances (in 1985, 1986, two in 1987, 1989, 1991, two in 1993, and 2003).[13]

In 1986 SamulNori began to expand their possibilities for genre crossing and international status by teaming up with two world-class musicians outside of Korea: a tour of Japan with Yamashita Yosuke—the pianist at the forefront of the Japanese free jazz movement—and a joint performance with the legendary studio drummer Steve Gadd at the Vancouver Expo. But it was 1987 that proved to be a breakthrough year for the Korean quartet. Under the direction of bass player and record producer extraordinaire Bill Laswell, SamulNori was invited to join an elite group of musicians to play a series of concerts in Japan during July and August. Calling themselves SXL under the billing "Live Under the Sky," it featured the talents of SamulNori, Bill Laswell (bass), Shankar (South Indian violinist), Ronald Shannon Jackson (American jazz and funk drummer), and Alyb (Aïyb) Dieng (Senegalese percussionist). Concerts held on August 1 and 2 drew in a combined audience of nearly 30,000 (Kim Hŏnsŏn 1995:210–11), events preserved in a live recording released by Sony (*SXL Live in Japan*, 1987). Other performances on the tour were released as *SXL: Into the Outlands* (Celluloid Records, 1987).[14]

After a couple of months back home to recuperate, SamulNori was back on the road to Western Europe. Under the auspices of Austrian percussionist and pedagogue Reinhard Flatischler, the quartet joined the project and tour titled "International Ethnic Percussion Project 'Megadrums'" from November 19 through December 1. Featuring the artists Dudu Tucci (Brazilian conga player), Aja Addy (Ghanaian *dondo* [talking drum] player), Wolfgang Puschnig (Austrian alto saxophonist), and Reinhard Flatischler—in addition to a battery of other percussionists and vocalists—SamulNori as part of Megadrums traveled extensively throughout Austria, Germany, and Switzerland, including the cities of Bremen, Munich, Hamburg, Cologne, Freiburg, Frankfurt, Bern, and Vienna (see figure 5.1 for their end-of-tour group photograph).[15] On November 29 in Rubingen, Switzerland, the group made a live recording featuring compositions/arrangements by Flatischler and SamulNori, released commercially as *Megadrums: Coreana* (Intuition, 1987).[16]

It was under these rather fortuitous conditions—speaking now from hindsight—that SamulNori was able to meet and interact with Wolfgang Puschnig. The lone reed player for the Megadrums project, Puschnig had from the age of eleven already developed a keen and passionate involvement with East Asian musics (albeit mostly secondhand from recordings), so the close and intimate contact with Kim and the quartet on his home turf was a profound experience on many levels. The Korean percussionists were equally enthralled with Puschnig and his professional activities, so much so that that winter, Puschnig and his longtime musical colleague, Linda Sharrock (American avant-garde jazz vocalist), traveled to Seoul at SamulNori's invitation to begin a more ambitious collaboration in earnest. Upon their return home, Puschnig and Sharrock formed a Western jazz counterpart to SamulNori, called "Red Sun," an ensemble that included the American Jamaaladeen Tacuma on bass and the Austrian Uli

Figure 5.1 Megadrums end-of-tour group photograph: Kim Duk Soo (seated, 2nd from left), Reinhard Flatischler (standing, 4th from left), Wolfgang Puschnig (standing, 2nd from right in front) (© SamulNori Hanullim).

Scherer on piano (to be replaced later by the American guitarist Rick Iannacone; Samstag and Lake 1994).

It was not just general cross-cultural exposure toward which both sides were striving; creative interaction and the fusion of styles, "*yin* and *yang*, east and west, rhythm and melody, harmony and modality" (Puschnig 1997), became the raison d'être and an ongoing passion for these new musical partners. Over a period of roughly nine years (1988–1997), SamulNori and Red Sun carried on this fruitful dialogue through meetings, workshops, and performances, culminating in the release of four joint recordings. At some point it occurred to the members of SamulNori that what they were attempting was the expansion of cultural and artistic limits in a manner that had striking parallels to the earlier world of their ancestors' *nanjang*. Initial evidence of such thought processes appeared in 1994 with the opening track of their second CD, titled "Nanjang (The Meeting Place)." By 1995 a newly renamed "Kim Duk Soo SamulNori" organization (after Ch'oe Chongshil's and Yi Kwangsu's departures, Kim was the only original member left; see appendix 2) chose the word "Nanjang" as the title of their new studio, record label, studio debut CD (recording 3), club (October 1998), and, later, production company. Tradition, it seems, had come full circle.

The Recordings

While "success" is difficult to assess when speaking about personal relationships or aesthetic decisions, especially when entertaining viewpoints borne of differing cultural perspectives, I have nevertheless chosen to examine the recordings made by SamulNori and Red Sun as a concrete, material record of a successful joint endeavor. When analyzing these documents I asked myself: To what extent were these musicians not only able to take advantage of but build upon compatible musical traits inherent in Korean percussion and jazz (syncretism)? And of course related and equally important to any cross-cultural collaborative effort was the quality of the interaction, the playing out of power relations: Was a balanced approach achieved with regard to the composition, recording, and representation of the various projects (after Stokes 2004:61)? I begin with an account of the production details, looking at factors such as personnel, choice of language and art on covers and liner notes, location of recording studio, and composition and mixing credits. I then briefly discuss structural considerations, the relationship between the Korean and Western contributions to the sonic whole in terms of timbral choices, foregrounding of vocal and/or instrumental lines, and musical form (related to kind and use of rhythmic cycle). This section concludes with analytical listening guides for two representative tracks revealing the special nature of the musical hybridization that emerged from this newly created sound world.

Production Details

Recorded only two years after their first meeting, the inaugural *Red Sun • SamulNori* (Polygram, DZ-2433, 1997 [1989]) was initially released by the Viennese Amadeo label in 1989 as an LP, to be remastered as a compact disc by Polygram in 1997. Recording details and the overall presentation, however, very much reflect a European orientation. All aspects of pre- and postproduction took place in Austria (Achau and Vienna), with the roles of producer and executive producer being played by Wolfgang Puschnig (Red Sun) and Wulf Müller respectively. Program notes suggest that all the musicians came together to jointly discuss each track (Yi Chonghak 1997), and compositional responsibilities are shared by all of the participants, yet Red Sun members are positioned in the foreground with regard to the placement of their photographs and quotes in the liner notes, their pairing with SamulNori performers on the front cover, and the listing of Red Sun before SamulNori on the title (although nearly all musicians appear in a joint performance photograph on the inner back cover). Red Sun featured the Austrians Wolfgang Puschnig (alto saxophone) and Uli Scherer (piano), alongside Americans Linda Sharrock (vocal) and Jamaaladeen Tacuma (electric bass); SamulNori was composed of Kim Duk Soo (*changgo*), Lee Kwang Soo (*kkwaenggwari*, vocal), Choi Jong Sil (*puk*), and Kang Min Seok (*ching*; Kang was SamulNori cofounder Kim Yongbae's replacement). Abstract cover art was provided by the vocalist Linda Sharrock (see figure 5.2); program notes are split evenly between English and Korean.

A substantial period of time—five years—separates the initial collaboration from the second offering, *Then Comes the White Tiger* (ECM Records, ECM-1499, 1994). Here the Red Sun lineup had become fixed with the replacement of Uli Scherer (piano) by Philadelphia native Rick Iannacone on electric guitar; SamulNori, on the other hand, continued to be in a state of flux, as in 1990 Choi

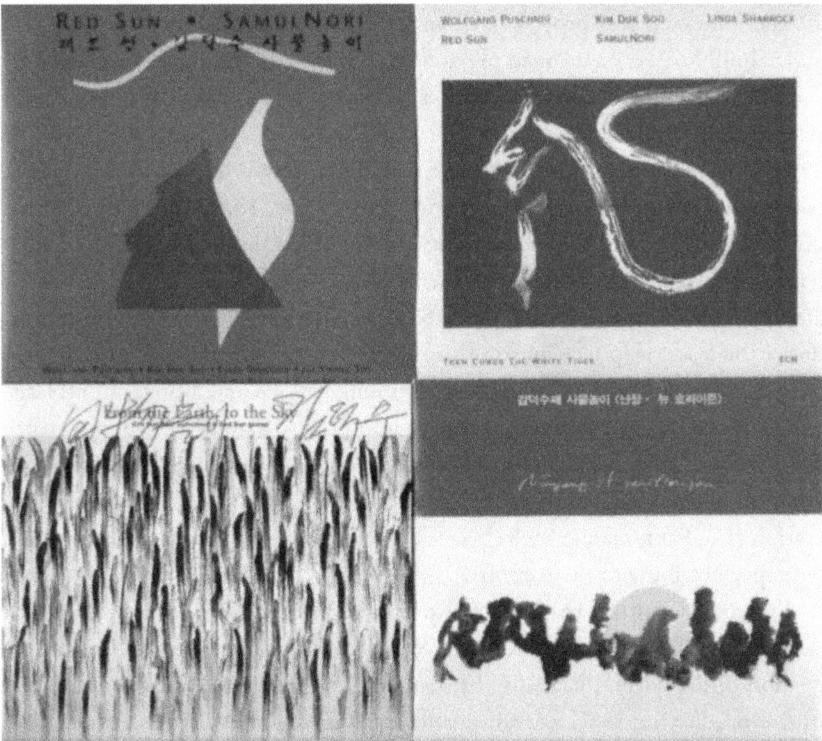

Figure 5.2 Cover art for the four joint Red Sun/SamulNori recordings, clockwise beginning with upper left corner: *Red Sun · SamulNori* (1989), *Then Comes the White Tiger* (1994), *Nanjang: A New Horizon* (1995), and *From the Earth, to the Sky* (1997) (© SamulNori Hanullim).

Jong Sil (from the early 1979 lineup) left the group to enter university and was replaced by Kim Woon Tae (Kim Unt'ae). Despite an extra Korean musician (the traditional zither player Kim Sung Woon) and the expansion in instrumentation by SamulNori members—additional woodwind and percussion instruments are added to the standard "*samul*" (two drums and two gongs) mix—, the recording in terms of production still leans in favor of their Euro-American counterparts. Significantly the raw recordings were made on the Koreans' home turf of Seoul, yet mixing and final producing were carried out in Munich by Wolfgang Puschnig. Red Sun members are still listed first on the title and personnel list, and they are given credit for composing the majority of the pieces, but interestingly the only photo included with the program notes is of SamulNori in full traditional costume performing while dancing (inside back cover). Linda Sharrock was again responsible for the cover design with a style evocative of Asian brush painting (see figure 5.2), and program notes are nicely balanced between Korean and English.

The following year proved to be an important milestone for Kim Duk Soo and SamulNori. As mentioned previously, 1995 was the year "Nanjang" became the title and emblem of the group's new studio, record label, and third joint release (and studio debut CD) *Nanjang: A New Horizon* (King, KSC-4150A, 1995). In the program notes we see for the first time reference to the quartet being called "Kim Duk Soo SamulNori," and, in fact, Kim is the only member given credit for composing/arranging the "traditional" tracks. This coincided with Lee Kwang Soo's departure—the last other remaining original member—and the establishment of the SamulNori foundation "SamulNori Hanullim" under the leadership of Kim (on this CD we are introduced to Kim Jung Hee [Kim Chŏnghŭi] on small gong and Kim Jung Kuk [Kim Chŏngguk] on large gong). Rising success and recognition at home led to SamulNori's performance the same year with the KBS Symphony Orchestra at the United Nations in celebration of the fiftieth anniversary of both the U.N.'s founding and Korea's liberation (Lee Sang-man 1995:82). Track #6 on this third project, "Celebration," pays special tribute to these events.

In striking contrast to the first two collaborations, it is perfectly clear with *Nanjang: A New Horizon* that SamulNori is now in firm control. With the exception of the cover illustration by Sharrock (see figure 5.2), nearly all aspects of the production took place in Seoul (mixing was split between Korea and London). Despite a certain amount of musical give-and-take between the two groups documented in the program notes, with all members of Red Sun contributing toward compositional duties (Hong 1995), the CD title and jacket oddly lists only SamulNori. This latter observation, however, almost certainly reflects the grace with which Red Sun decided to step back into the shadows so as not to steal any of the limelight or initial fanfare surrounding the opening of the Koreans' new production complex.[17] Program notes, also for the first time, now include Korean script for track titles alongside their English counterparts.

Viewed in isolation, the fourth and final release, *From the Earth, to the Sky* (Samsung, SCO-123NAN, 1997) seems to be an essentially Korean enterprise. All aspects of the production—recording, mixing, and postproduction—took place in Seoul, and Korean program notes are much more extensive and detailed than the English. Korean musicians outnumber Western ones by nine to four (Kim Duk Soo is joined by a battery of Korean traditional percussionists), cover art—breaking with tradition—is provided by the well-known Korean painter Lee Ufan (Yi Uhwan; see figure 5.2),[18] and SamulNori (now preceded officially by Kim Duk Soo's name) is listed before Red Sun in the title and on the personnel roster. Taken as the fourth and final puzzle piece of a complex whole, however, *From the Earth, to the Sky* completes a balanced picture: two recordings on European soil, two on South Korean. Program notes, track titles, and the overall feel of the CD intimate a sense of finality, the end of a certain phase in the creative lives of these two groups. The release is, furthermore, a tribute to Kim Duk Soo specifically, marking his fortieth anniversary as a performer (Howard 1999:76). In this context it is worth noting that along with Kang Min Seok (barrel drum), Kim is the only remaining member from the first recording made with Red Sun back in the late 1980s.

Structural Considerations

When moving beyond production details to examine specific compositional-structural choices, we see a similar trajectory in the fusion or meeting of artistic minds as equal partners, one that began in fits and starts but that quickly took on an exciting and purposeful direction. To help illustrate this process in brief, I have provided a concise (if not somewhat reductionist) overview of the four collaborative recordings in tables 5.1 and 5.3 according to SamulNori's evolving musical role in this overall transformation, using the following terms and criteria:

- background accompaniment: SamulNori (or, in some cases, accompanying Korean musicians) provides only basic rhythmic support in an unobtrusive or less prominent manner; frequently this entails the scaling back or elimination altogether of the small handheld gong (*soe*)

- featured: percussion lines (or other more Korean aspects) move sonically and/or compositionally to the foreground while Western instruments or voices continue to play/sing in a secondary role
- featured alone: percussion (or other Korean) instruments play alone
- equal partner: SamulNori and Red Sun members contribute to an equal and unified sonic whole—this is often accomplished by room given to the Korean percussion lines (compositionally and dynamically) and/or the modification of Western scales, timbres, or metrical frames in a Korean manner; or, conversely, the allowance of Western scale or harmonic structures in the overall texture.

I have also made note of the rhythmic base of each track as an additional tool for documenting the compositional strategies employed by both organizations (see table 5.2).

The first recording, *Red Sun • SamulNori*, strikes me in many ways as being fragmented in its overall approach. Korean percussion pieces are juxtaposed in regular alternation with "fusion" compositions, so that we hear the four core percussion instruments in isolation and a group *samul nori* piece on tracks #2, #4, #6, #8, and #10 (see table 5.1). An immediate and perhaps obvious explanation of this presentational format is that SamulNori is providing an introduction to Korean drumming for Western European audiences ostensibly unfamiliar with the music. This seems to be borne out as well by the wide sampling of rhythmic patterns used throughout the course of the recording: regional pieces from the core SamulNori repertoire on tracks #2, #5, #8, and #11; shaman rhythms on tracks #3 and #7; a rearranged movement from the *p'ungmul* repertoire on track #6; a pan-Korean rhythm on track #9; and modified or invented rhythms (unnamed in the program notes) on tracks #1, #4, #10, and #12 (see table 5.2). An examination of the remaining tracks (those with both groups participating), however, reveals a struggle to reconcile the two traditions. With the exception of track #12 (and briefly on tracks #7 and #11), it is as if the musicians do not know how to accommodate or integrate the powerful sound of the Korean drums and gongs. SamulNori is either employed as background accompaniment—frequently with a scaled-back small gong sound—or is featured alone, interaction easily equivalent to "I've taken my turn, now I'll let you take yours."

In spite of the five-year hiatus between the first two projects (implying the possibility of greater recognition of Korean traditional music on the part of European and/or American SamulNori fans), a cursory glance at the table of contents of *Then Comes the White Tiger* suggests that the Korean musicians still

Table 5.1: *Red Sun · SamulNori* (1989) and *Then Comes the White Tiger* (1994) compositional elements.

	Rhythmic base	Role of SamulNori
Red Sun • SamulNori		
Spirit Warriors	modified/invented rhythm	background accompaniment
The K'kwaenggwari	"Uttari p'ungmul"	featured alone
More than Ever	*p'unŏri*	background accompaniment; featured alone
The Buk	modified/invented rhythm	featured alone
Far Horizon	"Samdo sŏlchanggo karak"	background accompaniment; featured alone
Ho-Ho Kut	"Ho ho kut"	featured alone
O-Lim (Ascension)	*orimch'ae*	featured alone (briefly); background accompaniment; equal partner
The Changgo	"Samdo sŏlchanggo karak"	featured alone
Golden Bird	*chinyang*	background accompaniment
The Ching	modified/invented rhythm	featured alone
No Secrets	"Pinari"	featured alone (briefly); background accompaniment (moments as equal partner)
Places in Time (Pu-chong)	modified/invented rhythm	equal partner
Then Comes the White Tiger		
Nanjang (The Meeting Place)	"Pinari"	equal partner
Peaceful Question	modified/invented rhythm	equal partner
Kil-Kun-Ak	"Yŏngnam nongak"	featured alone
Hear Them Say	*pujŏng nori*	background accompaniment; equal partner (briefly)
Piri	*chungmori*	featured alone
Soo Yang Kol (The Valley of Weeping Willows)	"Samdo sŏlchanggo karak"	equal partner
Flute Sanjo	*chinyang*	equal partner
Komungo	*chungmori*	featured alone
Full House—Part I	"Samdo sŏlchanggo karak"	background accompaniment
Full House—Part II	"Samdo sŏlchanggo karak"	equal partner
Far Away / Arirang	*chungmori*	equal partner

Table 5.2: Rhythms incorporated in fusion recordings (roman numeral = project #; number in parentheses = number of occurrences on project).

Core Repertoire (Compositions): "Uttari p'ungmul" I (1), IV (2); "Samdo sŏlchanggo karak" I (2), II (3), III (1), IV (1); "Pinari" I (1), II (1); "Yŏngnam nongak" II (1), III (1), IV (2); "Honam nongak" IV (5)
P'ungmul Repertoire (Compositions): "Ho ho kut" I (1)
Shaman Repertoire (Compositions): "Shinawi" III (1)
Shaman Rhythms: *p'unŏri* I (1), III (1); *orimch'ae* I (1); *pujŏng nori* II (1); *tangak* III (1)
Pan-Korean Rhythms: *chinyang* I (1), II (1); *chungmori* II (3); *chajinmori* III (1); *ŏnmori* III (1); *insagut* IV (1)
Modified/Invented Rhythms (Unnamed): I (4); II (1); III (1)

felt a sense of duty in introducing their musical culture to foreign audiences, with solo tracks by SamulNori playing the opening rhythmic sequences of the piece "Yŏngnam nongak" on "Kil-Kun-Ak" (track #3), Kim Duk Soo playing the double-reed wind instrument *p'iri* on "Piri" (track #5), and Kim Sung Woon (Kim Sŏngun) playing the plucked-string zither *kŏmun'go* on "Komungo" (track #8; see table 5.1). And, in fact, the Korean program notes specifically identify the purpose of these latter two tracks as "introducing a Korean feeling to foreign countries" (Chu Chaeyŏn 1994). A broad range of rhythmic patterns is explored as well, with excerpts from the core repertoire (tracks #1, #3, #6, #9, and #10), shaman rhythms (track #4), pan-Korean rhythms (tracks #5, #7, #8, and #11), and modified/invented rhythms (track #2; see table 5.2). But unlike *Red Sun • SamulNori*, in which the remaining pieces wrestled with finding a common meeting ground, here we see a rapid and remarkable transformation toward equal partnership, as SamulNori plays the role of background accompaniment only on tracks #4 ("Hear Them Say") and #9 ("Full House—Part I"). It would seem that the time spent in gestation was beginning to bear fruit.

Bolstered by recording and production activity shifted away from Europe to Seoul, and in conjunction with their founding of the Nanjang studio and expanded enterprises, SamulNori felt free with *Nanjang: A New Horizon* to explore a wider range of themes and aural palettes. Red Sun members expand on previous instrumentation (Puschnig with bass clarinet, Iannacone with twelve-string guitar), and SamulNori is complemented by additional wind, string, and vocal artists from South Korea. The various tracks draw from a wide variety of predominantly Korean rhythms and performance traditions, representing samplings from the court and countryside, the secular and the sacred. Folk singing styles form the foundation of "Rabbit Story" (*p'ansori*; track #1) and "Arirang" (folk song; track #5), literati vocal genres in the vein of *shijo* or *kagok* are implied on "Meditation" (track #4), farmers' drumming and marching underpin "Celebration" (track #6), and shaman-inspired ritual and dance music is heard on "One Step to Never" (track #3), "Mother Child" (track #8), and "Shinawi" (track #9; see table 5.3). On track #2, "Things Change," which program notes

Table 5.3: *Nanjang: A New Horizon* (1995) and *From the Earth, to the Sky* (1997) compositional elements.

	Rhythmic base	Role of SamulNori
Nanjang: A New Horizon		
Rabbit Story	*chajinmori*	equal partner
Things Change	"Samdo sŏlchanggo karak"	background accompaniment
One Step to Never	*p'unŏri*	equal partner
Meditation	[not applicable]	featured
Arirang	*ŏnmori*	equal partner
Celebration	"Yŏngnam nongak"	equal partner
Water Drops	modified/invented rhythm	background accompaniment
Mother Child	*tangak*	equal partner
Shinawi	*shinawi*	equal partner/featured
From the Earth, to the Sky		
Prologue (Reaching Out)	"Honam nongak/Uttari p'ungmul"	featured
The Road Ahead	"Honam nongak"	equal partner
Burdens of Life	"Honam nongak"	equal partner
Going Places	"Honam nongak"	featured
Dance of Devotion	"Honam nongak"	equal partner
Another Step to the Sky	"Samdo sŏlchanggo karak/ Yŏngnam nongak"	equal partner
Round Up	"Yŏngnam nongak/Uttari p'ungmul"	equal partner/featured
Epilogue (The End is the Beginning)	*insagut*	equal partner

claim is based on the *tongsalp'uri* rhythmic pattern (found in the core repertoire piece "Samdo sŏlchanggo karak"; see table 5.2), we are even presented with a modified reggae beat, complete with rapping in Korean. Accordingly, this recording fulfills an introductory role reminiscent of its two predecessors, but with an important difference—SamulNori is now introducing Korean music *to Koreans*. Kim Duk Soo and his organization act as a much more proactive agent in this process; while Korean percussion does take second chair as background accompaniment on "Things Change" and "Water Drops," they meet in the middle as equal partners for the rest, even surpassing Red Sun on "Meditation" and "Shinawi," where SamulNori for the first time becomes the feature presentation.[19]

The final collaborative release, *From the Earth, to the Sky*, achieved a unified focus and balance that were lacking in the previous three attempts. It is as if the musicians met this one last time with the sole purpose of stripping away all extraneous and distracting details, moving beyond concerns of national or cultural identity to get down in earnest to the task at hand, the true "meeting of traditional Korean music and jazz, . . . a new [yet] completely natural music of our own" (Kim Duk Soo 1997). In its scaled-back instrumentation—the additional Korean musicians mostly doubling on gongs or drums, or providing backup vocals—and restricted rhythmic samplings (only two of the total six categories are represented; see table 5.2), each side finally felt free within this external simplicity to delve deeper and with more complexity into its own respective tradition. Red Sun is harmonically and melodically much more adventurous in spirit and practice, while SamulNori is sonically more at ease with the conventional full sound and resonance of the gongs. The "meeting" occurred in the realms of rhythm and improvisation: Red Sun exhibited their perhaps greatest awareness of Korean rhythmic frameworks, especially irregular meters (although they had previous practice on CD 1, track #7 [Western equivalent to 10/8], CD 2, track #4 [7/4], and CD 3, track #5 [also 10/8]); and both ensembles explored the possibilities and limits of improvisation at a new level, a shared core structural trait highlighted in previous discussion. Puschnig speaks to such issues in the program notes:

> From the clash of musical worlds (yet there is already a feeling of natural togetherness) on the first CD (Amadeo/Polygram), past the reflective but energetic mood of the second one (on ECM), to the third *Nanjang: A New Horizon* (opening up to more sounds of Korean voices and instruments) and finally to this latest one—*From the Earth, to the Sky*—we covered a vast field of musical possibilities and expressions by giving and taking from each other. Looking back, I can see that

they were all natural and logical steps in our development as a unity, leading us to now. (1997)

Representative Tracks

To help make this discussion more concrete, I have provided brief musical-structural analysis for two key tracks from the Red Sun/SamulNori oeuvre, included on the accompanying CD to this book: "Nanjang (The Meeting Place)" (from *Then Comes the White Tiger*, 1994) and "Burdens of Life" (from *From the Earth, to the Sky*, 1997). These compositions were chosen as representative examples of equal partnership (see tables 5.1 and 5.3), for their placement in the overall scheme (each track comes from the second of the "European" and "Korean" pairs of recordings, respectively), and for their adherence to traditional Korean and Western compositional approaches.

"Nanjang (The Meeting Place)" (track #3 on the accompanying CD) anticipates in name the title of the third joint CD released the following year (as well as SamulNori's new studio and label). Organizationally and temporally, however, it represents—at least by the Korean musicians—a straightforward performance of *pinari*/"Pinari," the sung ritual offering accompanied by percussion characteristic of fund-raising troupes and *namsadang* in the early twentieth century (see chapter 1).[20] Now a part of the SamulNori canon,[21] "Pinari" is divided into three parts: an opening ritual prayer (*sŏn'gosa*), a closing ritual prayer (*hugosa*), and a dramatic instrumental postlude (see table 5.4). Each section is played in a different rhythmic cycle (*sŏn'gosa* and *hugosa* refer to specific rhythms as well), with the opening prayer addressing how the earth was created, the naming of auspicious places in Seoul and Korea, the identification of geomantically powerful animals (the phoenix, the blue dragon, and the white tiger [hence the title of this album]), and the listing of spirits both in the home and in nature. In the closing prayer the soloist alternates with the other percussionists as a chorus in an extended prayer of blessing.[22]

The opening ritual prayer section (0:06–4:49) is characterized musically by verses sung in 6/8 meter, separated by cadences performed in 3/4 (a typical metrical strategy in many Korean folk percussion genres). The entire percussion quartet plays at full volume during the introduction and cadences, while the volume drops to barely audible during the singing of the texts (the small gong drops out here, because the vocalist is always the *soe* player). *Sŏn'gosa* as a rhythmic cycle is highly improvisatory, so that a model version of the rhythm is difficult to extrapolate; what is distinctive about the percussion part is the *ching* line, which

Table 5.4: Listening guide to "Nanjang (The Meeting Place)," from *Nanjang: A New Horizon* (track #3 on the CD accompanying this book).

Rhythmic cycle	Section	Timing
sŏn'gosa	introduction (instrumental)	0:06
	1st verse (Korean)	1:19
	cadence	1:41
	2nd verse (English)	1:48
	cadence	2:14
	3rd verse (Korean)	2:21
	cadence	2:49
	4th verse (English)	2:56
	cadence	3:34
	5th verse (Korean, with English overlay)	3:41
	cadence	4:42
hugosa	introduction (instrumental)	4:49
	1st verse (Korean)	5:28
	transition	6:08
	2nd verse (Korean)	6:13
	transition	7:05
	3rd verse (English)	7:09
	transition	7:40
	4th verse (Korean)	7:43
	transition	8:11
	5th verse (Korean, with English overlay)	8:15
chajin karak	postlude (instrumental)	10:14

acts as a more active and equal partner to the other instruments, when compared to its primarily time-keeping role in *p'ungmul* and other *samul nori* contexts (as seen in chapter 3). Figure 5.3 is a transcription of the opening sixteen phrases of track #3, showing the mallet hand of the hourglass drum (the circles in the boxes) and the highly agitated and syncopated large gong (bolded boxes; the gong is partially damped so that it can be heard at this rapid speed).

After this opening passage the rest of the combined ensemble enters—one by one, timbre by timbre—creating a dense and overlapping rhythmic texture that builds in intensity until its release with the onset of text: first the electric bass, followed by the electric guitar, barrel drum, small gong, and alto saxophone. The approach taken here in the opening (and, later, during the verses) by Red Sun is remarkably similar to that of late soul, early funk groups in the United States, who treated their "melodic" instruments in a percussive manner, playing repetitive short phrases or riffs over a static harmonic background. In "Nanjang" this is achieved by the bass playing a repeated slap bass figure that interweaves with the hourglass drum part, the guitarist providing short and static harmonic riffs, and Puschnig on alto saxophone imitating the small gong line through a limited melodic vocabulary. When the time comes for the cadences, both SamulNori and Red Sun respond appropriately by playing at full volume in a kind of rhythmic-melodic flourish that remains gesturally recognizable to each tradition.

Textually, this balance between East and West is found in the alternation

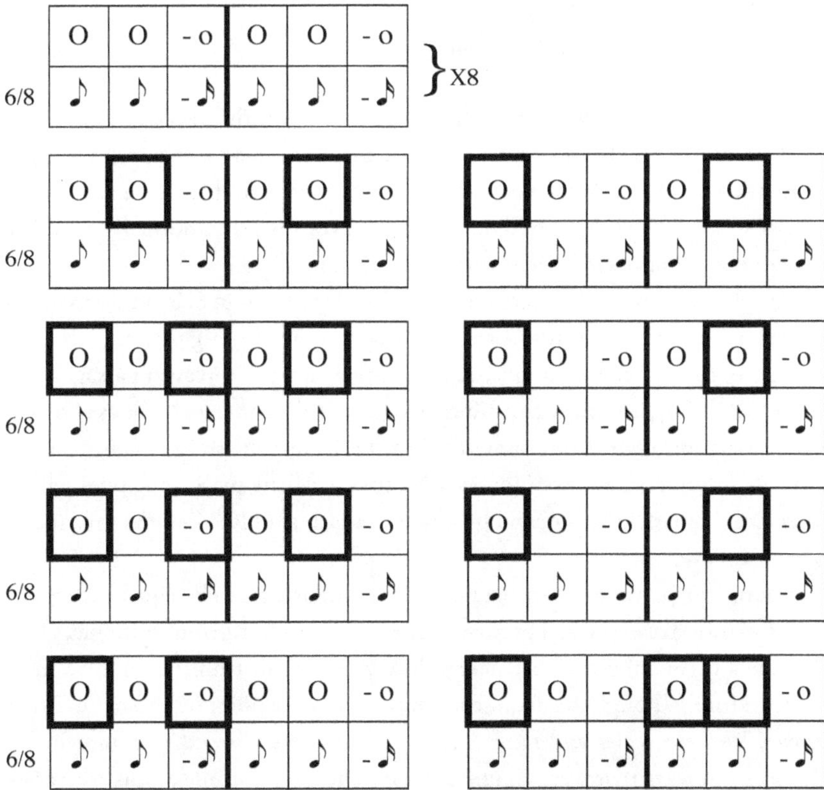

Figure 5.3 *Sŏn'gosa* opening passage from "Nanjang (The Meeting Place)" (until entrance of the electric bass). **Key:** O = louder *changgo* stroke, o = weaker *changgo* stroke.

of Korean and English verses (see table 5.4). In the second and fourth verses Linda Sharrock condenses and comments on the Korean text that precedes her entrances:

> Look at the sky, look at the sun from the sky
> and the ground that we tread on, though we'll never know why.
> The phoenix rose from the ashes,
> spreads his arms and all that it passes
> of flowers and blooms and great palaces come into view.
>
> Then comes the blue dragon,
> then comes the white tiger.
> Then comes the blue dragon,
> then comes the white tiger.
> Blossoms and secret palaces come into view.

In the fifth verse she overlays English fragments from the two previous verses on the Korean text. It is important to note that in all sung passages there exists an implied harmonic framework created by the (Western) pitched instruments, so that some pressure is exerted on the Korean vocalist, who normally wouldn't have to enter on the same pitch with the beginning of each verse.

The closing ritual prayer section (4:49–10:14) remains in 6/8 but slows down to approximately two-thirds of the opening tempo. Also highly improvisatory in nature, the same alternation occurs between sung and played passages and Korean and English texts; the difference here is that Sharrock chooses to use free association with themes unrelated to the Korean blessing (English that is difficult to understand, even for a native speaker). The piece concludes with a brief and dramatic instrumental postlude in a fast 4/4 (10:14–), the small gong playing on every beat.

I deem the partnership throughout this composition to be equal because of the give-and-take expressed between the two groups both compositionally and dynamically (our ability as listeners to hear all of the instruments in the overall sonic texture). Though the main structure or reference point was a Korean ritual prayer, Western scales and harmonic structures were allowed to comment on this form in ways that were complementary and often seamless. English verses made this vocal art approachable by non-Korean speakers—a strategy used in many "world music" crossover recordings—while at the same time prompting or even challenging audiences to see points of commonality between two other-

Table 5.5: Listening guide to "Burdens of Life," from *From the Earth, to the Sky* (track #4 on the CD accompanying this book).

Rhythmic cycle	Section	Timing
p'ungnyugut	introduction/head (instrumental)	0:00
kutkŏri	alto saxophone solo	0:30
	electric guitar solo	2:57
	SamulNori solo	5:51
	interlude (instrumental)	6:05
	vocal solo (English)	6:16
	coda (instrumental)	8:03

wise disparate vocal traditions. Other *samul nori* ensembles would soon record their own fusion versions of "Pinari," with the idea of integrating the electric guitar and bass with the percussion quartet lineup forming a separate but related canon among Korean urban youth of the early twenty-first century.[23]

In contrast to the highly structured and Korean form of "Nanjang," with "Burdens of Life" (track #4 on the accompanying CD) from the fourth and final recording, *From the Earth, to the Sky*, SamulNori and Red Sun approach the project as what might best be described as an old-fashioned Western jazz "jam session." The musicians follow a standard jazz format by opening with an introductory section, or "head," followed by solos taken by the various members in turn. Beginning with alto saxophone, then moving on to electric guitar, SamulNori alone, and finally Sharrock singing English text, each performer through improvisation explores rhythmic and melodic (for the Western participants) possibilities over an established meter (discussed below; see table 5.5). Harmonically and melodically one would characterize the "head" as loosely tonal, while the ensuing solos become free from the constraints of key signatures or conventional major/minor scales.

Throughout the composition SamulNori likewise improvises and interacts with the Western soloists in the role of a good jazz drummer (or an accomplished *p'ansori* accompanist, for that matter). After briefly opening with the rhythmic cycle *p'ungnyugut* (*chilgut*)—notice how the melodic instruments model their gestures after the Korean percussion line—the piece settles into the related slow 4-beat *kutkŏri* cycle from the *Honam nongak* core repertoire (because of the slower speed, I have rendered it as 12/4 instead of 12/8; see figure 5.4 for a simplified account of the small and large gong lines).[24] While 12/4 is not a com-

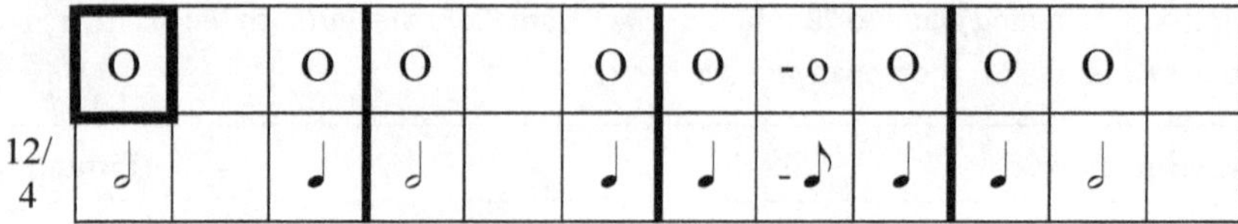

Figure 5.4 *Kutkŏri* rhythmic cycle ("Burdens of Life"). Key: O = louder *soe* stroke, o = softer *soe* stroke.

mon meter for jazz musicians, the choice is entirely appropriate from a Korean perspective, as *kutkŏri* is considered one of the best rhythms for improvisation in the entire *p'ungmul/samul nori* tradition (Hesselink 2004:425–26). SamulNori also brings Korean performance practice to the fore by increasing their playing dynamically in the leading up to the ends of solos, and in their heightened use of hemiola-like figures—changing into groupings of twos—as a means of further signaling a new section in the piece (a nice example of this sensitivity to Korean structures by Red Sun is heard at 1:52, when the bass plays in twos along with the barrel drum). The reassuring sound of the *ching* (large gong) on every beat one helps the listener stay rooted in the underlying cycle.

Two elements of the performance break with jazz tradition, though they don't interrupt the flow of the order or mood. The first is the inclusion of sung text in what is otherwise an instrumental form: Sharrock takes the place of what would normally be reserved for the bass player. The text, however, gives more concrete form to the ethos of the track (titled "Burdens of Life") by describing the transformation of an ideal(ized) world corrupted by wealth and war:

> Peace reigns in the valley,
> life has just begun.
> Oh, thank god in heaven
> we live in peace as one.
>
> Gold it glitters brightly,
> gleaming like the sun.
> Oh my god in heaven
> what has just begun?
>
> Brother against brother,
> father against son.
> Oh god, god in heaven
> what on earth have we done?

Mothers left with the daughters,
war clouds take the sons.
Oh my god in heaven
what on earth have we done?[25]

The performance ends with a brief coda, and while thematically it is unrelated to the head—again, unlike standard jazz practice—it mirrors it in instrumentation and general atmosphere, bringing the piece to a satisfying close.

With "Burdens of Life" we similarly experience an equal partnership between SamulNori and Red Sun. Seen as a kind of mirror image to "Nanjang," this time realized through a Western compositional structure, balance with the jazz idiom is achieved through dynamic and structural room given to the Korean percussion, and the modification of the metrical structures to match Korean rhythmic cycles. As I mentioned in the production details to this album, it was as if both sets of musicians were most at ease here with "just playing"—i.e., not worried with introducing "foreign" elements of their respective traditions to a widening audience base—in an effort at coming up with a music that was shared and without racial or national markers. Red Sun would officially disband after this project, and Kim Duk Soo and SamulNori would move on to other challenges, but the legacy of this meeting of Korean percussion and jazz continues to be felt in concert halls and recording studios throughout East Asia (and in the collective memories of SamulNori fans around the world).

Possibility in Cross-Cultural Collaboration

While four is an incomplete and superstitiously avoided number throughout much of East Asia, for SamulNori and Red Sun it marked the successful completion of nearly a decade of purposeful and meaningful action. On the earlier recordings it began as more of a creative struggle to join disparate—but not completely incompatible—musical structures and sounds, coupled to a perceived need to explain or introduce Korean music to both native and foreign audiences. Later efforts show the fruits of this labor as both sides, through mutual understanding and an ongoing process of give-and-take, emerge as equal partners engaged in a dialogue. This culminated in the uniformly most focused and balanced of the projects, *From the Earth, to the Sky*, in which a streamlined instrumentation and limited categorical use of rhythm made room for the most adventurous and yet respectful exploration of a creative middle ground, largely through the process of improvisation. The direction and use of the rhythmic patterns over the course of the four CDs reflect this focus and balance as well—slowly we see the move from more eclectic sampling and nontraditional patterns or cycles toward the more established regional or core repertoire where SamulNori musicians are most at home (see table 5.2).

I began this chapter with the idea of hybridity as a morally neutral designation when viewed in the abstract. But if hybridity leads to the breaking down of boundaries and the fostering of inclusion, especially in places or circumstances where rigidity and xenophobia have been the norm, then it becomes a powerful transformative tool for cross-cultural exchange and understanding (after Weiss 2008:233; see also Kapchan and Strong 1999:243–46). And when such hybridity is conceived of and generated internally under one's own conditions—as it was with SamulNori and their interactions with Red Sun—it has the potential for local empowerment and a way of defining oneself in the face of encroaching global forces (Winslow 2003; Stokes 2004:59–61).

SamulNori and Red Sun's efforts in most of the important particulars differed widely from the examples set previously by "elite pop artists" (such as Paul Simon or David Byrne) who have been accused of swooping in from on high and exploiting the "locals" (Erlmann 1996; Guilbault 1993). SamulNori was on a much more equal footing with Red Sun in terms of their socioeconomic status, their countries' financial and military power, and ease of international travel. All aspects of the recording process were shared equally by the two groups, including the composition of the pieces, the recording and mixing of the individual tracks, the choice of recording studio and engineer, the choice of language used in the program notes and advertising, and even the art created for the covers. Both groups traveled freely and willingly to each other's native lands, conducted joint workshops and master classes, and continued to interact long after the official events and projects had come to a close. What also distinguished their activities was the length of time they interacted—nearly ten years in total—and the respect that was shown in both directions as members of SamulNori learned Western instruments (piano and guitar) and harmonic structures, at the same time Puschnig and his cohorts studied Korean rhythmic structures and drumming techniques. As I mentioned previously—and as is documented further in this chapter and in appendix 4—musicians from both groups continue to work together, a sign of their deep and mutual respect.

The example set by SamulNori and Red Sun is very much in the vein of musical collaboration as conceived by the ethnomusicologist Louise Meintjes when viewing the positive aspects of the genesis of Paul Simon's *Graceland*, in that both stylistic features and power relations have been carefully negotiated and intertwined in terms of composition, production, and promotional processes (Meintjes 1990). Other such models of emulation have been documented by Timothy Taylor in South Africa, North America, and between Europe and Africa, specifically discussed within the parameters of cross-cultural collaboration (1997:173–96). And because the "economic stakes in this traffic are small" (Feld 1988:37)—to take a more sobering viewpoint—there have been no complaints or accusations of inequality or inequity from either side.

SamulNori and Red Sun's legacy is most strongly felt within the local Korean musical scene, efforts credited with spearheading the trend toward fusion projects employing traditional elements so common today on stages and festivals throughout South Korea (Kim Chŏngŭn 2008:75). SamulNori members remained at the forefront of this movement, releasing subsequent fusion CDs with European, Japanese, and American colleagues: *Eurasion Echoes*, 2000; *Kwang-Soo Lee & Red Sun* (*Wŏlhwa*), 1997; *Misŭt'a changgo [Mr. Changgo]: Kim Duk Soo with His Friends*, 1997; *On the Road: The 50th Anniversary of Kim Duk Soo's Debut*, 2007; *Salp'uri*, 2002; *Shinmyŏng*, 2000; *Yesanjok* (*Korean Song and Beat Project*), 2007. Red Sun Members also joined non-SamulNori Korean musicians for fusion projects within Korea: *Kim Sŏkch'ul: Kyŏlchŏng p'an* (*Kim Suk Chul: Final Say*), 1997; *Umezu Kazutoki: Dancing Winds*, 1997; *West End*, 1996. During the earlier stages of experimentation, SamulNori garnered the attention of the classical music world as well.[26]

Rival *samul nori* teams also joined the mix. Turep'ae Samulnori, one of the first professional teams established after the National Center's team (Kungnip Kugagwŏn Samulnori), released a predominantly fusion recording in 1993 (*Durae-Pae Samul Nori Che-3 chip* [volume 3]), while the 1990s and early 2000s saw the formation of Puri (P'uri)[27] and Gong Myoung (Kongmyŏng), two of the most influential and commercially successful of the new generation of *samul nori* performers (see the section "*Samul nori* fusion groups/projects" in appendix 4 for a listing of their recordings, as well as other artists inspired by their work). In addition to a myriad of other *samul nori* teams and related projects (see Howard 2006c:59–62), *samul nori* live or sampled has appeared on rap CDs (*Taiji Boys Live & Techno Mix*, 1992; *Ssai*: *Ssajib*, 2006), newly envisioned folk song renditions (*Chang Saik: Kich'im*, 1999), and industrial-electronica (*Chew and Swallow*, 2006), to name just a few of the many emerging contexts. In North America, the joining of *samul nori* with Western classical and/or rock instruments on university campuses has become a canon in its own right—many, like my own composition performed in 2008, captured on YouTube (http://www.youtube.com/watch?v=yj12yAJf-Lc).

The ideal of the *nanjang*—a safe forum for the interaction of different musical and cultural identities—is an attractive one for early twenty-first-century societies as they continue to grapple with problems of misunderstanding and indifference. SamulNori and Red Sun created such a space through *musical* conversation, bringing to the table a respect and understanding of each other's approaches and traditions. What they accomplished, through trial and error, was by no means a small or easy task. They succeeded, in the end, by establishing a new repertoire that acknowledged the sources rooted in Korean folk percussion and Western jazz, at the same time highlighting the flowering of something fresh and wondrous. In the process, they also touched on our shared humanity.

CONCLUSION

Pŏpko ch'angshin (Preserve the Old While Creating the New)

The Meanings of Tradition

If we were to count the number of faces that SamulNori has shown us in the past ten years, how many would that add up to? And of those faces, which one could we consider to be the real one?

Traditional musicians? Dancers? Minstrels? Jazz men? Contemporary musicians? New "mudang" [shamans]? Why is it that one face does not suffice? Eight years ago how was it possible that a joint performance with Indian percussion instruments, piano, and saxophone was conceived? Why is it that every year this group attempts to explore new worlds? Why is it that modern dancers want to dance "Yul Madang, Yuldu Kauri," a composition for piano and SamulNori? Why was SamulNori, a brass band, and choir composition the appropriate piece to mark the Pope's visit to Seoul? Why is it that as ancient as SamulNori's rhythms are we view it as modern music? How long will it be that we view Korea's traditional culture as merely a historical relic? Should it not be that what we consider to be of such value, should that not be given a new life now?

How many faces are still to be revealed by SamulNori in the future?

KANG JUN HYUK [KANG CHUNHYŎK] 1988:135

With the benefit of hindsight, it is apparent that the tale of the "children of wandering minstrels" was an unconditional success. Now in their fourth decade of activity, SamulNori as a group and genre is clearly considered traditional by the majority of the Korean population, as well as mainstream media, academia, and governmental agencies. *Samul nori* remains the default percussion genre at the National Center for the Korean Traditional Performing Arts, the flagship institution for the representation and promotion of Korean traditional arts both domestically and abroad, while recently the Korean Ministry of Culture, Sports, and Tourism launched a new workbook and DVD series in English titled "Encounters with Korean Traditional Music," of which the first volume is dedicated to *samul nori* (Lee, Young-Gwang 2009). This publication was included as part of a larger collection of traditional music CDs and DVDs (seventy-five in total) under the title of "Worldwide Presentation Project of Korean Traditional Music CDs," sent out by the ministry to foreign researchers; within this sampling only *samul nori* was included as an example of Korean percussion (an interesting choice, as there are now numerous government-sponsored CDs of *p'ungmul*). The genre is included in all recent major music histories (e.g., Yi Sŏngch'ŏn et al. 1997:180–81; Yun Myŏngwŏn et al. 2004:188–89; Song Pangsong 2007:716–19), and has become a catch phrase in Korean common parlance for any percussive genre employing the four core drums and gongs. And, as was mentioned previously, *samul nori* is now a regular offering at the primary, secondary, and university level throughout the peninsula.

When evaluating the effects of SamulNori's fusion projects it is equally clear that their presence has made a significant and long-lasting impact on the Korean traditional music world. Cross-cultural collaboration and hybridity are now the norm—as is amply evident in the regularly scheduled concerts and commercially released recordings of such work—to the extent that even the National Center includes such fusion compositions in its weekly concert series. Understood within the broader culture of presenting traditional music on the concert hall stage, SamulNori was a driving force in making tradition relevant again to modern Korean society, bringing back prestige, fame, and economic viability to generations of other traditional performing artists in the music and dance worlds. Their interactions with Wolfgang Puschnig and Red Sun also provided a safe and equitable model for engaging the outside world, both abroad and at home.

The relationship between SamulNori/*samul nori* and the cultural asset system is a more complex and problematic one. While it is obvious that the government will not officially bring the genre into its fold, such formalities have already been sidestepped by the National Center's activities and the efforts of the Korean Ministry of Culture, Sports, and Tourism, discussed above. A number of high-profile *samul nori* practitioners have joined the ranks of the cultural asset *namsadang* troupe in Seoul (such as National Center team members Ch'oe Pyŏngsam and Pak Ŭnha, not to mention long-standing *namsadang* member Nam Kimun), while for many years *p'ungmul* performers—including human cultural assets such as Iri Nongak's Kim Hyŏngsun (chapter 3)—have been called upon to serve as judges in *samul nori* competitions, often with the same or similar criteria used in regional *p'ungmul* festivals. Even back in the mid-1990s, when I was conducting fieldwork among rural *p'ungmul* communities in the Chŏlla provinces, many members of cultural asset teams knew the *samul nori* repertoire, some even incorporating aspects of its rhythms and playing techniques (either consciously or unknowingly). I had a similar experience in 2006 in Kangnŭng (a city in Kangwŏn province to the east), where the instructors for the main cultural asset *p'ungmul* group also taught *samul nori* pieces, though it never occurred to them to compose a *samul nori* version of their own tradition—the missing link to the canon (something I personally attempted to rectify; see Hesselink 2009).

More properly understood as the logical outgrowth of itinerant troupe performance culture and a worldview inclusive of the current, organic, and even foreign, however, SamulNori/*samul nori* rightly calls into question the very presence and future significance of a cultural asset system, policies that are increasingly emulated in other East Asian countries and the global organization of UNESCO in their category of the Masterpiece of the Oral and Intangible Heritage of Humanity. Earlier I wrote of the positive influences of this system and its appropriateness to the historical era in which it was born, one where wars and societal indifference had threatened the loss of much of what was considered distinctively Korean (Hesselink 2006:10–11). But with South Korea's emergence as a technologically advanced and globally savvy society—combined with a renewed pride in traditional culture—the example set by SamulNori seems closer to a twenty-first-century understanding of the meaning of tradition, one in which self-aware performers and creators are afforded agency and the freedom to choose their own identity, however complex and contested that might be.

The cultural asset system was in many ways from its very beginnings flawed in its privileging of the past and the resultant intellectual and philosophical belittling of the present. Numerous critics of the system and its processes have identified the inherent tension between preservation and promotion and the problematic nature of reenvisioning the past as "authentic" (nicely summarized and contextualized in Howard 2006b:27–48). Like hybridity, the choice to delimit the traditional is an act of historical perspective and interpretation, highly susceptible to politics, financial gain, and personal whim. But more importantly, cultural asset policy has ignored almost every significant musical event on the Korean peninsula of the twentieth century, including structural and aesthetic cross-fertilization between Koreans, Japanese, Americans, and Western Europeans. In doing so, it continues to promote a false sense of racial purity at the expense of the historical record and the rich interplay between Korea and her neighbors, including the activities of the *namsadang* and the touring and collaborative efforts of SamulNori. At some point in the not-so-distant future it will become painfully obvious that what cultural asset performers are doing today is not what their predecessors had done—however closely they might adhere to the "primary form" (*wŏnhyŏng*) as established by cultural asset documentation—and that for their art to continue to have relevance to themselves and the general public they must allow for their current, personal, and even idiosyncratic experiences to impinge on their performance and understanding of the traditional.

While I have spoken of the traditional only in positive terms throughout this book, the legitimization of authority and existing power structures is another function of tradition and the past. Looking to the examples set by one's elders is a notable feature of Korean culture, as is an almost unqualified reverence for anything borne of antiquity. Scholars of tradition have long noted the potency of the past as a historical and symbolic construct as a means of influencing and shaping current thought by those who are in power: "The mass of mankind, the majority of the population of most societies, are the recipients of tradition as a result of tradition-recommending initiative of some of their contemporaries, and above all the authorities of their society. The latter are more sensitive to the 'sacredness' of 'pastness,' and by their example and their recommendation they arouse the latent responses of their less 'dutiful' fellow countrymen" (Shils 1971:139–40; see also Russell 1945:xiii and Small 1998:87–93). Tradition as unchecked cultural phenomena can easily serve as an apparatus for hegemonic interests that threaten differing perspectives and individual voices, a powerful force for racism (aforementioned ideas of racial purity vs. what the *namsadang* and others represent), class distinction (court and other forms of elite culture vs. the "commoners"), and religious belief (Schroeder 2006:3–6; Leppert and McClary 1987).

If we are to understand any performance, musical or otherwise, as the exploration and affirmation of certain kinds of ideal relationships at the expense of others (Small 1998:183), then perhaps it is time to sympathetically yet critically examine the kinds of traditional culture that are being preserved in an effort to understand what aspects of Korea's past are still worth emulating in a society that has embraced democratic ideals (Kim, Samuel S. 2003; Moon, Chung-in and Jongryn Mo 1999). As the National Center and other governmental agencies prepare promotional materials and international tours showcasing Korean traditional culture, what face of Korea's past and present do they wish to present to the world? The inclusion of fusion projects and "newly composed" traditional works (*shin kugak*) marks a qualified acceptance of hybridity and outside cultural influences. But what about making plain the roots of the *namsadang* acts (including Manchurian and Chinese contributions), or the conditions under which professional female entertainers (*kisaeng*) developed their arts, especially during the Japanese occupation? There are not, of course, any simple solutions to these questions, but it is often in the asking or searching that progress is made toward openness, equity, and inclusion.

From my own perspective, the future of Korean traditional music seems to reside in groups such as Noreum Machi. Led by master vocalist and percussionist Kim Ju Hong (Kim Chuhong), a native of Chindo Island and pupil of Kim Duk Soo and Lee Kwang Soo, the self-avowed "New Wave Korean Music Group" was formed in 1993 as the next logical step in the development of *samul nori*. Envisioning the genre not so much as a particular repertoire or canon of works but rather as a medium through which to explore all forms of Korean traditional percussion, in 2003 Noreum Machi began a quest to integrate aspects of *samul nori* with Korean shaman and Buddhist drumming, as well as the vocal arts of *p'ansori* (narrative song accompanied by drum) and popular song. Like SamulNori, Noreum Machi has engaged in extensive touring and workshops around the globe (in 2009/2010 under the auspices of the World Music Institute); they have similarly drawn their inspiration from itinerant troupe performance culture. Long before the *namsadang* became immortalized in *The King and the Clown* (Kim Ju Hong was hired as a musician and actor for the film), Kim named his group in 1993 after *norŭm mach'i* (literally "play for high stakes"), the name of the top performer prize offered at a *namsadang* competition (see program notes to CD recording *Noreum Machi Kim Ju Hong*, 2007). Unencumbered by the dictates of the cultural asset system, Kim Ju Hong and his group continue to adapt and evolve in their "search for a harmony with modern musical trends without sacrificing their own [Korean] tradition" (Hong, Jimin 2009).

This book began with an account of SamulNori's genesis, and to them I now turn as a fitting conclusion. On January 9, 2009, in Seoul, SamulNori held the "30th Anniversary of SamulNori International Symposium," the culmination of a year of activities beginning in 2008 celebrating the accomplishments of the original team, subsequent members and institutional developments, and work with foreign artists (see figure C.1). In addition to bringing back surviving members Kim Duk Soo, Lee Kwang Soo (Yi Kwangsu), and Ch'oe Chongshil (see appendix 2), outside perspectives were also represented by numerous academics, an early tour manager and translator (Suzanna Samstag), an overseas coordinator (Katherine In-Young Lee), Kim Dong-Won (former director of education), Kim Duk Soo's wife (the dancer Kim Rihye), and brothers Kang Chunil (composer) and Kang Chunhyŏk (METAA founder and Space Theater manager). A generous gesture was also made with the invitation of three keynote speakers who represented the three prongs of SamulNori's early touring and fusion efforts: Japan (Hayashi Eitetsu, cofounder of Kodo and frequent collaborator with Kim Duk Soo), England/Europe (Keith Howard, professor of ethnomusicology at the University of London-SOAS), and North America (myself). The event came roughly a year after the release of Kim Duk Soo's solo CD honoring the fiftieth anniversary of his stage debut (*On the Road: The 50th Anniversary of Kim Duk Soo's Debut*, 2007).

In the midst of happy reunions, feelings of good will, and an abundance of congratulatory sentiments, however, there lingered a sense of urgency, of that which was yet to be accomplished. Kim Duk Soo said as much in his opening remarks in the program book: "In an era when much of the true nature of our traditional culture and spirit has been lost, at times I still feel there is much that needs to be done and I long for my youth of days past. But as always—until the day that I die—I plan on being right in there, stirring things up. And I look forward to celebrating the 40th and 50th anniversaries." It is because of this humility and passion, combined with the insight and conviction of a critic's words published twenty years ago, that I believe the legacy of SamulNori/*samul nori* is secure:

Figure C.1 Program book from the "30th Anniversary of SamulNori International Symposium," 2009 (© SamulNori Hanullim).

Just like its name, SamulNori is a traditional Korean percussion ensemble. And, of course, their first priority has been the perfection of their technique in gathering and organizing Korea's traditional rhythms. But these musicians refuse to permit us to become too comfortable with that role—they are musicians living for tomorrow. They are musicians who seek to constantly test themselves through encounters with musicians from other cultures. In free and open dialogue they ask themselves: "Can we survive when we contend with other means of expression?" In these encounters, however, they always seem to reassure us with their suppleness made strong by their deep historical roots. (Ku, Hee-seo 1989:75)

APPENDIX ONE

Minsokkŭkhoe Namsadang ("Folk Theater Association Namsadang") Founding Members

PERCUSSION MUSIC AND DANCE

Ch'oe Sŏnggu (small gong), Nam Hyŏngu/Unyong (small gong), Yang Toil (hourglass-shaped drum), Song Ch'angsŏn (double-reed wind instrument), Im Kwangshik (small gong), Ch'oe Ŭnch'ang (hourglass-shaped drum), Kim Munhak (small drum), Hwang Chŏmsŏk (large gong), Chi Sumun (barrel drum), Pak Chonghwi (barrel drum), Song Sun'gap (small drum), Chi Unha (small drum), Hong Hongshik (small drum), Pak Yongt'ae (dance), Nam Kihwan (dance), U Chongsŏng (dance), Kwak Pongnyŏl (dance), Nam Kidol (dance), Chŏng Ilp'a (double-reed wind instrument)

BOWL SPINNING

Nam Hyŏngu (bowl spinner), Kim Chaewŏn (bowl spinner), Yang Toil (jester)

ACROBATICS

Song Sun'gap (acrobat), Yang Toil (jester)

TIGHTROPE WALKING

Cho Songja (tightrope walker), Yang Toil (jester)

MASK DANCE

Ch'oe Sŏnggu (apostate monk), Yang Toil (gentleman scholar), Nam Hyŏngu (servant and prodigal servant), Cho Songja (aged parent), Pak Kyesun (niece), Nam Kihwan (niece), Pak Yongt'ae (monk with boil on face), Song Sun'gap (servant)

PUPPETRY

Nam Hyŏngu (main puppeteer), Yang Toil (vocalist), Ch'oe Sŏnggu (assistant puppeteer), Yi Suyŏng (assistant puppeteer), Pak Kyesun (assistant puppeteer), Pak Yongt'ae (assistant puppeteer), Ch'oe Ŭnch'ang (musician), Chi Sumun (musician), Song Ch'angsŏn (musician)

APPENDIX TWO

Major Divisions and Personnel Changes during the First Decade of SamulNori/*samul nori* Activity

1978: SAMULNORI

Kim Duk Soo (Kim Tŏksu), *changgo*: S, N, L
Kim Yongbae, *soe*: S, N
Yi Chongdae, *puk*
Ch'oe T'aehyŏn, *ching*: S

1979 (MARCH): SAMULNORI

Kim Duk Soo, *changgo*: S, N, L
Ch'oe Chongsŏk, *soe*: N
Kim Yongbae, *puk*: S, N
Ch'oe Chongshil, *ching*: S, P, L

1979 (MAY): SAMULNORI

Kim Duk Soo, *changgo*: S, N, L
Kim Yongbae, *soe*: S, N
Yi Kwangsu, *puk*: N
Ch'oe Chongshil, *ching*: P, L

1984: SAMULNORI

Kim Duk Soo, *changgo*: S, N, L
Yi Kwangsu, *soe*: N
Ch'oe Chongshil, *puk*: P, L
Kang Minsŏk, *ching*: P

KUNGNIP KUGAGWŎN SAMULNORI

Chŏn Sudŏk, *changgo*: P
Kim Yongbae, *soe*: S, N
Pang Sŭnghwan, *puk*: S
Pak Ŭnha, *ching*: L

1986: SAMULNORI

—same—

KUNGNIP KUGAGWŎN SAMULNORI

Nam Kimun, *changgo*: S, N, L
Kim Yongbae, *soe*: S, N
Pang Sŭnghwan, *puk*: S
Ch'oe Pyŏngsam, *puk*: S, P, L
Pak Ŭnha, *ching*: L

1987: SAMULNORI

—same—

KUNGNIP KUGAGWŎN SAMULNORI

Nam Kimun, *changgo*: S, N, L
Cho Kabyong, *soe*: P
Ch'oe Pyŏngsam, *puk*: S, P, L
Paek Chinsŏk, *ching*: P
[Pak Ŭnha rejoined in 1993]

Note: Primary associations indicated by S (Seoul Traditional Arts High School graduate), N (*namsadang* member), P (*p'ungmul* performer), and L (Little Angels member).

APPENDIX THREE

SamulNori Instrumentation

GONGS

Leading the ensemble in both rural *p'ungmul/namsadang* and *samul nori* contexts is the small handheld gong known as the *soe*, meaning literally "iron" or "metal." Alternatively known by its onomatopoeic designation *kkwaenggwari*, it is made of brass and is suspended by a rope threaded through two holes drilled in the lip of the instrument (further historical and bibliographic details for all of the instruments can be found in Hesselink 2006:49–66). *Soe* are produced by either pouring heated metal into a mold (*chumul*) or forging by hand (*pangja*), the latter process considered superior in quality and reflected in the considerably higher price. More recently it has also been common to mix in trace amounts of silver or gold, also adding to the end cost (see figure A3.1).

The gong is struck on its front surface by a mallet held with the free hand, while the hand holding the *soe* manipulates its sound through a number of damping techniques (*magŭmsoe*). *Soe* are commonly divided into male and female, the former generally associated with a higher and sharper toned pitch and the latter with a lower and more subdued one. General knowledge accords such matching with acoustics, such that the lead *soe* player who plays on a "male" *soe* should be heard above the second

Figure A3.1 The *soe* (photo by Nathan Hesselink).

soe player on a "female" *soe* (alternating in such a manner down through the rest of the section); the specific terminology doesn't provide any additional interpretive insight (*amsori*, literally "female sound," and *sussori*, "male sound"). This distinction is more important in large group settings where there is more than one *soe* player, not typical of most *samul nori* performances based on the precedent set by the original SamulNori group. The *soe* is most likely an import from the Chinese imperial court.

The metallic companion to the *soe* is the *ching*, a large handheld gong made of brass in the same manner as its smaller counterpart (the *ching* is suspended on a stand in a seated *samul nori* performance). The *ching* is struck with a padded beater, and in its older, rural form (a good instrument) is distinguished by an after-tone characterized by three undulations of sound referred to as *samp'aŭm* (three-wave sound). In recent years, however, there is some evidence of Kim Duk Soo and his organization commissioning *ching* with more limited resonance, generally reverberating for only one cycle of a rhythmic pattern to help with clarity needed at the faster tempos (Donna Kwon, personal communication, 2002). *Ching* strokes always mark the first beat of each cycle and are understood as the "sonic glue" that bind together the rest of the ensemble. In the past the sound of the *ching* was used as a signal for retreat in the military and as a means of sounding an alarm in village society. There is also the noteworthy but minority viewpoint of its sound being capable of changing the bone structure of an unborn child in the womb of a shaman (Kim Myŏnghwan 1992:71).

Figure A3.2 The *ching* (photo by Nathan Hesselink).

Also an import from the Chinese court, it is unclear when and how the *soe* and *ching* made their way from the upper to the commoner classes (see figure A3.2).

DRUMS

The most iconic and immediately recognized instrument of the percussion quartet is the *changgo* ("stick drum"), a double-headed, hourglass-shaped drum with historical roots still open to debate. The body of the *changgo* is hollow and is usually carved from a single piece of paulownia wood (*odong namu*), then spun on a lathe. The larger, lower-pitched side of the drum is struck with a mallet fashioned from the root of a bamboo tree and is associated with the earth and female energy. The smaller, higher-pitched side, in contrast, is struck with a stick carved from the stalk of the bamboo tree and is associated with the heavens and male energy (similar in conception to the gongs/drums and heavens/earth dichotomy presented above). *Changgo* vary in size and weight depending on genre, so that a *p'ungmul/samul nori* drum is lighter and louder than its court music counterpart and exhibits a slightly greater dynamic contrast between the low and high registers (Yi Yongshik et al. 2007:98–102; Yi Yongshik et al. 2008:72–74). Rural *p'ungmul* and *namsadang* perform-

Figure A3.3 The *changgo* (photo by Nathan Hesselink).

ers strap the instrument to the body securely with a white cotton cloth so that both hands are free to play while dancing; this cloth is obviously unnecessary for seated performances of *samul nori*. *Changgo* in the past were customarily finished with a clear varnish, though more recently many *samul nori* musicians have shown a preference for a deep red or maroon lacquer (see figure A3.3).

There is some indication that Kim Duk Soo's organization has begun to modify the structure of the *changgo*, shortening the mallet side bowl so that the mallet strokes are less resonant and hence easier to hear in fast passages (most likely in conjunction with their preference for *ching* with shorter sounding lengths). The stick side bowl is then lengthened in an effort to balance the sound between the two heads (Park, Shingil 2000:193–94). A more focused attention to the stick side of the *changgo* and registral differentiation in *samul nori* playing in general—a direct result of its increased technical demands—can also be seen in the types of drumheads employed. Rural *p'ungmul* and *namsadang* performers until recently tended to use matching heads made of cow, sheep, or dog leather, whereas *samul nori* players favored mixing skins (cow on the left [lower pitched], dog on the right [higher pitched]). According to my *namsadang* teacher An Chungbŏm, most *samul nori* players and *namsadang* players today have switched to using dog leather on the mallet side, and horse leather on the stick side for the increased clarity and vibrancy (personal communication, 2006).

The "earth" partner of the *changgo* is the *puk*, a double-headed, barrel-shaped drum. The only clearly indigenous percussion instrument in the quartet, today the body of the *puk* is constructed with interlocking slats of wood (in the past one also found single-unit bodies carved from a single tree trunk). Leather skins (usually cow) are stretched over both openings and laced together with rope, with tension maintained by optional wooden chucks wedged between the rope and the body of the instrument. In danced performances the *puk* is suspended from the performer's shoulder by a long cord of cotton cloth and is struck with a stick made of hardwood. Mythological tales imbue the *puk* with magical powers, and in the military this drum was used to signal advances (in contrast with the *ching* sound indicating retreats). SamulNori Hanullim has for years now commissioned its own instruments, marked by its logo stamped or burned into the side of the instrument (see figure A3.4). Hanullim drums and gongs are distributed through their own store in Seoul, and are also sold at the National Center for Korean Traditional Performing Arts (the Kungnip Kugagwŏn).

Beyond the core percussion quartet one also finds the *sogo* ("small drum"), a small, double-headed frame drum with a handle. Primarily used as a prop in danced perfor-

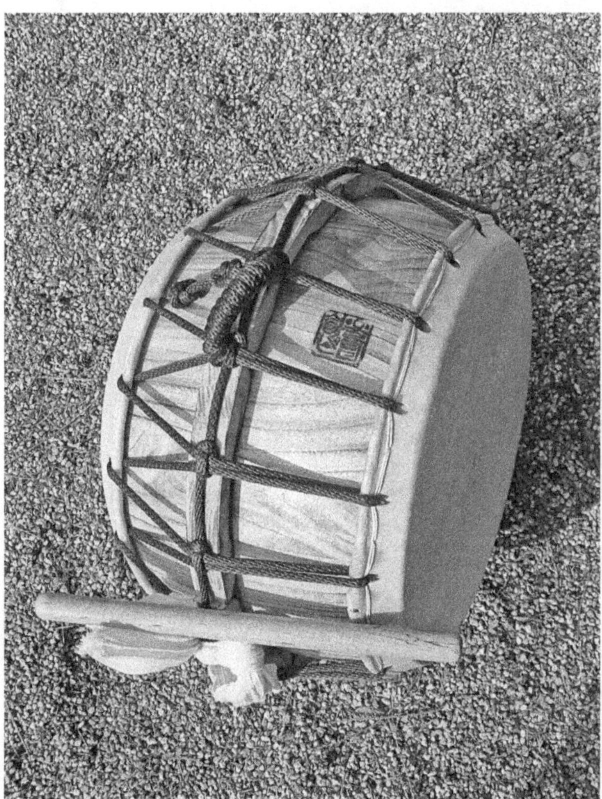

Figure A3.4 A *puk* made by SamulNori Hanullim, with logo burned into body of instrument (photo by Nathan Hesselink).

Figure A3.5 An Chungbŏm (*namsadang*) with *sogo* and *sangmo* hat, 2006 (photo by Nathan Hesselink).

Figure A3.6 The *t'aep'yŏngso* (photo by Nathan Hesselink).

mances by *p'ungmul/namsadang/samul nori* musicians manipulating spinning-tasseled hats (*sangmo*), the *sogo*'s method of construction and manner of playing results in very little sound production (see figure A3.5).

WIND INSTRUMENTS

It is worth briefly mentioning the use of the double-reed shawm known as the *t'aep'yŏngso/hojŏk* ("great peace pipe"/"barbarian pipe"; see figure A3.6). Originally the domain of rural *p'ungmul* and *namsadang* performances, the *t'aep'yŏngso* has also become a mainstay of the seated *samul nori* composition "Samul-kwa t'aep'yŏngso" (*Samul nori* and *t'aep'yŏngso*; see appendix 4), as well as the danced portion of a *samul nori* concert. In spite of its widespread use and ubiquitous appreciation across the various percussion genres, however, shawm music and musicians are generally independent of any group affiliation or provincial loyalty, and its melodic line contributes little or nothing to our understanding of *samul nori* rhythmic structure. To date there exists only one detailed study of the *t'aep'yŏngso* in English (Francis 2008).

APPENDIX FOUR

Electronic Media

AUDIO-VISUAL RECORDINGS

A SamulNori Class with Kim Duk-Soo: Learning Korean Culture Series Tape 1. VHS video, 120 minutes. Seoul: Overseas Koreans Foundation, Korean National University of Arts, 1999.

A SamulNori Class with Kim Duk-Soo: Learning Korean Culture Series Tape 2. VHS video, 50 minutes. Seoul: Overseas Koreans Foundation, Korean National University of Arts, 1999.

Han'guk ŭi hon: Kim Tŏksu SamulNori [The Soul of Korea: Kim Duk Soo SamulNori]. 3 DVDs. Seoul: Dawoori Entertainment, 2005.

P'ungmul-kwa samul nori [*P'ungmul* and *Samul nori*]. 2 CD-ROMs (ES199904–01). Pusan: Dream Wave, 1999.

P'ungmul mit samul nori punsŏk [An Analysis of *P'ungmul* and *Samul nori*]. 2 VHS videos (9703-V147), by Nam Kisu. Seoul: Namsadang yemaek yesultan, 1997.

Samul nori (Korean Traditional Folk Music & Performance: Ensemble for 4 Percussion Instruments). DVD (JMDVD-001) and CD (JCDS-0055). Seoul: Jigu, 2004.

SamulNori Ilbon Sant'ori Hol (Santory Hall) kongyŏn [SamulNori's

Performance at Japan's Santory (Suntory) Hall]. VHS video. Privately produced and distributed, [1987].

Wang ŭi namja (*The King and the Clown*). DVD. Seoul: Art Service, 2006.

CD RECORDINGS

Minsogakhoe Shinawi members

Minsogakhoe Shinawi 10th Regular Concert (March 1, 1979). Private recording of Kang Chunhyŏk.

P'ungmul nori. Shilla SUC 1794, 2000.

Sinawi Music of Korea. King Record Company KICC 5163, 1992.

SamulNori

A Week in the Real World Part 1. Real World CDRW25, 1992 (track #13).

After Ten Years . . . SamulNori: Master Drummers/Dancers of Korea. SKC SKCD-K-0236, 1988.

From the Earth, to the Sky: Kim Duk Soo SamulNori & Red Sun Group. Samsung SCO-123NAN, 1997.

Im Tongch'ang (Lim, Dong Chang). Syn-nara SYNCD-064B, 1993.

Kim Tŏksu Samulnori: Kyŏlchŏng p'an [Kim Duk Soo SamulNori: The Definitive Edition]. King SYNCD-114 (2 CDs), 1996.

Megadrums: Coreana. Intuition INT 2116 2, 1999 [1987].

Nanjang: A New Horizon. King KSC-4150A, 1995.

Red Sun • SamulNori. Polygram DZ-2433, 1997 [1989].

Samul nori. Oasis ORC-1426, 1994.

Samul-Nori: Drums and Voices of Korea. Oasis ORC-1041, 1991.

SamulNori "Record of Changes." CMP Records CMP CD 3002, 1990.

Samul-Nori: The Legendary Recording by Original Members in 1983. Nonesuch 7559–72093–2, 1984.

Spirit of Nature (*Ch'ŏngbae*). Nanjang Music TE004–01 (2 CDs), 2001.

SXL Live in Japan. Sony 32DH824, 1987 (tracks #2, #3, and #4).

SXL: Into the Outlands. Celluloid CELD 5017, 1987.

Taiji Boys Live & Techno Mix. Bando Records BDCD-015, 1992 (track #6).

The World is Full of Rhythms: 15 Years of Megadrums. Intuition INT 3225 2, 1999 (track #12).

Then Comes the White Tiger. ECM Records ECM-1499, 1994.

SamulNori solo projects

Drum Collection of Kim, Yong-bae (*Kim Yongbae sŏlchanggo karak moŭm*). Synnara NSSRCD-029, 2001.

Eurasion Echoes. Woongjin Media WJAC0378, 2000 (Yi Kwangsu).
Kwang-Soo Lee & Red Sun (*Wŏlhwa*). E & E Media SCO-139CSS, 1997.
Lee Kwang Soo: The Sounds of Arirang. Samsung SCO-100CSS, 1996.
Misŭt'a changgo [Mr. Changgo]: Kim Duk Soo with His Friends. ak SCO-137NAN, 1997.
On the Road: The 50th Anniversary of Kim Duk Soo's Debut (*Kil: Kim Tŏksu yein insaeng 50 chunyŏn kinyŏm*). Synnara NSC-175, 2007.
Salp'uri (*Salp'uli*). Starmax Media SMCD-040, 2002 (Yi Kwangsu, track #5).
Shinmyŏng. Woongjin Media WJAC0376, 2000 (Yi Kwangsu).
Yesanjok (Korean Song and Beat Project). Audioguy GOOD3106, 2007 (Yi Kwangsu).
Yi Kwangsu 40. Seoul Records SRCD-1388, 1997.
Yi Kwangsu ŭi sori kut "Pinari" [Yi Kwangsu's Recitation of "Pinari"]. Synnara NSSRCD-037, 2001.
Yi Kwangsu ŭi yesul segye [Yi Kwangsu's Art World]. Synnara NSSRCD-040 (2 CDs), 2001.

Red Sun Projects in Korea

Kim Sŏkch'ul: Kyŏlchŏng p'an (Kim Suk Chul: Final Say). E&E Media SCO-121CSS, 1997 (Wolfgang Puschnig).
Umezu Kazutoki: Dancing Winds. E&E Media SCO-138CSS, 1997 (Jamaaladeen Tacuma).
West End. Samsung Music SCO-105CSS, 1996 (Wolgang Puschnig, Jamaaladeen Tacuma, Linda Sharrock).

Kungnip Kugagwŏn Samulnori

Han'guk ŭi minsok ŭmak (Korean Folk Music). Jigu JCDS-0077, 1989.
Korean Folk Music (*Han'guk ŭi minsok ŭmak: Samul nori, kayagŭm pyŏngch'ang*). Jigu JCDS-0077, 1989 (tracks #1 and #2).
Korean Traditional Folk Music: Samullori. Jigu JCDS-0050, 1986.
Korean Traditional Music Volume II (Folk Music Highlights) (*Kugak chei chip* [*sogak*]). SKC SKCD-K-0005, 1987 (track #10).
Kungnip Kugagwŏn Samulnori (NCMI Samul Nori). Cantabile SRCD-1186, 1994.
Samul nori (Korean Traditional Folk Music Series No. 1). Jigu JCDS-0050, 1986.
Samul nori: Han'guk ŭmak sŏnjip 20 (Samullori: A Selection of Korean Traditional Music Volume 20). Jigu JCDS-0319, JCDS-0320 (2 CDs), 1992.

Turep'ae Samulnori

Durae-Pae Samul Nori Che-1 chip [Volume 1]. Sorimadang SCD-0008, 1993.
Durae-Pae Samul Nori Che-2 chip [Volume 2]. Sorimadang SCD-0009, 1993.
Durae-Pae Samul Nori Che-3 chip [Volume 3]. Sorimadang SCD-00010, 1993.

Durae-Pae Samul Nori: Drums and Voices of Korea. Oasis ORC-1349, 1993.
Dura Pae Samulnori: The Best Traditional Dance and Music Troupe of Korea (*Turaep'ae Samulnori*). Seorabul KCD-007, 1987.
Turep'ae Samulnori. O.K. Media OK-4138, 1999.

Other *samul nori* artists/groups

2007 Samul norian Yun Myŏngsu. RMS, 2007.
Cho Gap Yong Yŏngnam Sŏngju Gut, Taepyŏngso & Samul. Top TOPCD-023, 1999.
Cho Sanghun ŭi Kil (The Road). Synnara NSC-079, 2004.
Kil-ŭl kara, Kim Tongwŏn (Kim Dong-Won, On the Road). Sony BMG SB70195C, 2008.
Noreum Machi Kim Ju Hong. DaeShin Media, 2007.
Yi Yŏnggwang & Samulnori Mulgae: time-blend. Audioguy AGCD0019, 2009.

Samul nori pieces/artists on other collections

Sŏ Yongsŏk: Samul nori-wa t'aep'yŏngso, Taegŭm sanjo, Ajaeng sanjo [Sŏ Yongsŏk: "*Samul nori* and *T'aep'yŏngso*," "Solo Suite for Transverse Flute (*taegŭm*)," "Solo Suite for Eight-string Bowed Zither (*ajaeng*)"]. Soodo SDCD-3243, 2001 (track #1).
Yi Chongdae p'iri segye (Art World of Lee Jong-dae's Piri). Jigu TOPCD-060, 2003 (track #5).

Samul nori fusion groups/projects

3 ilgan ŭi chŏlmŭn ŭmakhoe: Sŏul kugak taegyŏngyŏn susangja + PURI + TriBe-HEaM [Three-day Youth Music Festival: Winners of the Seoul Traditional Music Competition + PURI + TriBe-HEaM]. Samsung SCO-098MUN, 1996.
Asura: Won Il. ak SCO-144WIN, 1997 (track #11).
Chang Saik: Kich'im [Chang Saik: Kich'im (Rise)]. Seoul Records SRCD-3532, 1999 (track #2).
Ch'angjak t'aak kŭrup P'uri (Percussion Ensemble Puri). Sori CMI CD-1005, 1999.
Chew and Swallow. Pussyfinger (Carson Day and Drucifer). Dielectric Records, 2006 (track #2).
Flying Korean: Korean Sound Beckoning Street Dance. Seoul Records SDT 0005, 2007 (tracks #1, #4, #8, and #9).
Gong Myoung (*Kongmyŏng: T'onghaeya [Understood]*). iDream DK 0185, 2001.
Gong Myoung: Deep Sea. Gongmyoung Entertainment , 2007.
Hon'go: Im Wŏnshik chŏnt'ong t'aak yŏnju kokchip [Soul Drum: A Collection of Im Wŏnshik's Traditional Percussion Performances]. Zero Power KTFC 1001, 2004.
King Yebi: Featuring Min Young-Chi. y b music RSYB-002, 2007 (track #1).
Puri: Neo-Sound of Korea, the 2nd. Mnet Media CMDC-0872, 2007.
Ssai [psy]: *Ssajib.* Seoul Records SRCD-3899, 2006 (track #10).

Non-*samul nori* artists

Black Roots. Woongjin Music WJAC0377, 2000.

Fretless Bass Rock Sanjo (*Kim Yŏngjin mu panju yŏngch'ŏn taeŭm*). Synnara NSC-081, 2004.

Kim Dae Hwan Black Rain. E & E Media SCO-022CSS, 1994.

Korean Jazz Music (*Han'guk ŭi tchaejŭ*). Jigu Records JCDS-0080, 1989.

Lee Seng Kang: The Song of Hope (*Yi Saenggang: Hŭimangga*). ene media SCO-171LSK, 2002.

Minsogak-kwa tchaejŭ [Folk Music and Jazz]. Oasis ORC-1043, 1989.

Namsadang ŭi hanŭl / Samgukki (The Heaven for Namsadang / Samguki). Music by Park Bum-hoon [Pak Pŏmhun]. Syn-nara SYNCD-049, 1993 (track #1).

Paek Inyŏng Chŭkhŭng (Improvisation). Synnara Music NSSRCD-014, 1999 (track #8).

Shin Joong Hyun not for Rock. Jigu Records JG-1 (4 CDs), 2002.

Shin Chunghyŏn Muwi Jayŏn [Shin Jung Hyun, Nature at Rest]. Nices (2 CDs), 1994.

Uri akki nadŭri [An Outing with Korean Instruments]. Gugak FM and Loen Entertainment SDT 0021, 2008 (track #1).

Wolfgang Puschnig: Mixed Metaphors. Amadeo 527 266–2, 1995.

Yi Saenggang "Nongak." Jigu JCDS-0391, 1993.

See also http://hearkorea.com, key word *samul nori* (web site of the National Phonograph Record Museum, Korean Music).

APPENDIX FIVE

Contents of the Compact Disc

Track #1: "Honam udo kut." Kim Yong-bae (*soe*), Nam Ki-mun (*changgo*), Bang Seung-hwan (Pang Sŭnghwan) (*puk*), and Park Eun-ha (Pak Ŭnha) (*ching*). *Samul nori* (Korean Traditional Folk Music Series No. 1). Jigu JCDS-0050, 1986 (11:25). © Jigu Records

Track #2: "The Road Ahead." Kim Duk Soo (Kim Tŏksu) (*changgo*), Kang Min Seok (Kang Minsŏk) (*puk*), Kim Bok Man (Kim Pongman) (*soe*), Jang Hyun Jin (Chang Hyŏnjin) (*ching*), Wolfgang Puschnig (alto saxophone), Rick Iannacone (electric guitar), Jamaaladeen Tacuma (electric bass), and Linda Sharrock (vocal). *From the Earth, to the Sky: Kim Duk Soo SamulNori & Red Sun Group*. Samsung SCO-123NAN, 1997 (5:31). © SamulNori Hanullim

Track #3: "Nanjang (The Meeting Place)." Kim Duk Soo (*changgo*), Lee Kwang Soo (Yi Kwangsu) (*soe*), Kang Min Seok (*puk*), Kim Woon Tae (Kim Unt'ae) (*ching*), Wolfgang Puschnig (alto saxophone), Rick Iannacone (electric guitar), Jamaaladeen Tacuma (electric bass), and Linda Sharrock (vocal). *Then Comes the White Tiger*. ECM Records ECM-1499, 1994 (11:10). © ECM Records

Track #4: "Burdens of Life." Kim Duk Soo (*changgo*), Kang Min Seok (*puk*), Kim Bok Man (*soe*), Jang Hyun Jin (*ching*), Wolfgang Puschnig (alto saxophone), Rick Iannacone (electric guitar), Jamaaladeen Tacuma (electric bass), and Linda Sharrock (vocal). *From the Earth, to the Sky: Kim Duk Soo SamulNori & Red Sun Group*. Samsung SCO-123NAN, 1997 (8:36). © SamulNori Hanullim

NOTES

INTRODUCTION

1. This same individual went so far as to say that "Kim Duk Soo's SamulNori has been responsible for an epoch with an impact as significant as Copernicus' discoveries" (Hahn, Myong-hee 1992:5).

2. These countries include the United States, Canada, England, Scotland, Sweden, Germany, France, Italy (for a PUMA commercial), Switzerland, Austria, Greece, Hungary, the Czech Republic, Israel, the (former) Soviet Union, China, Japan, Hong Kong, Thailand, and Australia. For a complete list of performances and dates through the 1990s, see SamulNori 1988; Samstag 1988b:45–47; Kim Hŏnsŏn 1994:249–56; University Musical Society 2002:10; Howard 2006a:18–19; and the web sites http://www.nanjangcultures.com/; http://www.kimduksoo.com/.

3. For two of the earliest reviews in full-text versions, see Jon Pareles, "Concert: 4 Percussionists from Korea," *New York Times*, November 23, 1983 (section C, p. 21, column 1); and Anna Kisselgoff, "Dance: The SamulNori Ensemble," *New York Times*, February 3, 1985 (section 1, part 2, p. 51, column 1).

4. Kim Tongwŏn and Chu Chaeyŏn 2007; http://www.culturebase.net/artist.php?1209, accessed July 15, 2008.

5. A notable success story of *samul nori* being used in kindergarten music education is found in Ch'oe Mihyang 2003. The importance of *samul nori* to the burgeoning field of music therapy in South Korea was demonstrated by

one researcher who found ten M.A. theses between 1998 and 2007 on the therapeutic effects of the percussion genre (Yi Chinwŏn 2008:83).

6. SamulNori was the official cheerleading group for the Seoul venue in 2002; they also produced two large-scale extravaganzas: (1) "Korea and Japan Supercussion Concert 2002"; and (2) "Kim Duk Soo's Dynamic Korea" (extremely positive reviews of these events are found in Kim Yongun 2002). *Samul nori* was taught every day in June at the Namsan-gol Hanok maŭl (Korean village) in conjunction with other World Cup events.

7. Further indicators of how ubiquitous SamulNori/*samul nori* has become in the past few years: (1) a recent article was written to educate South Koreans that the traditional percussion quartet of gongs and drums is also found in other genres, not just in *samul nori* (Kim Chŏngsu 2007); and (2) in a locally produced congratulatory concert the *samul nori* segment was advertised as "farmer's music," a clear indication of the conflation of the urban/presentational with the rural/participational ("The 45th Anniversary of Diplomatic Relations between Korea and Canada," Kay Meek Center, West Vancouver, June 6, 2008).

8. Many performers and academics in Korea have linked the genesis of the term *nongak* to the Japanese occupation, a choice on the part of the authorities believed to limit such activity to "music" by the "farmers," instead of its much broader contexts and significance among the colonized (see further Hesselink 2006:15).

9. From a Korean perspective: "How long will it be that we view Korea's traditional culture as merely a historical relic? Should it not be that what we consider to be of such value, should that not be given a new life now?" (Kang Jun Hyuk 1988); "Tradition is the past reborn in a shifting context" (Park, Chan E. 2003:20); "The path to creation . . . can only be discovered by understanding and harmonizing tradition with new ideas" (Cho, Chung Hyun 2004:8). And from other countries and disciplines: "[T]he dead convention can be restructured and revived, as it is in all authentic art. We recover its nature by an act of historical or artistic sympathy" (Hartman 1970:8); "It is a serious misconception to think that just by labeling something 'traditional,' it somehow should remain unchanged. It is the technique of the musicians and how well they craft the music in a contemporary setting that will ensure its future legacy" (Samstag 1988a [speaking directly about SamulNori]); "In this conception, tradition is not simply the reified emblems of authority but the immanence of the past in the cultural certainties of the present" (Coplan 1994:19); "Artists, no matter their cultural roots, confront a universal quandary—how to be vibrantly modern and eloquently historical" (Frederick 2004:9); "Traditional music provides a place for people to try out new approaches to their existing values, to experiment with new ideas, and to synthesize the new with the old" (Spiller 2004:xix); "[Tradition is] a process, in particular a process of creative transformation whose most remarkable feature is the continuity it nurtures and sustains" (Bakan 2007:27). Two longer passages by Laurent Aubert are also favorites: "There is no more 'music without history' than 'society without history': like every human fact, musical expression shows a constant dynamic between what proceeds from a cultural acquisition and what results in new creations, particular evolutions or external contributions. The nature of a tradition—musical in this case—is not to preserve intact a heritage from the past, but to enrich it according to present circumstances and transmit the results to future generations" (2007:10); "Some people hold in esteem the notion that tradition is opposed to all kinds of development or evolution. For them a traditional expression is thus of conservative definition: frozen, incapable of evolving, or even retrograde and reactionary. This opinion is widely contradicted by reality, and when it is applied to societies other than the West it offers a form of cultural ethnocentrism that is itself of a reactionary nature . . . . Traditional music is not in any case the picture of any original purity, or that of an intact musical past; alive,

and therefore subject to change like any organism, it always expresses the present, showing confluences and stages that have marked its course of production" (2007:22). See also Handler and Linnekin 1984:280 and Jackson 2000:12.

10. For Korean perspectives condemning SamulNori as popular, slick, and commercialized, and hence untraditional, see Chŏn Chiyŏng 2004:37–57; Choe, Yong-shik 1998; Hwang and Na 2001:209; and Kim Sangsŏp 2000.

11. This tension is implicit in Hobsbawm's sense of "invented tradition" (1983) and in Lord's analysis of epic song (1964); referring to "much of contemporary Korean cultural production," the ethnomusicologist Keith Howard saw a trend toward "steer[ing] a perilous path between tradition and innovation" (2006c:1).

12. Confucius in his *Analects* (book 2, chapter 11) speaks of the ideal teacher as one who cherishes the old while acquiring the new (Legge 1971:149). The modern folklorist Chu Kanghyŏn dedicated an entire book to the meaning of *pŏpko ch'angshin* (1999).

13. Currently (2011) there is a graduate student at Harvard University, Katherine Lee, who is conducting doctoral fieldwork on this missing record.

CHAPTER 1

1. For parallels in the Western world during the Middle Ages, see Attali 1985:14–16.

2. A nearly complete English translation of Shim's first chapter is found in Hesselink 2006 (translator).

3. Shim mentions specifically the *Haedong yŏksa* (History of Korea), *Koryŏsa* (History of Koryŏ), *P'yehaengjŏn* (Chronicle of the King), *Chŏnyŏngbojŏn* (Biography of Chŏn Yŏngbo), *Munhŏn t'onggo* (Thoughts on Literature), *Chibong yusŏl* (Topical Discourses of Chibong), and *Hŏbaektang shijip* (Collected Poems of Hŏ Paektang).

4. This literature includes material addressing their musical activity (Chang Hwiju 1999), relationships with other itinerant troupes and with Buddhist temples (No Tongŭn 1993; Yun Kwangbong 1998:335–36; Maliangkay 1999:88–90; Yi Nŭnghwa 1968:283; Son Inae 2004), activity during the Japanese occupation (Chang Sahun 1989; Song Sŏkha 1940), its existence in North Korea (Anonymous 2000).

5. For a further discussion of *pinarip'ae* and its musical composition, see Kim Hŏnsŏn 1995:75–116.

6. Local *p'ungmul* musicians not directly associated with *kŏllipp'ae* were also employed by Buddhist temples for special rites involving large instrumental ensembles during this period (Lee, Byongwon 1987:36).

7. Payment was called *hŏuch'ae* or *hwadae* (literally "flower fee"), a reference to the fee paid for the hiring of a professional female entertainer (*kisaeng*). Around the turn of the twentieth century the *hwadae* would be paid through an intermediary "clerk" (*sŏgi*; see Lee, Byongwon 1979:79–80 and Sŏ Chŏngbŏm and Yŏl Hanmyŏng 1977:73).

8. Earlier accounts by Rutt (1961:58–60, 1964:112) suggest that homosexuality was not viewed as particularly problematic by the commoner classes during the Chosŏn period (1392–1910).

9. Labor accompanied by *p'ungmul* was one of the oldest and most common social contexts for *p'ungmul*'s production (Shin Yongha 1985; Chŏng Pyŏngho 1994:25, 119, and 211; Chu Kanghyŏn 1997:200–246).

10. Shim's text specifically mentions Chinwi subcounty (P'yŏngt'aek city) of Kyŏnggi province, Tangjin city and Hoedŏk district (Taejŏn city) of South Ch'ungch'ŏng province, Kangjin subcounty of North Chŏlla province, Kurye city of South Chŏlla province, Chinyang

and Namhae cities in South Kyŏngsang province, and Songhwa and Ŭnyul cities of South Hwanghae province (modern-day North Korea).

11. These include *insagut, tollim pŏkku, sŏnsori p'an, tangsan pŏllim, yangsangch'igi, hŏt'ŭn sangch'igi, obang kamgi, obang p'ulgi, mudong nollim, ssangjulbaegi, sat'ongbaegi, kasae pŏllim, chwau ch'igi, nejulbaegi, madang ilch'ae*, and *milch'igi pŏkku*. See Yang Kŭnsu 1998 for a more detailed discussion of these rhythmic patterns.

12. The term *ch'ebak'wi* in Shim's text should be changed to *ch'eppak'wi*, which gives us the proper meaning provided here.

13. Shim's *Koreana* article (Sim Woo-sung 1997:49) tells us that *ŏrŭm* means "ice" and that it was so named because of how slippery the rope was. The spelling for ice, however, is *ŏl + ŭm*, not *ŏ + rŭm* (meaning "crossing") as it is found in this translation. The ice reference is absent in Shim's later 2000 full-length publication (with Song Ponghwa).

14. These are all standard masks from the *t'al ch'um* repertoire, though they are a sampling from various regional traditions (see Yi Tuhyŏn 1986:35–75 and Chŏng Pyŏngho 1995:305–80).

15. More recent analyses of mask dance within *namsadang* troupes, as well as related folk drama groups, are found in Han Kisuk 1989 and T'oegyewŏn sandae nori pojonhoe 1999.

16. Information in English on the story line and characters is found in Choe, Sang-su 1974 and Yi Tuhyŏn 1986:76–80.

17. An entire work has been devoted to puppetry and itinerant troupe performance culture (Yun Kwangbong 1994). The folklorist Song Sŏkha has also written on the topic (1960:162–68).

18. Shin Kinam, a well-known and respected *p'ungmul changgo* performer active in the mid- to later twentieth century, directly identified *kŏllipp'ae* with the *namsadang* (1992:62).

19. Yi Wŏnbo was succeeded by Kim Kibok, who now leads the reconstructed *namsadang* troupe (regional cultural asset team) in Ansŏng (see Ch'oe Pyŏngjun 1999).

20. The Minsogakhoe Shinawi ("Folk Music Association Shinawi"), a group responsible for promoting and performing traditional and new works of music and dance in the 1970s and 1980s in and around Seoul, based their name and much of their aesthetic philosophy on the Minsokkŭkhoe Namsadang (see Ch'oe T'aehyŏn 1991). This is further addressed in chapter 2.

21. The highly influential Chŏlla-province percussionist-dancers Pak Hyŏngnae (recorded in Hesselink 1998:316–18) and Shin Kinam (1992:62) saw performances by this troupe in the 1960s firsthand. Both of these men spoke about the impressiveness of the aural and visual components of the *namsadang*'s drumming and dancing.

22. Pak Kyesun and Nam Kihwan are directly related to one of the earliest holders of the genre (now deceased), the esteemed Nam Hyŏngu/Unyong (Pak is his wife, Nam is his son; see further Yi Kyuwŏn and Chŏng Pŏmt'ae 1995:588–92).

23. A website in English describing the content of the musical and its history is at http://eng.baudeogi.com/festival/festival_01_3.asp.

24. These include Yi Kyuwŏn and Chŏng Pŏmt'ae (1995:580–83) on the bowl spinner Kim Chaewŏn; Kim Wŏnmi (2000) on the puppeteer Yi Suyŏng, a direct disciple of the puppeteer Pak Kyesun; and Yi Chŏngu (1999) on Pak Kyesun, the current cultural asset holder for puppetry.

25. *The King and the Clown* was allowed to be distributed only by DVD in China, not screened in theaters, because of its homosexual content (Cho Chungshik 2006).

26. In January 2009, Kwŏn Wŏnt'ae shared a stage with Kim Duk Soo in Seoul for a one-day festival promoting dried persimmons from the county of Wanju in North Chŏlla province.

27. Two other high-profile tightrope walkers include Kim Dae-Gyun (Kim Taegyun), the designated holder for National Important Intangible Cultural Asset No. 58 (folk genre), and Park Hoi Seung (Pak Hoesŭng), a self-designated promoter of court-style rope walking (Chu, Miok 2004).

CHAPTER 2

1. Son later wrote a master's thesis on *nongak* dance (Son Pyŏngu 1988).

2. For photo documentation and further historical details in English, see Provine 1998.

3. Three days later, on March 12, 1984, the Center's team formally recorded "Samul-kwa t'aep'yŏngso shinawi" (it was later released on *Sinawi Music of Korea*, 1992).

4. Chŏn Sudŏk is the son of the famous (and now deceased) *Honam udo p'ungmul changgo* great Chŏn Sasŏp from Chŏngŭp (Hesselink 2006:26; Yi Kyuwŏn and Chŏng Pŏmt'ae 1995:92–95).

5. Pak Ŭnha, like Kim Duk Soo, had studied *changgo* with the esteemed Yang Toil (*namsadang*) and was similarly a member of the touring group Little Angels.

6. Pang wrote a master's thesis on Kim Yongbae's *soe/kkwaenggwari* playing in 1998 (Pang Sŭnghwan 1998). A later MA thesis on Kim Yongbae's *kkwaenggwari* performance was published by Cho Sanghun (2002).

7. Nam Kimun's parents were Nam Hyŏngu and Pak Kyesun (both *namsadang*), his older brother is Nam Kihwan (currently a "human cultural asset" along with their mother for *namsadang* arts), and his younger brother is Nam Kisu (also involved in *p'ungmul* and *namsadang* activities).

8. Pak Ŭnha, Ch'oe Chongshil, and Kim Duk Soo were all members of the Little Angels. The Little Angels performance team was founded in 1962 and comprised primarily girls under the age of sixteen. Founded and funded by the Reverend Moon (Sun Myung) of the Unification Church, the Little Angels represented Korea on international stages through the performance of mostly traditional genres of music and dance. As of 2003 they had performed 3,500 times in forty-five different countries (Rhonda Sewell, "Korean Culture Takes the Stage," *Toledo Blade*, February 28, 2003, section D, p.11; see also Ku Hee-seo 1994:25–26).

9. A book celebrating Kim Yongbae's life and work was published in 1998 (Kim Hŏnsŏn 1998). Three years later an accompanying CD was released highlighting Kim's singing and percussion skills (*Drum Collection of Kim, Yong-bae*, 2001).

10. These included Paek Chinsŏk on *ching* (Paek played in Ami Nongak, the Pusan *p'ungmul* troupe from which Ch'oe hailed) and Cho Kabyong on *soe* (another Pusan-area *p'ungmul* performer). Cho Kabyong was featured in a June 26, 2001, performance at the National Center, showcasing his talents on the *soe* (small gong), *ajaeng* (eight-string bowed zither), *hojŏk* (double-reed, conical wooden oboe), and the *yŏltubal* (spinning-tasseled hat). Cho has also released a solo CD (*Cho Gap Yong Yŏngnam Sŏngju Gut* 1999).

11. For a more recent overview of performing arts venues in and around Seoul, see Anonymous 1997.

12. Both Ch'oe T'aehyŏn and Kim Duk Soo were graduates of the Seoul Traditional Arts High School. In addition to this 1991 article on the Minsogakhoe Shinawi, Ch'oe also authored a book on the compositional elements of Korean music (1993).

13. Performers included Pak Pŏmhun on *p'iri* (oboe), Yi Ch'ŏlchu on *taegŭm* (large transverse flute), Kim Panghyŏn on *sogŭm* (small transverse flute), Ch'oe T'aehyŏn on *haegŭm* (two-string bowed fiddle), Kim Mugyŏng on *ajaeng* (eight-string bowed zither), Pak Miryŏng on *kayagŭm* (twelve-string plucked zither), and Kim Kyŏnghŭi on *changgo* and as a dancer

(Kim Sejung, Pak Hŏnbong, and Chi Yŏnghŭi were also listed as planners or consultants; the first two pages of this first concert program are reproduced in Chŏn Chiyŏng 2005:293).

14. Chang Tŏkhwa would go on to a distinguished career in *sanjo* (solo instrumental suite) accompaniment, working with master artists such as Yi Saenggang (*taegŭm* [transverse flute]), Ch'oe Kyŏngman (*p'iri* [double-reed wind instrument]), and Pak Chongsŏn (*ajaeng*).

15. Further historical and bibliographic details for all of the instruments can be found in Hesselink 2006:49–66.

16. There is some confusion here with regard to naming and chronology: Minsogakhoe Shinawi 1999 lists this concert as both "Konggan's Evening of Traditional Music" and the "10th Regular Concert," but it then omits the March 1, 1979, performance. Similarly, in Yi Sŏngch'ŏn's account of the traditional music scene of 1979 (1980:341) he lists the March 1, 1979, performance as the "11th Regular Concert." What I have presented in table 2.2 is what I believe to be the accurate listing, backed up by Ch'oe T'aehyŏn's seminal account (1991:33, 36), later documentation by the Minsogakhoe Shinawi (2000), and a 1979 personal recording I secured titled *Minsogakhoe Shinawi 10th Regular Concert*.

17. While there is some debate with regard to who first came up with the name "Samul-Nori," most accounts credit it to a joint effort spearheaded by Shim Usŏng (Yi Hyŏngyŏng 2004:36). Shim should receive some attribution for this because of his early use of the word *samul* to refer to *p'ungmul* instruments, rather than its use for the Buddhist quartet (see Shim Usŏng 1968:700).

18. The *namsadang soe* player Ch'oe Chongsŏk and his younger brother Ch'oe Chong-shil (a rural *p'ungmul* performer) were brought in temporarily for this performance; the younger brother would stay on, while the older would return to the *namsadang* (see appendix 2).

19. Ch'oe Chongshil's fiftieth birthday was celebrated in a special commemorative performance held at the National Center on August 8, 2007. Yi Kwangsu's personal website, with great photo documentation, can be found at www.samulnori.com; a list of his individual recordings is listed in appendix 4.

20. This included *Sinawi Music of Korea* (1992) recorded on March 12, 1984, with original 1969 society members Pak Pŏmhun (*p'iri*) and Ch'oe T'aehyŏn (*haegŭm*) on tracks #2 and #3, and later members Kim Kwangbok (*p'iri/t'aep'yŏngso*), Chang Tŏkhwa (*changgo*), and Nam Kimun (*kkwaenggwari*) on track #4, "Poong-mool nori & taepyongso sinawi" (Nam, a friend of Kim Yongbae, was recruited from the *namsadang* to join the center *samul nori* team in 1986). This essentially *samul nori* lineup was reproduced exactly, almost reunion style, on track #1 of the CD recording by the society titled *P'ungmul nori* (2000): Kim Kwangbok (*t'aep'yŏngso*), Chang Tŏkhwa (*changgo*), Nam Kimun (*kkwaenggwari*), Pak Pŏmhun (*puk*), and No Chongak (*ching*).

CHAPTER 3

1. Many of these parameters informed an earlier study of mine on traditional Japanese performance behavior in the late twentieth century (Hesselink 1994).

2. These ensembles are (in order of recognition): Chinju Samch'ŏnp'o Nongak (1966), P'yŏngt'aek Nongak (1985), Iri Nongak (1985), Kangnŭng Nongak (1985), and Imshil P'ilbong Nongak (1988).

3. For the debates surrounding the use of these competing terminologies, see Hesselink 2006:15–17.

4. For a political and structural analysis of a typical *p'ungmul* performance, see Hesselink 2008.

5. Kim, Jin-Woo (2003a and 2003b) has analyzed some ways promoters in Korea have staged *p'ungmul*-based performances in concert halls for local and foreign audiences.

6. Korean scholars have been fascinated with village life and its effect on communal consciousness (Kim Hŭngju 1993; Kim Inu 1993; Kim Chaeŭn 1987; Yun T'aerim 1964). My own ruminations on the topic are found in Hesselink 2011.

7. For more detailed information regarding the individual *samul nori* instruments, refer to appendix 3.

8. The first piece played by SamulNori that February evening in 1978 was titled "Uttari p'ungmul" (*uttari*, literally "upper bridge/leg," is an older designation for the northern areas of Kyŏnggi and Ch'ungch'ŏng provinces), or, alternatively, "Chungbu nongak." Its performance was based on the *p'ungmul* rhythms of the "center region" (*chungbu*) or *uttari* area of South Korea, a choice that made sense as these rhythms were the bread and butter of the extant *namsadang* troupes (see chapter 1). To this were added two more regionally based compositions—"Yŏngnam nongak" (rhythms from the Kyŏngsang provinces) in April 1978 and "Honam nongak/Honam udo kut" (rhythms from the "right" or western counties of the Chŏlla provinces) in May 1979—as well as a Kyŏnggi province narrative prayer ("Pinari," September 1980) and a piece for four *changgo* combining rhythms from the three geographical areas mentioned above ("Samdo sŏlchanggo karak," June 1982; see Howard 2006c:18). (In an attempt to make room for a danced piece on the second half of their program ["P'an kut," September 1980], SamulNori developed an arrangement that combined the three regional pieces into one, titled "Samdo nongak" [rhythms from the three provinces, premiered November 1979], a practice that had become standardized by 1988 [Samstag 1988b:48]).

9. A roughly equivalent performance transcription is provided in Ch'oe Pyŏngsam et al. 1992:168–204; see also Hesselink 2004.

10. The effect of indoor venues and the larger issue of urban consumption in the realm of Korean folk performing arts has been documented and analyzed by one of Korea's leading musicologists (Hahn, Man-young 1991:219–31).

11. Originally the domain of rural *p'ungmul* and *namsadang* performances, the *t'aep'yŏngso* has also become a mainstay of the seated *samul nori* composition "Samul-kwa t'aep'yŏngso" (*Samul nori* and *t'aep'yŏngso*; see appendix 4), as well as the danced portion of a *samul nori* concert. In spite of its widespread use and ubiquitous appreciation across the various percussion genres, however, shawm music and musicians are generally independent of any group affiliation or provincial loyalty, and its melodic line contributes little or nothing to our understanding of *samul nori* rhythmic structure. To date there exists only one detailed study of the *t'aep'yŏngso* in English (Francis 2008).

12. See, for example, the compact discs *Samullori* (Ensemble for Four Percussion Instruments; Jigu JCDS-0050, 1986, track #1), *After ten years . . . SamulNori: Master Drummers/Dancers of Korea* (SKC SKCD-K-0236, 1988, track #3), and *Korean Folk Music* (Jigu JCDS-0077, 1989, track #1).

13. The first SamulNori competition (*kyŏrugi*) was held in 1989. Throughout the 1990s and into the 2000s a "foreigner" division was opened every other year, attracting groups from around the globe. Photo documentation is provided in chapter 4.

14. The other three are: *Red Sun • SamulNori* (Polygram DZ 2433, 1989), *Then Comes the White Tiger* (ECM 1499, 1994), and *Nanjang—A New Horizon* (King KSC-4150A, 1995). These recordings are further discussed in chapter 5.

CHAPTER 4

1. Three other sets of pedagogical audio-visual materials have been released by non-SamulNori organizations: *P'ungmul mit samul nori punsŏk* (An Analysis of *P'ungmul* and *Samul nori*), 2 VHS videos, 1997; *P'ungmul-kwa samul nori* (*P'ungmul* and *Samul nori*), 2 CD-ROMs, 1999; and *Samul nori*, DVD and CD, 2004.

2. Throughout this chapter I use a more general understanding of the term "cosmology," referring to both the shape and size of the heavens and the earth and their motions, as well as "any theory of how the universe works in a more metaphysical sense" (Cullen 1996:xi; here Cullen calls the former "cosmography," the latter "cosmology").

3. A similar practice is found in Korea in the Ch'ŏnmach'ong burial mound from the fifth century CE, located in the (then) Shilla capital city of Kyŏngju (Gyeongju).

4. The earliest extant record of *wuxing* is found in the *Shang shu* (The Book of Documents), dated during the Zhou period (first millennium BCE), though its full theorizing and explication occurred during the Han dynasty (Chen, Cheng-Yih 1996:200–201). Further discussion of its origins and contexts throughout East Asia is found in Graham (1986, 1989), Sivin (1987), Feuchtwang (2002), and Hesselink and Petty (2004).

5. An artifact in two parts excavated from a second-century BCE tomb revealed a round heaven-disc that pivoted at the center of a square earth-plate beneath it (Cullen 1996:44–45).

6. The image of the cosmos as contained within the square and circle is found in ancient Vedic thought (Vatsyayan 1983:103; 2003:83–86), as well as Balinese ritual associations (Tenzer 2000:33–38).

7. In the fourth-century BCE Taoist classic the *Dao de jing* (stanza 25), we have the written and thus highly formalized account of the interrelationships between heaven, earth, and man: "Man models himself on earth, earth on heaven, heaven on the way [*dao*], and the way on that which is naturally so" [人法地, 地法天, 天法道, 道法自然] (Lau 1982: 39; for an alternative translation, see Roberts 2001:82).

8. And from Mencius himself: "Heaven sees through the eyes of the people. Heaven hears through the ears of the people" (Hinton 1999:169; see also Kŭm Changt'ae 2000:37).

9. In chapter seven of the Taoist commentary *Huinanzi* (c. 120 BCE) there is the clear structure beginning with *tao* at the top, bifurcating to *yin* and *yang*, then branching to heaven, earth, and human (*tian*, *di*, and *ren*), followed by the five elements (*wuxing*; see Tsao Penyeh 2000:64–67). It is also interesting to note that the symphony written by the New York based Chinese composer Tan Dun celebrating Hong Kong's reunification with China was titled "Symphony 1997: Heaven, Earth, Man" (the piece also contained *wuxing* elements; see Wah, Yu Siu 2004).

10. Remarkably similar imagery from Europe is provided by Michael Maier, a seventeenth-century physician, alchemist, composer, music theorist, and reformer. In his *Atalanta Fugiens* (1617) and its later abridged version *Secretioris naturae secretorum scrutinium chymicum* (1687), Maier set fifty fugues to texts and accompanying engravings to illustrate alchemical truths. Of particular salience to this chapter is emblem 21, which reads: "Make a circle around a man and woman, then a square, now a triangle; make a circle, and you will have the Philosophers' Stone" (Godwin 1987:117).

11. According to Anicus Manlius Severinus Boethius (c. 475–525), one of the founding fathers of Western music theory, the three realms of musical activity included music of the heavens, music made by man, and music from the natural world (Bower 1989:9–10).

12. Shaman rituals performed by specialists and local musicians in the countryside similarly drew on the power and efficacy of music (Choi, Changjo 2003), a theme taken up by SamulNori in its educational materials discussed later in this chapter.

13. A certainly related understanding of this sacred geometry informed the work of the early nineteenth-century Zen master Sengai, who in his calligraphic work titled "The Universe" simply painted a square, triangle, and circle (reproduced in Suzuki 1999:36; importantly, the modern commentator equated the triangle with humans).

14. Im Tongch'ang, the pianist and theorist who worked with SamulNori on the notation for their workbooks, also regularly used this phrase (see Kim Hŏnsŏn 1995:219).

15. *Hana-a*, *wŏn-pang-kak*, and *umjigim* as used in the workbooks are primarily SamulNori theoretical constructs; the concept of *hohŭp* is more readily found in research on traditional vocal music, both folk and aristocratic genres (Chŏng Sŏnhye 1996; Yi Hwanhŭi 1998), and as a pedagogical aid in dance instruction (Van Zile 2008:82–83). An example of a Korean music educator employing *samul nori* instruments and some of these techniques in the kindergarten classroom is found in Ch'oe Mihyang 2003.

16. This textbook represents an excerpt from a larger work published in Korean the previous year (Kim Tongwŏn 1998).

17. SamulNori's Web site (http://203.252.231.26/kukak_information/samulnori/nanjang-samulnori.pdf) uses similar wording:

> SamulNori's music is based on the rhythms of traditional Korean folk percussion music. The name SamulNori literally means "the play of four things." The four things refer to the four percussive instruments. Each instrument is associated with an element in nature. They play the harmony of cosmos linking up nature and human being in accordance with the rule of Yin and Yang's change. . . . As each instrument is associated with an element in nature, the *k'kwaenggwari* is related to lightening. The *Ching* . . . should make an osculating sound, imitating the shape of the valleys of Korea. Thus, *Ching* is associated with the wind. The *JangGo* [*changgo*] . . . is associated with rain.

18. Anecdotal evidence suggests that at least one performer used the terms *wŏn-pang-kak* informally in private lessons during the 1980s to illustrate rhythmic concepts (Keith Howard, personal communication, 2007).

19. The ambitious reader is referred to the writings of the Korean folklorist and musical theorist Yi Pohyŏng, who has written extensively on the rhythmic levels and hierarchies implied by such *wŏn-pang-kak* theorizing (a convenient English summary of most of his work to date on this topic is found in Lee, Bo hyung 2003). Pak Shin'gil 1997 analyzes *samul nori* rhythms largely through the prism of *ŭm* and *yang*, overlaid on Charles Seeger's (1977) divisions of pitch dynamics, timbre, proportion, tempo, and accent.

20. The *samt'aegŭk* and its implied relationship of heaven, earth, and man (*samjaesang*) was the central organizing metaphor and symbol of the Seoul 1988 Olympics. An excerpt from one of the first working drafts of the organizing committee matches SamulNori's intent almost word for word: "By reviving the sublime, transcendental, and cosmological dimensions, we can make sacred space as if the world were being created anew. People all over the world will feel utter nobility because heaven, earth, and humans now harmonize with each other in the fresh morning of God's city" (Yi Ŏryŏng, cited in Dilling 2001:176–77).

21. It is worth reiterating that technically speaking the actual meaning of *kak* (角) is angle, not triangle as SamulNori and other Korean theorists have misinterpreted it. *Kak*, or *jue* in

Chinese, does properly refer to the trysquare in older Chinese sources, as well as the related character *ju* (矩) used in the *Zhou bi* (see Chen, Cheng-Yih 1996:45–65, 110–11).

22. The English translation of these terms in the textbook is incorrect; my own translation is based on the Korean text provided earlier in this work.

23. A number of folk and ritual rhythmic patterns do, however, use duple division (2) and mixed division (2 + 3 or 3 + 2) beats.

24. Earlier intimations of his cosmological theorizing are found in Han Myŏnghŭi (1994:74–77).

CHAPTER 5

1. In the West one would look to the carnival as an equivalent phenomenon, its focus on play and subversion while blurring the boundaries of the sacred and profane (Brottman 2005:2, 10).

2. The word *t'ŭrot'ŭ* is the Koreanized pronunciation of the second half of the name of the Western social dance "fox trot," a common and popular rhythmic accompaniment in *t'ŭrot'ŭ* songs. An alternative and contested term is *ppongtchak*, an onomatopoeic rendering of this rhythmic accompaniment: "*ppong tchak ppong tchak*" (akin to "*boom chick boom chick*").

3. The following information is taken from an interview conducted with Paek during the summer of 2006.

4. Paek's collaborative CD (1999) is titled *Chŭkhŭng*, meaning "Improvisation." Im Tongch'ang's earlier debut recording featured SamulNori on every track (*Im Tongch'ang*, 1993).

5. Other notable recordings by Lee Saenggang include a 1989 CD for *taegŭm*, saxophone, and *samul nori* ensemble (*Minsogak-kwa tchaejŭ* [Folk Music and Jazz]), and a studio recording of *p'ungmul/nongak* dance music (*Yi Saenggang "Nongak,"* 1993).

6. This song today is found more readily on *Shin Joong Hyun not for Rock*, 2002, disc 1, track #1.

7. This idea of applying a *sanjo* structure or aesthetic to rock was further taken up by Shin's bass player from his Music Power group of the late 1970s, Kim Yŏngjin, in an entire CD dedicated to the solo electric bass (*Fretless Bass Rock Sanjo*, 2004).

8. Kim continued to perform and record with Yamashita and Umezu well into the 1990s and early 2000; see the albums *Kim Dae Hwan Black Rain*, 1994, and *Black Roots*, 2000.

9. For the truly adventurous, I refer listeners to the recording *Korean Jazz Music* (1989). Recorded in 1987 in anticipation of the Seoul '88 Olympics, it was an effort to combine Korean folksongs with African traditional and Western pop music, something the composers called "Afro-Koro" (an ambitious mix of traditional folk song realized through a West African pop and disco aesthetic, played on African drums, Western strings and brass, and Korean drums and wind instruments).

10. Everett (2004:15) seems to use "syncretism" in the way others (such as Sutton and Weiss) have described hybridity, such that "syncretism is here interpreted as a case where cultural idioms may be combined yet the cultural elements remain distinguishable." And according to the philosopher Simon Blackburn, syncretism is "a movement aimed at establishing a harmony between apparently opposing positions in philosophy or theology" (2006:358).

11. The full title of this video is *SamulNori Ilbon Sant'ori Hol (Santory Hall) kongyŏn* (SamulNori's performance at Japan's Santory Hall). The video has never acquired a formal publisher or distributor, but is rather sold at locations around Seoul.

12. The year 1985 is also significant in that it marked the founding of Sulkidoong (Sŭlgidung), a group dedicated to reinterpreting and recomposing the folksong repertoire

through the lens of lighter classical and popular music influences (a kind of revisiting of the *shin minyo* movement of the 1930s). A similar (and rival) group Ŏullim was founded in 1989.

13. A 1994 offshoot of *Ult'arigut* with SamulNori is discussed at some length in Howard 2006a.

14. In February 1988 Bill Laswell recorded SamulNori in New York during their Asia Society Tour, an improvisatory and shaman-influenced disc titled *SamulNori "Record of Changes"* (1990).

15. Extensive photographic documentation and interviews with musicians from both the "Live Under the Sky" and "Megadrums" tours are found in SamulNori 1988. A year later SamulNori rejoined Puschnig, Tucci, and Yamashita Yosuke (Japanese pianist) for a series of concerts in Japan and Korea titled "SamulNori vs. Mu," to celebrate the tenth anniversary of SamulNori's founding (see Ku, Hee-seo 1989 for a concert review).

16. Flatischler would later include a track from this CD on his compilation *The World is Full of Rhythms: 15 Years of Megadrums* (Intuition, 1999). For a review of the various Megadrums projects and recordings, see Pinto 1989.

17. An essentially Red Sun lineup would release their own CD that same year under the title *Wolfgang Puschnig: Mixed Metaphors* (Amadeo, 1995).

18. Lee is a Korean who lives and works in Japan, but who is best known and appreciated in Europe. His creative philosophy and transcendence of borders made him an ideal candidate for SamulNori's cover art: "Nation and tradition are not fixed entities formed long ago and handed down unchanged ever since. Rather, they are open and flexible concepts, constantly redefined with the changing times" (Lee Ufan, quoted in Lee, Dong-seok 2003:56).

19. According to the current CEO of Nanjang Cultures, this CD is their best seller, having sold more than 500,000 copies (an astronomical amount in the traditional music world; Chu Chaeyŏn, personal communication, 2009). A Korean perspective on this recording is found in Yi Changjik 1995.

20. For a further discussion of this performance and its musical composition, see Kim Hŏnsŏn 1995:75–116. A slightly different version of "Pinari" performed by Kungnip Kugagwŏn Samulnori rendered in Western notation is found in Ch'oe Pyŏngsam et al. 1992:206–62.

21. A chronological sampling of "Pinari" recordings includes: track #1, *Samul-Nori: The Legendary Recording by Original Members in 1983*, 1984; track #1, *After Ten Years . . . Samul-Nori: Master Drummers/Dancers of Korea*, 1988; track #1, *Samul-Nori: Drums and Voices of Korea*, 1991; track #1, *Samul nori*, 1994; an entire CD dedicated to "Pinari" (*Yi Kwangsu ŭi sori kut "Pinari"*, 2001); tracks #2 and #3, *Cho Sanghun ŭi Kil* (The Road), 2004; and track #2, *Noreum Machi Kim Ju Hong*, 2007.

22. Three variants of the Korean text for "Pinari" can be found at http://www.koreartnet.com/wOOrII/umak/samulnori/binari.html.

23. At least three other fusion versions of "Pinari" exist: track #2, *Puri: Neo-Sound of Korea, the 2nd*, 2007; track #5, *2007 Samul norian Yun Myŏngsu*, 2007; and track #2, *Yesanjok* (Korean Song and Beat Project), 2007. See the fusion group/projects section in appendix 4.

24. The first five pieces on this recording essentially follow the rhythms and their ordering of "Honam udo kut": track #1 mimics the opening section of the *p'ungmul p'an kut*; track #2 features *och'ae chilgut, chajin och'ae chilgut*, and *chwajilgut*; track #3 features *p'ungnyugut* and *kutkŏri*; (track #4 reproduces a vocal section based on a different part of the *p'ungmul* repertoire); and track #5 features *samch'ae*.

25. Liner notes to this recording include some textual errors.

26. Kang Chunil (brother of Kang Chunhyŏk) wrote *Concerto for Samul and Orchestra* in 1983 (accompanied by Western orchestra), and in 1988 Pak Pŏmhun (an original Minsogakhoe Shinawi member) wrote *Shin modŭm (Gathering the Spirits)* for *samul nori* accompanied by Korean orchestra (Pak also wrote a musical theater piece in honor of the *namsadang*, captured on the recording *Namsadang ŭi hanŭl*, 1993). For a rhythmic analysis of *Shin modŭm*, see Yi Chuhŭi 1994.

27. A discussion of P'uri appears in Yi Soyŏng 1999.

BIBLIOGRAPHY

Abelmann, Nancy. 1996. *Echoes of the Past, Epics of Dissent: A South Korean Social Movement*. Berkeley: University of California Press.

Allan, Sarah. 1991. *The Shape of the Turtle: Myth, Art, and Cosmos in Early China*. Albany: State University of New York Press.

An Hosang. 1994. "Segye ŭmak-e hamnyuhan uri ŭmak samul nori" [*Samul nori* (Our Music) Meets World Music]. *Yesul ŭi chŏndang* 7:20–22.

An Pyŏngt'ak. 198?. "Samul nori shidae-e kut-ŭl saenggak handa" [Thoughts on *Kut* in the Age of *Samul nori*]. In *Honam chwado: P'ilbong maŭl p'ungmulgut* [Chŏlla Province "Left Side" Style: *P'ungmulgut* of P'ilbong Village], by Yang Chinsŏng, 17–18. Namwŏn: Honam chwado p'ungmul p'an kut palp'yohoe shilmut'im.

Anonymous. 1997. "Performing Arts Venues." *Koreana* 11.2:36–43.

———. 2000. *Chosŏn ŭi minsok chŏnt'ong: Minsok ŭmak* [Korean Folk Traditions: Folk Music]. Seoul: Taesan ch'ulp'ansa.

Atkins, E. Taylor. 2001. *Blue Nippon: Authenticating Jazz in Japan*. Durham: Duke University Press.

Attali, Jacques. 1985. *Noise: The Political Economy of Music*. Translated by Brian Massumi, foreword by Frederic Jameson, afterword by Susan McClary. Minneapolis: University of Minnesota Press.

Aubert, Laurent. 2007. *The Music of the Other: New Challenges for Ethnomusicology in a Global Age*. Translated by Carla Ribeiro, with a foreword by Anthony Seeger. Aldershot: Ashgate.

Bakan, Michael B. 2007. *World Music: Traditions and Transformations*. New York: McGraw Hill.

Baldinger, Wallace S. 1954. "Takeuchi Seihō: Painter of Post-Meiji Japan." *Art Bulletin* 36.1:45–56.

Barnes, Gina L. 1999. *The Rise of Civilization in East Asia: The Archaeology of China, Korea, and Japan*. London: Thames and Hudson.

Blackburn, Simon. 2006. *The Oxford Dictionary of Philosophy*. 2nd ed. New York: Oxford University Press.

Blesser, Barry, and Linda-Ruth Salter. 2007. *Spaces Speak, Are You Listening? Experiencing Aural Architecture*. Cambridge, MA: MIT Press.

Bohlman, Philip V. 2002. *World Music: A Very Short Introduction*. New York: Oxford University Press.

———. 2008. "Other Ethnomusicologies, Another Musicology: The Serious Play of Disciplinary Alterity." In *The New (Ethno)Musicologies*, edited by Henry Stobart, 95–114. Lanham, Md.: Scarecrow Press.

Boissevain, Jeremy. 1974. *Friends of Friends: Networks, Manipulators, and Coalitions*. London: Basil Blackwell.

Bourdieu, Pierre. 1984. *Distinction: A Social Critique of the Judgement of Taste*. Translated by Richard Nice. Cambridge: Harvard University Press.

Bower, Calvin M., trans. 1989. *Fundamentals of Music: Anicus Manlius Severinus Boethius*. Edited by Claude V. Palisca. New Haven: Yale University Press.

Brottman, Mikita. 2005. *High Theory/Low Culture*. New York: Palgrave Macmillan.

Broyles, Michael. 1992. "Music of the Highest Class": Elitism and Populism in Antebellum Boston. New Haven: Yale University Press.

Buenconsejo, José S., ed. 2003. *A Search in Asia for a New Theory of Music*. Quezon City: University of the Philippines Center for Ethnomusicology.

Bussell, Jennifer L. 1997. "A Life of Sound: Korean Farming Music and its Journey to Modernity." B.A. thesis, University of Chicago.

Buswell, Robert E., and Timothy S. Lee, eds. 2005. *Christianity in Korea*. Honolulu: University of Hawai'i Press.

Buzo, Adrian. 2002. *The Making of Modern Korea*. New York: Routledge.

Ch'ae, Hyun-kyung [Ch'ae Hyŏn'gyŏng]. 2000. "Newly-Composed Korean Music: Westernization, Modernization, or Koreanization?" *Tongyang Ŭmak* 22:141–51.

Chang Hwiju. 1999. "Sadangp'ae sori kalkka poda yŏn'gu" [A Study of the Female Itinerant Troupe Song "Kalkka poda"]. *Han'guk ŭmak yŏn'gu* 27:111–28.

Chang Kwangyŏl. 1996. "SamulNori: Han'guk ŭi ŭmak-i segye ŭmakkye-rŭl kangt'a handa" [SamulNori: Korean Music Makes an Impact on the World Music Community]. *Kaeksŏk* 143:34–37.

Chang Sahun. 1986. *Han'guk ŭmaksa* [A History of Korean Music]. Seoul: Segwang ŭmak ch'ulp'ansa.

———. 1989. *Yŏmyŏng ŭi kugakkye* [The Closing Days of the Traditional Music World]. Seoul: Segwang ŭmak ch'ulp'ansa.

———. 1995 [1986]. *Han'guk akki taegwan* [Korean Musical Instruments]. Seoul: Sŏul taehakkyo ch'ulp'anbu.

Chen, Cheng-Yih. 1996. *Early Chinese Work in Natural Science: A Re-examination of the Physics of Motion, Acoustics, Astronomy, and Scientific Thoughts*. Hong Kong: Hong Kong University Press.

Chen, Yingshi. 2002. "Theory and Notation in China." In *East Asia: China, Japan, and Korea*, edited by Robert C. Provine, Yoshihiko Tokumaru, and J. Lawrence Witzleben, 115–26. New York: Routledge.

Chin Nara. 2006. "Namsadang! Hallyu ŭi chungshim-ŭro segye-ro hyanghara!" [*Namsadang*! The Korean Wave Taking on the World]. *Wŏlgan munhwajae* 261:10–11.

Cho, Chung Hyun [Cho Chunghyŏn]. 2004. "From the Fire: Contemporary Korean Ceramics." In *From the Fire: A Survey of Contemporary Korean Ceramics*, edited by Penny Kiser, 4–8. Washington, DC: International Arts & Artists.

Cho Chungshik. 2006. "Chung 'Wang ŭi namja sangyŏng malla'" [Screening of *The King and the Clown* Banned in China]. *Chosŏn ilbo* A9, July 4.

Cho Sanghun. 2002. "Chŏlla udo p'ungmul karak-e kwanhan yŏn'gu: Kim Yongbae ŭi kutkŏri (kkwaenggwari) karak-ŭl chungshim-ŭro" (A Study on Folk Rhythm in Western Jeolla Province: Focused on the Rhythm by Kim Yong-bae). Master's thesis, Chŏnbuk University.

Ch'oe Chongmin. 2002. "P'ungmul ŭi hyŏndaejŏk chŏn'gae yangsang" [*P'ungmul*'s Present-day Developmental Phase]. In *Saeroun chŏnt'ong ŭmak-ŭrosŏ ŭi p'ungmul* [*P'ungmul* as New Traditional Music], 11–20. Yesan: Yesan kukche p'ungmulche chojik wiwŏnhoe.

Ch'oe Ikhwan. 1995. *P'ungmul nori kyobon* [A Manual for Playing *P'ungmul*]. Seoul: Tosŏ ch'ulp'an p'ungmul.

Ch'oe Mihyang. 2003. "Ch'wihakchŏn yua ŭi t'a akki-rŭl iyonghan kugak suŏp" (Traditional Music Education of Kindergarten by Percussion Instrument). *Han'guk ŭmaksa hakpo* 30:725–48.

Ch'oe Pyŏngjun. 1999. "In'gan munhwajae chijŏng toen 60nyŏn yurang insaeng majimak namsadang Kim Kibok" [Human Cultural Asset and the Last of the *Namsadang* Kim Kibok: Sixty Years of Itinerant Life]. *Kyŏnghyang shinmun*, July 5.

Ch'oe Pyŏngsam. 2000. *Samul nori paeugi: Wŏlli-esŏ yŏnju-kkaji* [Learning *Samul nori*: From Principles to Performance]. Seoul: Hangminsa.

Ch'oe Pyŏngsam, Ch'oe Hŏn, Yi Pohyŏng, and Kang Yewŏn. 1992. *Han'guk ŭmak che 27 chip: Samul nori* (Anthology of Korean Traditional Music 27: Samullori Percussion Ensemble). Seoul: Kungnip kugagwŏn.

Choe, Sang-su [Ch'oe Sangsu]. 1974. "Puppet Play." In *Survey of Korean Arts: Folk Arts*, 166–216. Seoul: National Academy of Arts.

Ch'oe T'aehyŏn. 1991. " 'Minsogakhoe shinawi' ŭi hoego-wa chŏnmang" [Reflections on and Prospects for the "Folk Music Association Shinawi"]. *Han'guk ŭmaksa hakpo* 7:27–47.

———. 1993. *Kusŏng yoso-ro ponŭn kugak kok* [A Look at Traditional Music Pieces through Their Compositional Elements]. Seoul: Hyŏndae ŭmak ch'ulp'ansa.

Choe, Yong-shik [Ch'oe Yongshik]. 1998. "Traditional Music Has Universal Appeal across Time, Border." *Korea Times*, Monday, August 31, p.9.

Choi, Changjo [Ch'oe Ch'angjo]. 2003. "Study of How Koreans View and Utilize Nature." In *Korean Anthropology: Contemporary Korean Culture in Flux*, edited by the Korean National Commission for UNESCO, 69–93. Seoul: Hollym.

Chŏn Chiyŏng. 2004. *Kathin chonjae ŭi yesul, yŏllin yesul: Chŏn Chiyŏng ŭi kugak p'yŏngnon* [Imprisoned Art, Free Art: Chŏn Chiyŏng's Criticism of Korean Traditional Music]. Seoul: Puk k'oria.

———. 2005. *Kŭndaesŏng ŭi ch'imnyak-kwa 20 segi Han'guk ŭi ŭmak* [The Invasion of Modernity and Korean Music in the Twentieth Century]. Seoul: Puk k'oria.

Chŏng Haeim. 2004. "Maehwajŏm changdan-kwa ŭm-yang" [The *Maehwajeom* (Apricot-stroke) Rhythmic Cycle and *Yin-yang*]. In *The Korean Beat: In Search of the Origins of*

Korean Culture, compiled by Kim Tschung-Sun and Sem Vermeersch, 131–54. Daegu: Academia Koreana of Keimyung University.

Chŏng Pyŏngho. 1994 [1986]. *Nongak*. Seoul: Yŏrhwadang.

———. 1988. "*Norip'an ŭi kusŏng-kwa kinŭng*" [The Composition and Functions of the *Norip'an*]. In *Nori munhwa-wa ch'ukche* [Play Culture and Festivals], edited by Yi Sangil, 9–23. Seoul: Sŏnggyun'gwan taehakkyo ch'ulp'anbu.

———. 1995. *Han'guk ŭi minsok ch'um* [Korean Folk Dance]. Seoul: Samsŏng ch'ulp'ansa.

Chŏng Sŏnhye. 1996. "Han'guk ch'um-kwa hohŭp ŭi unyong-e kwanhan yŏn'gu" [A Study of the Use of Breath in Korean Dance]. Master's thesis, Chungang University.

Chŏng Un'gil, ed. 1998. *Han'guk minsok taesajŏn* [A Dictionary of Korean Folk Customs]. Seoul: Minjung sŏgwan.

Chu Chaeyŏn. 1994. Korean program notes to *Then Comes the White Tiger*, ECM, ECM-1499.

Chu Kanghyŏn. 1996. *Uri munhwa ŭi susukkekki* [The Enigma of Korean Culture]. Seoul: Han'gyŏre shinmunsa.

———. 1997. *Han'guk ŭi ture* [Communal Labor of Korea], volume 2. Seoul: Chimmundang.

———. 1999. *21 segi uri munhwa: Uri munhwa paengnyŏn, waepŏpko ch'angshin in'ga* [Korean Culture in the Twenty-first Century: One Hundred Years of Korean Culture, Why "Preserve the Old while Creating the New"?]. Seoul: Han'gyŏre shinmunsa.

Chu, Miok. 2004. "Putting His Foot on the Rope Where His Mind Is." *Seoul* 10:14–15.

Coplan, David B. 1994. *In the Time of Cannibals: The Word Music of South Africa's Basotho Migrants*. Chicago: University of Chicago Press.

Cullen, Christopher. 1996. *Astronomy and Mathematics in Ancient China: The Zhou bi suan jing*. Cambridge: Cambridge University Press.

Cumings, Bruce. 1997. *Korea's Place in the Sun: A Modern History*. New York: W. W. Norton.

deBary, Wm. Theodore, Bary Bloom, and Irene Bloom, comps. 1999. *Sources of Chinese Tradition, Volume I: From Earliest Times to 1600*. 2nd ed. New York: Columbia University Press.

Delissen, Alain. 2002. "The Aesthetic Pasts of *Space* (1960–1990)." *Korean Studies* 25.2:243–60.

DeNora, Tia. 1995. *Beethoven and the Construction of Genius: Musical Politics in Vienna, 1792–1803*. Berkeley: University of California Press.

Deuchler, Martina. 1992. *The Confucian Transformation of Korea: A Study of Society and Ideology*. Cambridge: Council on East Asian Studies, Harvard University.

Diamond, Beverly, M. Sam Cronk, and Franziska von Rosen. 1994. *Visions of Sound: Musical Instruments of First Nations Communities in Northeastern America*. Chicago: University of Chicago Press.

Dilling, Margaret. 2001. "The Script, Sound, and Sense of the Seoul Olympic Ceremonies." In *Contemporary Directions: Korean Folk Music Engaging the Twentieth Century and Beyond*, edited by Nathan Hesselink, 171–234. Berkeley: Institute of East Asian Studies, University of California.

Durant, Alan. 1984. *Conditions of Music*. London: Macmillan.

Erlmann, Veit. 1996. "The Aesthetics of the Global Imagination: Reflection on World Music in the 1990s." *Public Culture* 8.3:467–87.

Everett, Yayoi Uno. 2004. "Intercultural Synthesis in Postwar Western Art Music: Historical Contexts, Perspectives, and Taxonomy." In *Locating East Asia in Western Art Music*, edited by Yayoi Uno Everett and Frederic Lau, 1–21. Middletown: Wesleyan University Press.

Feld, Steven. 1988. "Notes on World Beat." *Public Culture Bulletin* 1.1:31–37.

———. 1994. "From Schizophonia to Schismogenesis: On the Discourses and Commodification Practices of 'World Music' and 'World Beat.'" In *Music Grooves: Essays and Dialogues*, by Charles Keil and Steven Feld, 257–89. Chicago: University of Chicago Press.

Feuchtwang, Stephan. 2002. *An Anthropological Analysis of Chinese Geomancy*. Bangkok: White Lotus Press.

Finchum-Sung, Hilary. 2003. "From Rhetoric to Practice: Korean Composers Speak." *Ŭmak-kwa munhwa* 8:89–118.

———. 2006. "New Folksongs: Shin Minyo of the 1930s." In *Korean Pop Music: Riding the Korean Wave*, edited by Keith Howard, 10–20. Folkstone: Global Oriental.

Francis, Aaron. 2008. "Drinking Straws and Shaman Melodies: A Historical and Analytical Study of the *Taepyeongso*." Master's thesis, University of British Columbia.

Frederick, Warren. 2004. "Forging Fresh Yet Resonant Ceramics." In *From the Fire: A Survey of Contemporary Korean Ceramics*, edited by Penny Kiser, 9–13. Washington, D.C.: International Arts & Artists.

Frith, Simon, ed. 1989. *World Music, Politics, and Social Change*. Manchester: Manchester University Press.

Godwin, Joscelyn, ed. 1987. *Michael Maier's Atalanta Fugiens (1617)*. With an introductory essay by Hildemarie Streich. Tysoe, Warwickshire: Magnum Opus Hermetic Sourceworks.

Goldin, Paul R., and Victor H. Mair. 2005. "Early Discussions of Music and Literature." In *Hawai'i Reader in Traditional Chinese Culture*, edited by Victor H. Mair, Nancy S. Steinhardt, and Paul R. Goldin, 130–33. Honolulu: University of Hawai'i Press.

Graham, A. C. 1986. *Yin-yang and the Nature of Correlative Thinking*. Singapore: Institute of East Asian Philosophies.

———. 1989. *Disputers of the Tao*. LaSalle, Ill.: Open Court.

Guilbault, Jocelyne. 1993. "On Redefining the 'Local' through World Music." *World of Music* 35.2:33–47.

Guo, Qitao. 2003. *Exorcism and Money: The Symbolic World of the Five-Fury Spirits in Late Imperial China*. Berkeley: Institute of East Asian Studies, University of California.

Hahn, Man-young [Han Manyŏng]. 1991. *Kugak: Studies in Korean Traditional Music*. Translated and edited by Inok Paek and Keith Howard. Seoul: Tamgu Dang.

Hahn, Myong-hee [Han Myŏnghŭi]. 1992. "What Is Samulnori?" In *Korean Traditional Percussion: Samulnori Rhythm Workbook I, Basic Changgo*, Korean Conservatorium of Performing Arts, SamulNori Academy of Music, 5–6. Seoul: Sam-Ho Music.

Han Kisuk. 1989. "Namsadang tŏppoegi ch'um-e kwanhan yŏn'gu" [A Study of the *Namsadang's Tŏppoegi* (Mask Dance) Dance]. Master's thesis, Chungang University.

Han Myŏnghŭi. 1990. "Samul nori." *Ŭmak tonga* 77: 156–59.

———. 1992a. "Changgang ŭi yŏulmok: 80 nyŏndae ŭi kugakkye" [Neck of the Rapids on the Long River: The World of Traditional Music in the 1980s]. *Han'guk ŭmaksa hakpo* 9:13–28.

———. 1992b. "Samul-kwa chaejŭ" [*Samul nori* and Jazz]. *Yesul segye* 11:14–15.

———. 1994. *Uri karak uri munhwa* [Our Music, Our Culture]. Seoul: Chosŏn ilbosa.

Han Myŏnghŭi, Song Hyejin, and Yun Chunggang. 2001. *Uri kugak 100 nyŏn* [One Hundred Years of Our Korean Traditional Music]. Seoul: Hyŏnamsa.

Han, Myung-hee [Han Myŏnghŭi]. 1993. "SamulNori: Providing a Musical Release." *Koreana* 7.4:34–35.

Han Pŏmt'aek. 2003. "Ansŏng namsadang p'ungmulp'ae ŭi kwanhan yŏn'gu" [A Study of Ansŏng Namsadang P'ungmulp'ae]. Master's thesis, Chungang University.

Handler, Richard, and Joycelyn S. Linnekin. 1984. "Tradition, Genuine or Spurious." *Journal of American Folklore* 97:273–90.

Han'guk chŏngshin munhwa yŏn'guwŏn [Academy of Korean Studies], ed. 2002. *Ch'ŏnjamun* [The Thousand Character Classic]. Seoul: Kyŏngin munhwasa.

Hartman, Geoffrey H. 1970. *Beyond Formalism: Literary Essays, 1958–1970*. New Haven: Yale University Press.

Hesselink, Nathan. 1994. "Kouta and Karaoke in Modern Japan: A Blurring of the Distinction Between *Umgangsmusik* and *Darbietungsmusik*." *British Journal of Ethnomusicology* 3:49–61.

———. 1998. "Of Drums and Men in Chŏllabuk-do Province: Glimpses into the Making of a Human Cultural Asset." *Korea Journal* 38.3:292–326.

———. 2001. "On the Road with 'Och'ae Chilgut': Stages in the Development of Korean Percussion Band Music and Dance." In *Contemporary Directions: Korean Folk Music Engaging the Twentieth Century and Beyond*, edited with an introduction by Nathan Hesselink, 54–75. Berkeley: Institute of East Asian Studies, University of California.

———. 2002. "Modernization, Urbanization, and the Re-emergence of the Professional Korean Folk Musician." *Han'guk ŭmaksa hakpo* 29:717–46.

———. 2004. "*Samul nori* as Traditional: Preservation and Innovation in a South Korean Contemporary Percussion Genre." *Ethnomusicology* 48.3:405–39.

———. 2006. *P'ungmul: South Korean Drumming and Dance*. Chicago: University of Chicago Press.

———, trans. 2006. "'The Formation of *Namsadang* (Korean Itinerant Performer) Troupes': Chapter One of *A Study of Namsadang Troupes*," by Sim Usŏng. Translated, edited, and with an introduction by Nathan Hesselink. *Acta Koreana* 9.2:31–57.

———. 2008. "Taking Culture Seriously: Democratic Music and Its Transformative Potential in South Korea." *World of Music* 49.3:75–106.

———. 2009. " 'Yŏngdong Nongak': Mountains, Music, and the SamulNori Canon." *Acta Koreana* 12.1:1–26.

———. 2011. "Rhythm and Folk Drumming (*P'ungmul*) as the Musical Embodiment of Communal Consciousness in South Korean Village Society." In *Analytical and Cross-Cultural Studies in World Music*, edited by Michael Tenzer and John Roeder, 263–87. New York: Oxford University Press.

Hesselink, Nathan, and Jonathan C. Petty. 2004. "Landscape and Soundscape: Geomantic Spatial Mapping in Korean Traditional Music." *Journal of Musicological Research* 23.3–4:265–88.

Hinton, David, trans. 1999. *Mencius*. Washington, D.C.: Counterpoint.

Hobsbawm, Eric. 1983. "Introduction: Inventing Traditions." In *The Invention of Tradition*, edited by Eric Hobsbawm and Terence Ranger, 1–14. Cambridge: Cambridge University Press.

Hong, Charles. 1995. English program notes to *Nanjang: A New Horizon*, King, KSC-4150A.

Hong, Jimin [Hong Chimin]. 2009. "Wakening the DNA of Our Sound! The 24th *Noreum Machi* Festival." *Seoul Shinmun*, June 22, page 23.

Howard, Keith D. 1999. *Korean Music: A Listening Guide*. Seoul: National Center for Korean Traditional Performing Arts.

———. 2006a. "Imploding the Percussion Gestalt: Samulnori and Emerging Korean Tradition." *Acta Koreana* 9.1:13–33.

———. 2006b. *Preserving Korean Music: Intangible Cultural Properties as Icons of Identity*. Perspectives on Korean Music Volume 1. Aldershot: Ashgate.

———. 2006c. *Creating Korean Music: Tradition, Innovation, and the Discourse of Identity*. Perspectives on Korean Music Volume 2. Aldershot: Ashgate.

Hwang, Byung-ki [Hwang Pyŏnggi] and Hyo-shin Na [Na Hyoshin]. 2001. *Hwang Pyŏnggi-wa ŭi taehwa* (Conversations with Kayageum Master Byung-ki Hwang). Seoul: P'ulbit.

Idema, Wilt, and Stephen H. West. 1982. *Chinese Theater, 1100–1450: A Sourcebook*. Wiesbaden: Steiner.

Jackson, Shannon. 2000. *Lines of Activity: Performance, Historiography, Hull-House Domesticity*. Ann Arbor: University of Michigan Press.

Joo, Young-Ja [Chu Yŏngja]. 2008. "An Analysis of 'Sujeochun' Based on the Philosophies of 'Tiandiren' and 'Yin and Yang.'" *Journal of the Asian Arts* 2:121–84.

Jung, C. G. 1976. *The Symbolic Life: Miscellaneous Writings*. Translated by R. F. C. Hull. Princeton: Princeton University Press.

Kang Chunhyŏk. 2009. "SamulNori kongyŏn yangshik ŭi yŏksa: Kim Tŏksu-wa SamulNori-rŭl chungshim-ŭro" [A History of SamulNori's Performance Style: With Regard to Kim Tŏksu and SamulNori]. In *SamulNori t'ansaeng 30 chunyŏn kinyŏm kukche shimp'ojiŏm (30th Anniversary of SamulNori International Symposium)*, 91–97. Seoul: SamulNori t'ansaeng 30 chunyŏn kinyŏm saŏphoe.

Kang Jun Hyuk [Kang Chunhyŏk]. 1988. "The Faces of SamulNori . . . ." In *SamulNori*, edited by SamulNori, 135. Seoul: Art Space Publications.

Kang Muhak. 1991. *Tan'gun Chosŏn ŭi wŏn-pang-kak munhwa* [The "Circle-Square-Triangle" Culture of Tan'gun's Korea]. Seoul: Myŏngmundang.

Kapchan, Deborah A., and Pauline Turner Strong. 1999. "Theorizing the Hybrid." *Journal of American Folklore* 112.445:239–53.

Kartomi, Margaret J. 1981. "The Process and Results of Musical Culture Contact: A Discussion of Terminology and Concepts." *Ethnomusicology* 25:227–50.

Keightley, David. 2000. *The Ancestral Landscape: Time, Space, and Community in Late Shang China (ca. 1200–1045 B.C.)*. Berkeley: Institute of East Asian Studies, University of California.

Keil, Charles. 1984. "Music Mediated and Live in Japan." *Ethnomusicology* 27.1:91–96.

Killick, Andrew P. 2001. "The Traditional Opera of the Future? *Ch'anggŭk*'s First Century." In *Contemporary Directions: Korean Folk Music Engaging the Twentieth Century and Beyond*, edited by Nathan Hesselink, 22–53. Berkeley: Institute of East Asian Studies, University of California.

Kim Chaeŭn. 1987. *Han'gugin ŭi ŭishik-kwa haengdong yangshik* [Consciousness and Behavioral Patterns of Koreans]. Seoul: Ihwa yŏja taehakkyo ch'ulp'anbu.

Kim Chiwŏn and Yun Ch'un'gil. 1994. "Samul-i kanda, param-i inda" [*Samul nori* Moves, the Wind Rises]. *Wŏlgan ŭmak* 270:94–97.

Kim Chŏngsu. 2007. "Samul nori-e man ssŭiji annŭnda" (Korean Traditional Percussion Quartet Instruments, Which Are Not Used Only for Samulnori). *Kugak nuri* 89:30–31.

Kim Chŏngŭn. 2008. "Music Without Borders." *Morning Calm* 32.11:72–78.

Kim Duk Soo [Kim Tŏksu]. 1992. "Author's Introduction." In *Korean Traditional Percussion: Samulnori Rhythm Workbook I, Basic Changgo*, Korean Conservatorium of Performing Arts, SamulNori Academy of Music—Kim Duk Soo [Kim Tŏksu], Lee Kwang Soo [Yi Kwangsu], Kang Min Seok [Kang Minsŏk], 7–11. Seoul: Sam-Ho Music Publishing Company.

———. 1997. Opening quote in program notes to *From the Earth, to the Sky*, Samsung, SCO-123NAN (in Korean).

Kim, Duk Soo, ed., Dong-Won Kim, writer, and Shin-Gil Pak, trans. 1999. *Samulnori Textbook*. Seoul: Overseas Koreans Foundation, Korean National University of Arts.

Kim Hŏnsŏn. 1988. *Samul nori-ran muŏshin'ga* [What Is *Samul nori*?]. Seoul: Kwiinsa.

———. 1994 [1991]. *P'ungmulgut-esŏ samul nori-kkaji* [From *P'ungmulgut* to *Samul nori*]. Seoul: Kwiinsa.

———. 1995. *Kim Hŏnsŏn ŭi samul nori iyagi* [Kim Hŏnsŏn's Account of *Samul nori*]. Seoul: P'ulbit.

———. 1998. *Kim Yongbae ŭi salm-kwa yesul: Kŭ widaehan samul nori ŭi sŏsashi* [The Life and Art of Kim Yongbae: The Epic of That Grand *Samul nori*]. Seoul: P'ulbit.

Kim Hŭngju. 1993. "Nongmin ŭi kajok-kwa kongdongch'e saenghwal" [The Family and Communal Life of the Farmer]. In *Han'guk nongmin ŭi puran-kwa hŭimang: 1992 nyŏn Han'guk nongmin ŭishik chosa* [The Anxieties and Aspirations of the Korean Farmer: An Examination of the Korean Farmer's Consciousness in 1992], by Kim Ilch'ŏl, Kim T'aehŏn, and Kim Hŭngju, 9–47. Seoul: Sŏul taehakkyo ch'ulp'anbu.

Kim Inu. 1993. "P'ungmulgut-kwa kongdongch'ejŏk shinmyŏng" [*P'ungmulgut* and Communal Spirit]. In *Minjok-kwa kut: Minjok kut ŭi saeroun yŏllim-ŭl wihayŏ* [Folk and Ritual: Towards a New Understanding of Folk Ritual], 102–44. Seoul: Hangminsa.

Kim, Jin-p'yŏng [Kim Chinp'yŏng]. 1983. "The Letterforms of Han'gŭl: Its Origin and Process of Transformation." In *The Korean Language*, edited by the Korean National Commission for UNESCO, 80–102. Seoul: Si-sa-yong-o-sa.

Kim, Jin-Woo [Kim Chinu]. 2003a. "The Influence of Tourism on the *P'ungmul* Performance at Chongdong Theater." *Ŭmak-kwa munhwa* 8:145–59.

———. 2003b. "The Presentations and Reactions of the Saturday Regular Performance of Korean Music and Dance at the National Center for Korean Traditional Performing Arts." *Han'guk ŭmaksa hakpo* 30:813–35.

Kim Kyŏnghŭi, ed. 2001. *Kŏnwŏn 1400 nyŏn, kaewŏn 50 nyŏn: Kungnip kugagwŏnsa* [Established 1400 Years (Ago), Opened 50 Years (Ago): A History of The National Center for Korean Traditional Performing Arts]. Seoul: Kungnip kugagwŏn.

Kim Myŏnghwan. 1992. *Nae puk-e aenggil sori-ka ŏpsŏyo* [There Is No Voice That Can Match My Drum(ming)], edited by Kim Haesuk, Pak Chonggwŏn, Paek Taeung, and Yi Ŭnja. *Ppuri kip'ŭn namu minjung chasŏjŏn 11: Kosu Kim Myŏnghwan ŭi hanp'yŏngsaeng* (The Deep-rooted Tree Oral Histories (11): The Life of the *P'ansori* Drummer Kim Myŏnghwan). Seoul: Ppuri kip'ŭn namu.

Kim Rihye. 1988. "Playing As They Go . . . ." In *SamulNori*, edited by SamulNori, 5–7. Seoul: Art Space Publications.

Kim, Samuel S., ed. 2003. *Korea's Democratization*. Cambridge: Cambridge University Press.

Kim Sangsŏp. 2000. "Samul nori-rŭl t'onghae pon saeroun chŏnt'ong ŭi ch'angch'ul-kwa kŭ sahoejŏk ŭimi" (Revival of the Tradition and the Social Meaning of Samulnori). Master's thesis, Andong University.

Kim Taegyun. 1990. "Samul nori-e kwanhan yŏn'gu: Anjŭnban karak-ŭl chungshim-ŭro" [A Study of *Samul nori*: With Regard to the Seated Forms of Rhythmic Patterns]. Master's thesis, Sŏnggyun'gwan University.

Kim Tŏksu. 1998. "Sangmo ŭi kibon" [Spinning-tasseled Hat Fundamentals]. In *Han'guk chŏnt'ong yŏnhŭi ŭi ihae-wa shilche II* [The Practice and Appreciation of Korean Traditional Performing Arts II], edited by Kim Tŏksu, 3–21. Seoul: Han'guk yesul chonghap hakkyo.

Kim Tongwŏn. 1998. "Han'guk chŏnt'ong changdan ŭi kusŏng wŏlli" [Organizational Principles of Traditional Korean Rhythmic Patterns]. In *Han'guk chŏnt'ong yŏnhŭi ŭi ihae-wa shilche I* [The Practice and Appreciation of Korean Traditional Performing Arts I], edited by Kim Tŏksu, 95–149. Seoul: Han'guk yesul chonghap hakkyo.

———. 2002. *Shwiun changgo ch'ŏkkŏrŭm* (Easy *Janggo* Textbook). Seoul: Samho myujik.
———. 2003. *Samulnori uttari p'ungmul* [SamulNori's "Uttari p'ungmul" (composition)]. Taejŏn: Ch'ungch'ŏng namdo kyoyuk kwahak yŏn'guwŏn.
Kim Tongwŏn and Chu Chaeyŏn. 2007. Liner notes to CD recording *On the Road: The 50th Anniversary of Kim Duk Soo's Debut*. Translated by Yang Jong Sung, supervised by Suzanna Samstag. Synnara, NSC-175.
Kim Ŭisuk. 1993. *Han'guk minsok cheŭi-wa ŭm-yang ohaeng: Minsok cheŭi ŭi hyŏngsŏng iron* [Korean Folk Ritual and the Concept of *Ŭm-yang* and the Five Elements: A Formative Theory of Folk Ritual]. Seoul: Chimmundang.
Kim Wŏnho. 1999. *P'ungmulgut yŏn'gu* [A Study of *P'ungmulgut*]. Seoul: Hangminsa.
Kim Wŏnmi. 2000. "Namsadang ŭi majimak yurang yein Yi Suyŏng" [Yi Suyŏng, *Namsadang*'s Last Itinerant Artist]. In *Tasŭrŭm: Han'guk yesul chonghap hakkyo chŏnt'ong yesulwŏn hakpo* [Introduction: Journal of the School of Korean Traditional Arts, The Korean National University of Arts], 242–46. Seoul: Han'guk yesul chonghap hakkyo chŏnt'ong yesulwŏn.
Kim, Yang-kon [Kim Yanggon]. 1967. "Farmers Music and Dance." *Korea Journal* 7.10:4–9, 29.
Kim Yongun. 2002. "Wŏldŭ k'ŏp-ŭl Han'guk ŭi shinmyŏng mudae-ro talgunda" [Heating Up the World Cup with Korea's Enthusiasm]. *Joseon ilbo*, Arts section, June 1, p.46.
Kim, Young Ja [Kim Yŏngja]. 1981. "The Korean *Namsadang*." *Drama Review* 25.1:9–16.
Ko Susanna, author, and Yi Chŏnggyu, illustrator. 2005. *Ŏlssu chŏlssu samul nori* [Exciting *Samul nori*]. Seoul: Munwŏn, SamulNori Hanullim.
Koo, Hagen [Ku Hagen]. 1993. "The State, *Minjung*, and the Working Class in South Korea." In *State and Society in Contemporary Korea*, edited by Hagen Koo, 131–62. Ithaca: Cornell University Press.
Korean Conservatorium of Performing Arts, SamulNori Academy of Music—Kim Duk Soo [Kim Tŏksu], Lee Kwang Soo [Yi Kwangsu], Kang Min Seok [Kang Minsŏk] (with Im Dong Ch'ang [Im Tongch'ang], transcriptions and additional research/synthesis). 1990. *SamulNori: Changgo ŭi kibon* [SamulNori: *Changgo* Fundamentals]. Seoul: Samho ch'ulp'ansa.
———. 1992. *Korean Traditional Percussion: Samulnori Rhythm Workbook I, Basic Changgo*. Translated by Suzanna M. Samstag. Seoul: Sam-Ho Music Publishing Company.
———. 1993. *Kim Tŏksu p'ae SamulNori-ga yŏnju hanŭn samdo sŏlchanggo karak, haksŭp p'yŏn* (SamulNori: Korean Traditional Percussion SamulNori Rhythm Workbook 2, samdo sul changgo karak). English text by Suzanna M. Samstag. Seoul: Sam-Ho Music Publishing.
———. 1995. *Kim Tŏksu p'ae SamulNori-ga yŏnju hanŭn samdo sŏlchanggo karak, yŏnju p'yŏn* (SamulNori: Korean Traditional Ppercussion SamulNori Rhythm Workbook 3, samdo sul changgo karak). Seoul: Sam-Ho Music Publishing.
Korean Overseas Information Service. 2003. *Guide to Korean Cultural Heritage*. Seoul: Hollym.
Ku, Hee-seo [Ku Hŭisŏ]. 1989. "SamulNori vs. Mu: The Tenth Anniversary of SamulNori." *Koreana* 3.1:74–75.
———. 1994. "SamulNori: Taking Korean Rhythms to the World." *Koreana* 8.3:24–27.
Kŭm Changt'ae. 2000. *Yugyo ŭi sasang-kwa ŭirye* (The Confucian Thoughts and Rites). Seoul: Yemun sŏwŏn.
Kuttner, Fritz A. 1990. *The Archaeology of Music in Ancient China: 2000 Years of Acoustical Experimentation ca. 1400 B.C.–A.D. 750*. New York: Paragon House.
Kye Yŏnsu, comp. 2006 [1911]. *Handan kogi* [Chronicles on Korean History]. Translated and edited by Im Sŭngguk. Seoul: Chŏngshin segyesa.

Lau, D. C., trans. 1982. *Tao Te Ching*. Hong Kong: Chinese University Press.

Ledyard, Gari. 1997. "The International Linguistic Background of the Correct Sounds for the Instruction of the People." In *The Korean Alphabet: Its History and Structure*, edited by Young-key Kim-Renaud, 31–87. Honolulu: University of Hawai'i Press.

Lee, Bo hyung [Yi Pohyŏng]. 2003. "The Rhythmic Formation of the *Changdan*'s Syntactical Structure in Music with an Underlying Deep Structure." In *A Search in Asia for a New Theory of Music*, edited by José S. Buenconsejo, 99–129. Quezon City: University of the Philippines Center for Ethnomusicology.

Lee, Byong Won [Yi Pyŏngwŏn]. 1979. "Evolution of the Role and Status of Korean Professional Female Entertainers (*Kisaeng*)." *World of Music* 21.2:75–84.

———. 1981. "Concept, Practice, and Repertoires of Traditional Improvisatory Music of Korea." *Journal of the Asian Music Research Institute* 4:21–36.

———. 1987. *Buddhist Music of Korea*. Seoul: Jungeumsa.

———. 1997. *Styles and Esthetics in Korean Traditional Music*. Seoul: National Center for Korean Traditional Performing Arts.

Lee, Dong-seok [Yi Tongsŏk]. 2003. "A Dot Opens Up a World: Painter Lee Ufan." *Koreana* 17.1:54–57.

Lee, Ki-baek [Yi Kibaek]. 1995. *A New History of Korea*. Translated by Edward W. Wagner with Edward J. Schultz. Seoul: Ilchokak.

Lee, O-Young. 1992. "Preface." In *Korean Traditional Percussion: Samulnori Rhythm Workbook I, Basic Changgo*, by Korean Conservatorium of Performing Arts, 3. Seoul: Sam-Ho Music Publishing.

Lee, Sang-man [Yi Sangman]. 1995. "Drums of Peace: KBS Orchestra Plays at the U.N." *Koreana* 9.4:80–82.

Lee, So-young [Yi Soyŏng]. 2003. "Reading New Music in the Age of Fusion Culture: Focused on Korean Fusion Music (*Gugakfusion*)." Translated by Chung Heewon. *Tongyang Ŭmak* 25:189–214.

Lee, Young-Gwang [Yi Yŏnggwang]. 2009. *Samulnori Percussion Ensemble: Encounters with Korean Traditional Music 1*. Translated and edited by Ha Ju-Yong (with DVD). Seoul: Ministry of Culture, Sports, and Tourism Republic of Korea.

Legge, James, trans. 1971 [1893]. *Confucius: Confucian Analects, The Great Learning, and the Doctrine of the Mean*. New York: Dover Publications.

Leppert, Richard, and Susan McClary, eds. 1987. *Music and Society: The Politics of Composition, Performance, and Reception*. New York: Cambridge University Press.

Li, Ying-chang. 1994. *T'aishang Kan-ying P'ien: Lao-tzu's Treatise on The Response of the Tao*. Translated with an introduction by Eva Wong. San Francisco: HarperCollins Publishers.

Livingston, Tamara E. 1999. "Music Revivals: Towards a General Theory." *Ethnomusicology* 43.1:66–85.

Lord, Albert B. 1964. *The Singer of Tales*. Cambridge: Harvard University Press.

Lysloff, Ren, T.A. 1997. "Mozart in Mirrorshades: Ethnomusicology, Technology, and the Politics of Representation." *Ethnomusicology* 41.2:206–19.

Mackerras, Colin, ed. 1983. *Chinese Theater: From Its Origins to the Present Day*. Honolulu: University of Hawai'i Press.

Maliangkay, Roald H. 1999. "Handling the Intangible: The Protection of Folksong Traditions in Korea." Ph.D. dissertation, University of London, School of Oriental and African Studies.

———. 2008. "Their Masters' Voice: Korean Traditional Music SPs (Standard Play Records) under Japanese Colonial Rule." *World of Music* 49.3:53–74.

McClary, Susan. 1991. *Feminine Endings: Music, Gender, and Sexuality*. Minneapolis: University of Minnesota Press.

Meintjes, Louise. 1990. "Paul Simon's Graceland, South Africa, and the Mediation of Musical Meaning." *Ethnomusicology* 34.1:37–73.

Middleton, Richard. 2003. "Locating the People: Music and the Popular." In *The Cultural Study of Music: A Critical Introduction*, edited by Martin Clayton, Trevor Herbert, and Richard Middleton, 251–62. New York: Routledge.

Minsogakhoe Shinawi. 1977. Program to *Minsogakhoe "Shinawi" Folk Music Festival* (December 24, 1977, at the Korean Culture and Arts Foundation).

———. 1999. Program to *Minsogakhoe "Shinawi" Thirty-Year Commemorative Performance* (November 26, 1999, at Tongsung Art Center's Tongsung Hall).

———. 2000. Liner notes to CD recording *P'ungmul nori*, Shilla, SUC-1794.

Mitchell, J. Clyde, ed. 1969. *Social Networks in Urban Situations: Analyses of Personal Relationships in Central African Towns*. Manchester: Manchester University Press.

Mitchell, Tony. 1993. "World Music and the Popular Music Industry: An Australian View." *Ethnomusicology* 37.3:309–38.

Moon, Chung-in [Mun Chungin] and Jongryn Mo [Mo Chongnin]. 1999. *Democratization and Globalization in Korea: Assessments and Prospects*. Seoul: Yonsei University Press.

Murray, Stephen O. 2002. *Pacific Homosexualities*. Lincoln: Writers Club Press.

Nam Hwajŏng. 2008. Liner notes to CD *Kugak pangsong ch'uch'ŏn aidŭl norae: Uri akki nadŭri* [Gugak Broadcasting System's Recommended Songs for Children: A Visit with Korean Traditional Instruments]. SDT-0021, Loen Entertainment.

Nam, Sang-suk [Nam Sangsuk], and Gim, Hae-suk [Kim Haesuk]. 2002. *Introduction to Korean Traditional Performing Arts*. Seoul: Kungnip han'guk yesul chonghap hakkyo chŏnt'ong yesulwŏn.

Nettl, Bruno, ed. 1978. *Eight Urban Musical Cultures: Tradition and Change*. Urbana: University of Illinois Press.

———. 1983. *The Study of Ethnomusicology: Twenty-nine Issues and Concepts*. Urbana: University of Illinois Press.

———. 2005. *The Study of Ethnomusicology: Thirty-one Issues and Concepts*. Urbana: University of Illinois Press.

No Poksun. 1993. *Nongak*. Chŏnju: Chŏlla puktorip kugagwŏn.

No Tongŭn. 1993. "No Tongŭn ŭi uri nara ŭmaksa kyoshil" [No Tongŭn's Classroom on Korean Music History]. *Nangman ŭmak* 19:25–61.

———. 1995. *Han'guk kŭndae ŭmaksa 1* [Modern Korean Music History I]. Seoul: Han'gilsa.

No Ŭnuk, ed. 1991. *Pak Chiwŏn chakp'um chip* [The Works of Pak Chiwŏn]. P'yŏngyang: Munye ch'ulp'ansa.

O Changhyŏn, Pak Chinu, and Shim Usŏng. 2000. *Minsok nori chido charyo* [A Guide to Folk Entertainments]. Seoul: Taegwang munhwasa.

Pak Hŏnbong and Yi Tuhyŏn. 1964. *Kkoktugakshi norŭm* [Puppetry]. *Muhyŏng munhwajae chosa pogosŏ 1* [Intangible Cultural Asset Report of Investigation #1]. Seoul: Munhwajae kwalliguk.

Pak Kihwan. 1987. *Kugak t'ongnon* [A Survey of Traditional Music]. Seoul: Hyŏngsŏl ch'ulp'ansa.

Pak Sangguk, Kim Hohwan, Ch'ŏn Chin'gi, and Sŏ Hŏn'gang. 1996. *P'yŏngt'aek nongak*. Seoul: Kungnip munhwajae yŏn'guso.

Pak Shin'gil. 1997. "Samul nori ŭi changgo karak yŏn'gu: Ch'alsŭ Shigŏ ŭi akkongnon-e ipkak hayŏ" [A Study of *Samul nori*'s *Changgo* Rhythms: Based on Charles Seeger's Method of Understanding Musical Compositions]. *Han'guk ŭmaksa hakpo* 19:85–106.

Pang Sŭnghwan. 1998. "Samul nori-e nat'anan kutkŏri changdan-e kwanhan yŏn'gu: Kim Yongbae ŭi kkwaenggwari ridŭm-ŭl chungshim-ŭro" [A Study of *Samul nori's Kutkŏri* Rhythmic Pattern: With Regard to Kim Yongbae's *Kkwaenggwari* Rhythm]. Master's thesis, Danguk [Tan'guk] University.

Park, Chan E. 2003. *Voices from the Straw Mat: Toward an Ethnography of Korean Story Singing*. Honolulu: University of Hawai'i Press.

Park, Shingil [Pak Shin'gil]. 2000. "Negotiating Identities in a Performance Genre: The Case of *P'ungmul* and *Samulnori* in Contemporary Seoul." Ph.D. dissertation, University of Pittsburgh.

Pihl, Marshall R. 1994. *The Korean Singer of Tales*. Cambridge: Council on East Asian Studies, Harvard University Press.

Pinto, Tiago de Oliveira. 1989. "Review of Megadrums Live: Reinhard Flatischler and the International Ethnic Percussion Project." *The World of Music* 31.2:151–52.

Provine, Robert C. 1988. *Essays in Sino-Korean Musicology: Early Sources for Korean Ritual Music*. Seoul: Il Ji Sa Publishing.

———. 1998. "My Experiences with the 'Institute.'" *Koreana* 12.4:28–31.

Puschnig, Wolfgang. 1997. English program notes to *From the Earth, to the Sky*, Samsung, SCO-123NAN.

Rice, Timothy. 1994. *May It Fill Your Soul: Experiencing Bulgarian Music*. Chicago: University of Chicago Press.

Roberts, Moss, trans. 2001. *Dao De Jing: The Book of the Way*. Berkeley: University of California Press.

Rockwell, John. 1999. "Serious Music." In *Democracy and the Arts*, edited by Arthur M. Melzer, Jerry Weinberger, and M. Richard Zinman, 92–102. Ithaca: Cornell University Press.

Russell, Bertrand 1945. *A History of Western Philosophy*. New York: Simon and Schuster.

Rutt, Richard. 1961. "The Flower Boys of Shilla (*Hwarang*), Notes on their Sources." *Transactions of the Royal Asiatic Society, Korea Branch* 28:1–66.

———. 1964. *Korean Works and Days: Notes from the Diary of a Country Priest*. Rutland: Tuttle.

Said, Edward W. 1979. *Orientalism*. New York: Vintage Books.

Samstag, Suzanna. 1988a. Liner notes to *Samulnori: Record of Changes*, CMP CD 3002.

———. 1988b. "SamulNori." *Koreana* 2.3:43–49.

Samstag, Suzanna M., and Steve Lake. 1994. English program notes to *Then Comes the White Tiger*, ECM, ECM-1499.

SamulNori, ed. 1988. *SamulNori*. Photographs by Ichiro Shimizu, translations by Suzanna M. Samstag, Kim Ri-hae [Kim Rihye], and Kwak Hye-song [Kwak Hyesŏng]. Seoul: Art Space Publications.

SamulNori Hanullim Yŏn'gu Kyoyukpu [SamulNori Hanullim Department of Research and Education]. 1994a. *Honam udo nongak* [Chŏlla Province *Nongak* of the Western Counties]. Seoul: SamulNori Hanullim.

———. 1994b. *Samul nori ŭi kich'o: Yŏngnam nongak, Uttari p'ungmul* [*Samul nori*'s Foundations: "Yŏngnam nongak," "Uttari p'ungmul"]. Seoul: SamulNori Hanullim. Reprinted as *Samul nori kyobon* [*Samul nori* Textbook], Seoul: Sori narae.

———. 1994c. *Changgo ŭi kibon: Changdan yŏnsŭp* [*Changgo* Fundamentals: Rhythm Practice]. Seoul: SamulNori Hanullim.

———. 1994d. *Sŏlchanggo karak: Kich'op'yŏn* [*Sŏlchanggo* Rhythms: Beginner]. Seoul: SamulNori Hanullim.

———. 1994e. *Sŏlchanggo karak: Chunggŭpp'yŏn* [*Sŏlchanggo* Rhythms: Intermediate]. Seoul: SamulNori Hanullim.

———. 1994f. *Samdo sŏlchanggo karak: Yŏnjup'yŏn* [*Sŏlchanggo* Rhythms from Three Provinces: Performance Version]. Seoul: SamulNori Hanullim.

Schroeder, Ralph. 2006. "Introduction: The IEMP Model and Its Critics." In *An Anatomy of Power: The Social Theory of Michael Mann*, edited by John A. Hall and Ralph Schroeder, 1–16. New York: Cambridge University Press.

Seeger, Charles. 1977. *Studies in Musicology 1935–1975*. Berkeley: University of California Press.

Sejong munhwa hoegwan chŏnsa p'yŏnjip wiwŏnhoe [*A Complete History of the Sejong Center for the Performing Arts* Compilation Committee]. 2002. *Sejong munhwa hoegwan chŏnsa* [A Complete History of the Sejong Center for the Performing Arts]. Seoul: Maru.

Senelick, Laurence. 2000. *The Changing Room: Sex, Drag, and Theater*. New York: Routledge.

Shen, Zaihong. 2001. *Feng Shui: Harmonizing Your Inner and Outer Space*. New York: Dorling Kindersley.

Shils, Edward. 1971. "Tradition." *Comparative Studies in Society and History* 13.2:122–59.

Shim Hyesŭng. 1987. "Chindo madang noriyo-e kwanhan yŏn'gu: Namsadangp'ae-wa ŭi kwallyŏnsŏng yŏbu-rŭl chungshim-ŭro" [A Study of Chindo Field Songs: Whether or Not There is a Relationship with the *Namsadang*]. Master's thesis, Seoul National University.

Shim Usŏng. 1968. *Namsadang. Muhyŏng munhwajae chosa pogosŏ 40* [Intangible Cultural Asset Report of Investigation #40]. Seoul: Munhwajae kwalliguk.

———. 1975. *Han'guk ŭi minsokkŭk* [Korean Folk Theater]. Seoul: Ch'angjak-kwa pip'yŏng.

———. 1978. *Minsok munhwa minjung ŭishik* [Folk Culture, People's Rituals]. Seoul: Taehwa ch'ulp'ansa.

———. 1994 [1974]. *Namsadangp'ae yŏn'gu* [A Study of *Namsadang* Troupes]. Seoul: Tosŏ ch'ulp'an tongmunsŏn.

———. 1998. *Minsok munhwaron sŏsŏl* [An Introduction to Discussions of Folk Culture]. Seoul: Tongmunsŏn.

———. 1999. "30 chunyŏn-ŭl hoego hamyŏ" [Looking Back on Thirty Years]. In program to *Minsogakhoe "Shinawi" Thirty-Year Commemorative Performance* (November 26, 1999, at Tongsung Art Center's Tongsung Hall).

Shim Usŏng and Song Ponghwa. 2000. *Namsadang nori* [*Namsadang* Entertainments]. Seoul: Hwasan munhwa.

Shin Kinam. 1992. *Ŏttŏk'e hŏmŏn ttokttok hŏn cheja han nom tugo chugŭlkko*? [What Do I Have to Do to Get a Single Smart Disciple Before I Die?], edited by Kim Myŏnggon. *Ppuri kipŭn namu minjung chasŏjŏn 3: Imshil "sŏlchanggu chaebi" Shin Kinam ŭi hanp'yŏngsaeng* (The Deep-rooted Tree Oral Histories (3): The Life of the Korean Drummer, Sin Ki-nam). Seoul: Ppuri kip'ŭn namu.

Shin Yongha. 1985. "A Social History of *Ture* Community and *Nongak* Music." *Korea Journal* 25.3:4–17, 25.4:4–18.

Sim U-sŏng [Shim Usŏng]. 1974. "Namsadang." In *Survey of Korean Arts: Folk Arts*, 455–71. Seoul: National Academy of Arts.

Sim Woo-sung [Shim Usŏng]. 1997. "Namsadang: Wandering Folk Troupes." *Koreana* 11.2:44–49.

Simmel, Georg. 1950. "The Metropolis and Mental Life." In *The Sociology of Georg Simmel*, edited with an introduction by Kurt H. Wolff, 409–24. Glencoe, Ill.: Free Press of Glencoe.

Sivin, Nathan. 1987. *Traditional Medicine in Contemporary China*. Ann Arbor: University of Michigan Press.

Small, Christopher. 1998. *Musicking: The Meanings of Performing and Listening*. Hanover: Wesleyan University Press.

Sŏ Chŏngbŏm and Yŏl Hanmyŏng, eds. 1977. *Sumŏsanŭn oet'olbagi I: Chŏnt'ong sahoe ŭi hwanghon-e sŏn saramdŭl* [Outcasts in the Shadows I: People in the Twilight of Traditional Society]. Seoul: Ppuri kip'ŭn namu.

Sohn, Tae-soo [Son Taesu]. 1997. "'Samul Nori Has Roots in Spirit of Koreans': Kim Duk-soo Celebrates 20th Anniversary of His Percussion Quartet." *Korea Newsreview* 26.5:31.

Solís, Ted. 2004. "Teaching What Cannot Be Taught: An Optimistic Overview." In *Performing Ethnomusicology: Teaching and Representation in World Music Ensembles*, edited by Ted Solís, 1–19. Berkeley: University of California Press.

Son Inae. 2004. "Sadangp'ae sori panga t'aryŏng yŏn'gu: Sŏnamhae tosŏ chiyŏk ŭi namsadangp'ae sori-rŭl chungshim-ŭro" [A Study of the *Sadangp'ae* Song "Panga t'aryŏng": With Regard to the *Namsadangp'ae* Songs of the Southwest Coast Islands]. *Han'guk minyohak* 15:177–214.

Son, Min-jung. 2004. "The Politics of the Traditional Korean Popular Song Style T'urot'u [*t'ŭrot'ŭ*]." Ph.D. dissertation, University of Texas at Austin.

Son Pyŏngu. 1988. "Nongak hyŏngshik-e issŏsŏ chinp'uri-e kwanhan yŏn'gu" [A Study of Form and Ground Formations in *Nongak*]. Master's thesis, Chungang University.

Song, Bang-Song [Song Pangsong]. 1980. *Source Readings in Korean Music*. Seoul: Korean National Commission for UNESCO.

———. 2000. *Korean Music: Historical and Other Aspects*. Seoul: Jimoondang Publishing Company.

———. 2001. "The Historical Development of Korean Folk Music." In *Contemporary Directions: Korean Folk Music Engaging the Twentieth Century and Beyond*, edited with an introduction by Nathan Hesselink, 5–21. Berkeley: Institute of East Asian Studies, University of California.

Song Hye-jin [Song Hyejin]. 1994. "Music: East Meets West/Foreigners Find Fulfillment in Korea's Traditional Music." *Koreana* 8.3:28–32.

———. 2000. *A Stroll Through Korean Music History*. Seoul: National Center for Korean Traditional Performing Arts.

Song Pangsong. 2007. *Chŭngbo Han'guk ŭmak t'ongsa* [An Expanded Broad History of Korean Music]. Seoul: Minsogwŏn.

Song Sŏkha. 1940. "Sadang ko" [A Study of the *Sadang*]. *Chosŏn minsok* 3:65–74.

———. 1960. *Han'guk minsokko* [Studies on Korean Folklore]. Seoul: Ilshinsa.

Spiller, Henry. 2004. *Gamelan: The Traditional Sounds of Indonesia*. Oxford: ABC-CLIO.

Stock, Jonathan P. J. 2008. "New Directions in Ethnomusicology: Seven Themes toward Disciplinary Renewal." In *The New (Ethno)Musicologies*, edited by Henry Stobart, 188–206. Lanham, Md.: Scarecrow Press.

Stokes, Martin, ed. 1994. Ethnicity, Identity and Music: The Musical Construction of Place. Oxford : Berg.

———. 2004. "Music and the Global Order." *Annual Review of Anthropology* 33:47–72.

Sutton, R. Anderson. 2002. *Calling Back the Spirit: Music, Dance, and Cultural Politics in Lowland South Sulawesi*. New York: Oxford University Press.

———. 2003. "Innovation and Accessibility: Towards a Typology of Fusion Music in Korea." *Tongyang Ŭmak* 25:227–50.

———. 2009. "Korean Fusion Music on the World Stage: Perspectives on the Aesthetics of Hybridity." *Acta Koreana* 12.1:27–52.

Suzuki, Daisetz T. 1999. *Sengai: The Zen of Ink and Paper*. Boston: Shambala.

Taylor, Timothy D. 1997. *Global Pop: World Music, World Markets*. New York: Routledge.

Tenzer, Michael. 2000. *Gamelan Gong Kebyar: The Art of Twentieth-Century Balinese Music*. Chicago: University of Chicago Press.

Titon, Jeff. 1995. "Text." *Journal of American Folklore* 108:432–48.

T'oegyewŏn sandae nori pojonhoe [T'oegyewŏn Sandae Nori Preservation Society]. 1999. *T'oegyewŏn sandae nori: Yŏnhŭi taebon* [T'oegyewŏn *Sandae nori*: A Performance Manual]. Seoul: Ilwŏn.

Tsao Penyeh. 2000. "Soundscape of Daoist Rituals: 'Musical' Values from the Insider's Perspective." *Tongyang Ŭmak* 22:63–88.

U Shirha. 2004. *Chŏnt'ong ŭmak ŭi kujo-wa wŏlli: Samt'aegŭk ŭi ch'um, tongyang ŭmak* [The Structures and Principles of Traditional Music: The Dance of the *Samt'aegŭk*, Asian Music]. Seoul: Sonamu.

University Musical Society, Youth Education Program. 2002. *SamulNori: Teacher Resource Guide*. Ann Arbor: University Musical Society.

Van Zile, Judy. 2001. *Perspectives on Korean Dance*. Middletown: Wesleyan University Press.

———. 2008. "Visible Breathing: The Use of the Breath in Korean Dance." *Society and Culture* 10:80–89.

Vatsyayan, Kapila. 1983. *The Square and the Circle of the Indian Arts*. New Delhi: Roli Books International.

———. 2003. "The Biological and Mathematical Foundation of Indian Theories of Art." In *A Search in Asia for a New Theory of Music*, edited by José S.Buenconsejo, 77–87. Quezon City: University of the Philippines Center for Ethnomusicology.

Wah, Yu Siu. 2004. "Two Practices Confused in One Composition: Tan Dun's Symphony 1997: Heaven, Earth, Man." In *Locating East Asia in Western Art Music*, edited by Yayoi Uno Everett and Frederick Lau, 57–71. Middletown: Wesleyan University Press.

Waterman, Christopher Alan. 1990. *Jùjú: A Social History and Ethnography of an African Popular Music*. Chicago: University of Chicago Press.

Weiss, Sarah. 2008. "Permeable Boundaries: Hybridity, Music, and the Reception of Robert Wilson's *I La Galigo*." *Ethnomusciology* 52.2:203–38.

Whang In-joung [Hwang Injŏng]. 1981. *Management of Rural Change in Korea: The Saemaul Undong*. Seoul: Seoul National University Press.

Wi Hosŏn. 1994. "Chungguk kodae ŭm-yang ohaengsŏl ŭi chŏn'gae-wa kŭ sasangjŏk t'ŭksŏng" [The Development of the Ancient Chinese Theory of *Ŭm-Yang* and the Five Elements and Its Ideological Characteristics]. Master's thesis, Yŏngnam University.

Williams, Sean. 2001. *The Sound of the Ancestral Ship: Highland Music of West Java*. New York: Oxford University Press.

Winslow, Deborah. 2003. "Potters' Progress: Hybridity and Accumulative Change in Rural Sri Lanka." *Journal of Asian Studies* 62.1:43–70.

Wolff, Janet. 1987. "Foreword: The Ideology of Autonomous Art." In *Music and Society: The Politics of Composition, Performance and Reception*, edited by Richard Leppert and Susan McClary, 1–12. Cambridge: Cambridge University Press.

Wright, Edward Reynolds, and Man Sill Pai [Pae Manshil]. 2000. *Traditional Korean Furniture*. New York: Kodansha International.

Yang Jongsung [Yang Chongsŭng]. 2003. *Cultural Protection Policy in Korea: Intangible Cultural Properties and Living National Treasures*. Seoul: Jimoondang.

Yang Kŭnsu. 1998. "Namsadang 'p'ungmulgut'-e naejae toen hyŏndaejŏk suyong kach'i-e yŏn'gu" [A Study of the Inherently Modern Reception Value of the *Namsadang*'s Percussion Music and Dance]. Master's thesis, Sejong University.

Yi Chaesuk, ed. 1998. *Chosŏnjo kungjung ŭirye-wa ŭmak* [Chosŏn Dynasty Court Ceremonies and Music]. Seoul: Sŏul taehakkyo ch'ulp'anbu.

Yi Changjik. 1995. "Kugak ŭi segyehwa-e ttarŭn myŏngam: SamulNori-wa kaeryang kugakki" [Different Perspectives on the Globalization of Korean Music: SamulNori and Modified Traditional Instruments]. *Munhwa yesul* 192:74–77.

Yi Chinwŏn. 2008. "21 segi minsok ŭmakhak yŏn'gu hyŏnhwang-gwa chŏnmang" [The Present Condition and Future Prospects for Folk Music Research in the 21st Century]. In *21 segi kugakhak yŏn'gu kwaje-wa chŏnmang: Han'guk kugak hakhoe ch'angnip 60 chunyŏn kinyŏm haksulhoe* [Themes and Prospects for Traditional Music Research in the 21st Century: A Conference in Honor of the 60th Anniversary of the Founding of the Korean Musicological Society], 71–100. Seoul: Han'guk kugak hakhoe.

Yi Chonghak. 1997. Korean program notes to *Red Sun • SamulNori*, Polygram, DZ-2433.

Yi Chongsul. 1997. *T'oegye Yulgok chŏrhak yŏn'gu* [A Study of the Philosophies of T'oegye and Yulgok], volume I: *T'aegŭk-igisŏl non'gu* [A Discussion of the Theories of the "Great Absolute" and the "Basic Principles and Atmospheric Force of Nature"]. Seoul: Han'guk sasang yŏn'guwŏn, Pusŏl sudŏk munhwasa.

Yi Chŏngu. 1999. "Ch'ŏnnyŏn ŭi hŭng maek innŭn 3tae namsadang, majimak yenŭng poyuja Pak Kyesun-sshi ilga" [Master Pak Kyesun, Third-Generation *Namsadang* Performer Possessing the Heartbeat of a Millennium, The Last Performing Arts Cultural Asset Holder]. *Han'gyŏre*, July 2.

Yi Chuhŭi. 1994. "Samul nori-wa changgo karak punsŏk: Shin modŭm-esŏ kutkŏri • chajinmori • hwimori changdan-ŭl chungshim-ŭro" [*Samul nori* and an Analysis of *Changgo* Rhythms: With Regard to the Rhythms *Kutkŏri*, *Chajinmori*, and *Hwimori* in the Composition "Shin modŭm"]. Master's thesis, Chungang University.

Yi Haerang, ed. 1985. *Han'guk ŭmaksa* [A History of Korean Music]. Seoul: Taehan min'guk yesulwŏn.

Yi Hwanhŭi. 1998. "Palsŏng kigwan ŭi kujo mit olbarŭn palsŏng-kwa hohŭppŏp-e kwanhan yŏn'gu" [A Study of the Structure of the Vocal Cords with Proper Voice and Breathing Technique]. Master's thesis, Chosŏn University.

Yi Hyŏngyŏng. 2004. *Shwipke paeunŭn samul nori* [Easy-to-Learn *Samul nori*]. Seoul: Hangminsa.

Yi Kyuwŏn and Chŏng Pŏmt'ae. 1997 [1995]. *Uri-ka chŏngmal araya hal uri chŏnt'ong yein paek saram* [One Hundred of Our Traditional Artists We Should Know]. Seoul: Hyŏnamsa.

Yi Nŭnghwa. 1968 [1927]. *Chosŏn haehwasa* [A History of Korean *Kisaeng*]. Seoul: Shinhan sŏrim.

Yi Sangil. 1987. *Han'gugin ŭi kut-kwa nori* [Ritual and Play of the Korean People]. Seoul: Munŭmsa.

Yi Sŏngch'ŏn. 1980. "Kugak kaegwan mit charyo: 1979 nyŏndo" [A Survey of Traditional Music and Its Materials in 1979]. *Han'guk yesulchi* 15:335–55.

Yi Sŏngch'ŏn, Kwŏn Tŏgwŏn, Paek Ilhyŏng, and Hwang Hyŏnjŏng. 1997 [1994]. *Algi shwiun kugak kaeron* [An Easy-to-Understand Introduction to Traditional Music]. Seoul: P'ungnam.

Yi Sŏngjae. 1999 [1994]. *Chaemi innŭn kugak killajabi* [An Interesting Guide to Traditional Music]. Seoul: Seoul Media.

Yi Soyŏng. 1999. "P'uri-wa SamulNori" [P'uri and SamulNori]. In *Na-nŭn tarŭge tŭnnŭnda—Han'guk ŭmak ŭi saeroun chip'yŏng-ŭl hyanghayŏ: Yi Soyŏng ŭi ŭmak pip'yŏng* [I Hear It Differently—Toward New Horizons in Korean music: The Music Criticism of Yi Soyŏng], 55–70. Seoul: Yesul.

———. 2005. *Han'guk ŭmak ŭi naemyŏnhwa toen orient'allijŭm-ŭl nŏmŏsŏ* [Overcoming Internalized Orientalism in Korean Music]. Seoul: Minsogwŏn.

———. 2007. "Ilche kangjŏmgi shin minyo ŭi honjongsŏng yŏn'gu" (The Hybridity of Korean New-Folk Song (Sinminyo) during the Japanese Colonial Period). Ph.D. thesis, Academy of Korean Studies.

Yi Tuhyŏn. 1986. "Mask Dance-Dramas." In *Traditional Performing Arts of Korea*, edited by The Korean National Commission for Unesco, 35–80. Seoul: Seoul Computer Press.

Yi Yŏngmi. 1997. "Hwan p'ŏp'omŏnsŭ ŭi *Nant'a*: Samul nori-ka taejung munhwa kyŏnghyang-gwa chŏmmok hayŏ mandŭrŏnaen tto hana ŭi hwallo" [*Nant'a* as Fun Performance: *Samul nori* as a Pop Culture Trend and the Creation of a New Genre and Way of Life]. *Munhwa yesul* 220:97–99.

———. 1999. *Han'guk taejung kayosa* [A History of Korean Popular Song]. Seoul: Shigongsa.

Yi Yongshik, Sŏ Inhwa, Han Chŏngwŏn, Kim Sori, Chŏng Hwanhŭi, Pak Sangji, Pak Kiman, and Kim Yongshik. 2007. *Kugakki yŏn'gu pogosŏ 2007* (2007 Report on the Study of Korean Traditional Musical Instruments). Seoul: Kungnip kugagwŏn.

Yi Yongshik, Sŏ Inhwa, Yi Sukhŭi, Kim Sori, Chŏng Hwanhŭi, Pak Sangji, Yi Arŭm, Kim Yongshik, Yun Kwŏnyŏng, and Pak Sanghyŏp. 2008. *Kugakki yŏn'gu pogosŏ 2008* (2008 Report on the Study of Korean Traditional Musical Instruments). Seoul: Kungnip kugagwŏn.

Yoo, Meoung-jong [Yu Mŏngjong], and Choi, Hang-young [Ch'oe Hangyŏng]. 2002. "Shin Joong-hyun: Living Chronicle of Korean Rock Music." *Koreana* 16.4:42–47.

Yoon, Yee-Heum [Yun Ihŭm]. 1997. "The Contemporary Religious Situation in Korea." In *Religion and Society in Contemporary Korea*, edited by Lewis R. Lancaster and Richard K. Payne, 1–17. Berkeley: Institute of East Asian Studies, University of California.

Yu Minyŏng, Kim Sŏnghŭi, Chŏn Sŏnghŭi, Yi Ŭn'gyŏng, Kim Tonggwŏn, and Kim T'aehun. 2000. *Kungnip kŭkchang 50 nyŏnsa* [A Fifty-Year History of the National Theater]. Seoul: T'aehaksa.

Yu Yŏngnyŏl. 2000. "Ansŏng namsadang p'ungmul nori chŏnsŭng pangan yŏn'gu" [A Study of Ansŏng Namsadang's Transmission Method of *P'ungmul*]. Master's thesis, Yongin University.

Yun Kwangbong. 1994. *Yurang yein-kwa kkoktugakshi norŭm* [Itinerant Artists and Puppetry]. Seoul: Miral.

———. 1998. *Chosŏn hugi ŭi yŏn'gŭk* [Theater of the Late Chosŏn Period]. Seoul: Pagijŏng.

Yun Myŏngwŏn, Hŏ Hwabyŏng, Cho Ch'anggyu, Kim Tonghyŏn, and Kim Yosŏp. 2004.

Han'guk ŭmak-ron: Uri ŭmak ŭi mŏt-kwa chŏngshin [A Discussion of Korean Music: The Character and Soul of Our Music]. Seoul: Ŭmak segye.

Yun T'aerim. 1964. *Han'gugin ŭi sŏnggyŏk* [The Character of Korean People]. Seoul: Hyŏndae kyoyuk ch'ongsŏ ch'ulp'ansa.

Zo, Zayong [Cho Chayong]. 1982. Guardians of Happiness: Shamanistic Tradition in Korean Folk Painting. Seoul: Emileh Museum.

———. 1988. "The Old Woman and Her 'Duduri.'" In *SamulNori*, edited by SamulNori, 38–39. Seoul: Art Space Publications.

INDEX-GLOSSARY

www.ingramcontent.com/pod-product-compliance
Lightning Source LLC
Chambersburg PA
CBHW032135020426
42334CB00016B/1178
9780226330976